The Lesbian Pillow Book

Edited by Alison Hennegan

FOURTH ESTATE • London

First published in Great Britain in 2000 by
Fourth Estate Limited
6 Salem Road
London W2 4BU
www.4thestate.co.uk

1 3 5 7 9 10 8 6 4 2

A catalogue record for this book is available from the British Library.

ISBN 1-85702-323-4

Typeset by Rowland Phototypesetting Limited,
Bury St Edmunds, Suffolk
Printed in Great Britain by Mackays of Chatham plc
Chatham, Kent

The Lesbian Pillow Book

To Caroline,
to my mother
and to the memory of my father

Contents

In the Beginning . . . ?

Betwixt and Between

In Foreign Parts

Courts, Courtesans and Whores

Dealings with the Enemy

Breeches Parts

Marriage Lines and Family Matters

Just Friends?

Romantic Agonies

Self or Other?

Sisters

Lessons for Life

Of Women's Gardens

Glimpses

Two Legs Good, Four Legs Better?

Farewells

Coda

Thanks

A number of people have helped in the making of this book and it is a pleasure to thank them. I am grateful to Georgia Brown who initially pointed the way to some of the sixteenth-century works which appear here; to Peter Cochran, who is currently transcribing and editing the Diaries of Byron's friend John Cam Hobhouse, and who made me a gift of the intriguing little snippet from them which concerns Madame Vestris and a number of over-excited Regency ladies; to Geoffrey Kantaris for help with Renaissance Spanish; to Richard Dance for his modernisation of Marie Maitland's poem; to Andrew Webber for tracking down birth and death dates for 'Marie-Madeleine'; and to Anne Barton who has lent books, enquired kindly and fed me, magnificently and often, very often (I apologise to her here and now for the fact that cats are not quite as well represented in this book as dogs).

Michael Kerrigan fed me books and occasionally much-needed moral support at regular intervals; Jane Liddell-King has discussed, suggested and encouraged over many months; Peter Parker calmed terrors, compared notes and gave me a very necessary sense that I was not alone in the grisly business of trying to complete a long-term project; Michael Mason cheered at regular intervals from the sidelines; Sue Gilbert, as usual, steadily refused to acknowledge the possibility of defeat, either for the book or its editor. My warmest thanks to all of them.

The staff of several of Cambridge University Library's reading rooms have given punctilious and courteous help, namely those in the West Room, the Rare Books and Manuscripts Room, the Microfilm Room and the Anderson Room; my thanks to them all.

Thanks for permission to reprint copyrighted material usually appear under Acknowledgements but a handful of people have been so very generous I want to thank them here: Professor François Lafitte (for Havelock Ellis), Helena Whitbread (for the Anne Lister Diaries), Lis Whitelaw (for Rosemary Manning) and Serena Thirkell (for Angela Thirkell).

I am particularly indebted to the cheerful generosity of three fellow-anthologisers: Emma Donoghue and Gillian Spraggs are themselves editors of fine collections of women's love-poetry, *What Sappho Would have Said* and *Love Shook My Senses*. Emma gave me a great deal of extremely practical advice and information when I was beginning work on this book, and her own *Passions Between Women: British Lesbian Culture, 1668–1801* has been a source of constant pleasure and enlightenment. Gill not only steered me through some of the more maddening complications of recent changes in local and international copyright law, but also drew my attention to a number of early texts and, moreover, provided her own translations of many of them. Throughout, she has taken an intelligently enthusiastic and practically helpful interest in the enterprise. That she has done much of this at a time when she has had her own pressing commitments and deadlines makes her kindness all the greater and all the more appreciated. Jane Stevenson, co-editor with Peter Davidson of the forthcoming *Early Women Poets: An Anthology*, most generously sent me some splendid texts by sixteenth- and seventeenth-century women poets, answered queries and provided additional information, all with remarkable speed, wit and good humour.

It is also a source of considerable pleasure that so much of the more recent work that appears in this book should be the work of friends. It is now more than twenty-five years since I first came to know Christine Donald and Gill Spraggs, and more than twenty since I first met Suniti Namjoshi and Gillian Hanscombe: all of them remain important over the years, as friends, allies and touchstones. Gill Hanscombe, in particular, has, during the creation of this book, fielded even more dispirited telephone calls than usual in the small hours of the morning. Rosemary Manning and Tom Wakefield, sadly, will not see *The Lesbian Pillow Book*, but – *absint omina* – Maureen Duffy, Esther Isaac, Kate Charlesworth, Emma Donoghue, Ellen Galford and Sally Cline will. My thanks to all of them.

My thanks go too to my editor at Fourth Estate, Christopher Potter, who has seen me miss two deadlines, without, apparently, ceasing to believe that this book would happen. (If he *did* stop believing in it, he never said so to me, which is at least as important.)

I am extremely grateful to my inspired copy-editor, Monica Schmoller, whose scrupulous attention to detail, combined with unfailing tact and most welcome wit, turned a task which I had been dreading into a most unexpected pleasure.

My greatest debt of gratitude, however, is to Caroline Gonda who has from the very beginning helped shape both the contents and spirit of this book. It is no exaggeration to say that without her it would not have seen the light of day, especially in its taxing final stages. And it is true to say that, in the best tradition of collaborative lesbian writing, I can no longer always tell where my phrases end and hers begin. I would like to say that this book is for her but find myself wondering, like so many sixteenth-century love-poets, how I can give her what is so largely hers already.

Introduction

This book has its origins in one particular aspect of my own long love-affair with reading. *The Lesbian Pillow Book* is a very personal anthology, whose roots go back to the late 1950s when, as a young homosexual woman emerging into a seemingly undocumented world, I scanned every book for hints and clues that might explain me to myself. In doing so, I uncovered the traces of other, rather similar women who had passed this way before. Many of them, I discovered, had also spent their formative years haunting libraries and bookshops in search of predecessors and kindred spirits. Some of them you will encounter in this volume. I've called it a Pillow Book as a respectful gesture to another passionate woman reader (though not, as far as I know, a lesbian one). At the turn of the tenth and eleventh centuries, Sei Shonagon, a highly literate lady of the Japanese court, compiled for her own delight and edification a commonplace book, her own personal anthology, filled with material to read when she retired for the night, to slip under her pillow when she was ready for sleep, to have by her when she woke in the morning. Its contents – pen-portraits, social vignettes, sayings, thoughts, anecdotes heard or recounted, even lists of words which intrigued or pleased her – were as varied in genre, mood and function as I have tried to make the contents of this book. And, like this book, hers included the overtly erotic but was not in any way confined to it.

Reading, as this anthology should make abundantly clear, has for a very long time had a particular importance for lesbians. Over the centuries, many women who love and desire other women have turned to books, hoping to find there some answering echo of their own, often confusing, sometimes perilous, emotions and experience. They have sought enlightenment, affirmation, evidence of a past and a pedigree. At the most basic level, they have quite simply been looking for company, women they'd like to spend time with, somebody else like them. Those lucky enough to be both literate and learned trawled widely, not limited to their own time or to a single language or culture. They found real women (Sappho, whose life and legend resurface time and again in this book), and mythical beings (Hippolyta, the Amazon Queen). Some were immortals – goddesses such as Diana, and all her many half-sisters who shared with her a preference for virginity and a maiden band; others, mere mortals who had had immortality conferred upon them by their creators – Shakespeare's Rosalind and Viola – were adopted early as 'honorary sisters', however disappointing their eventual 'dwindling into a wife'.

Some likenesses proved better than others; some were barely recognisable, the product of unskilled hands or wildly disordered imaginings. Rage (such as Martial's or Juvenal's) might distort; so too might frustrated and uncomprehending desire of the sort that has inspired many a fictional 'lesbian' in centuries' worth of pornography written by and for heterosexual men; or in the literature and painting of the late nineteenth century where 'Beautiful Evil', that most exotic form of (rarely encountered) lesbian life, abounds.

Women of earlier ages, however, could not afford to be as selective as many of us have since become, insisting upon our right to be so; they found ways to take what they needed from the books they could find, and to leave or re-work less palatable matter. Long before theories of 'the reader as author' became modish, many a lesbian was, perforce, an adept. (I have included later in this book, in the section called 'Glimpses', an extract from an earlier essay which describes my own juvenile perfecting of the art.) Even the beastliest authors may have their uses. Juvenal, for example, may be horrid about lesbians, but, as Anne Lister discovered, in the last years of the eighteenth century, an awful lot of lesbians seemed to read him. Which leads us to another useful tip. Always inspect other women's bookshelves closely. (And we do, of course, we do. When my own lover first came out, very tentatively, to a friend, she found her confidante distinctly underwhelmed. When challenged, the friend replied: 'Well, you can hardly expect it to be a surprise. You forget, I've seen your books.') Moreover, many a lesbian's life is further mapped by the inscriptions written in her books by those who gave them to her: some of my own books contain miniature novels on their fly leaves, where I can trace a procession of owners and their changing relations with each other.

We can watch some of the earlier women in this anthology reading and sifting what they have found in books, taking it and reworking it for their own needs. The sixteenth-century Scottish poet, Marie Maitland, constructs her own litany of same-sex lovers, drawn from the Bible, ancient history and classical literature. Anne Lister (in real life) cons her Ovid, and Fanny Derham (in Mary Shelley's fiction) studies her Plato; and both of them learn Latin and Greek so that they may read these authors in the original, free from censorship and bowdlerised translations. (Homosexuality, as I myself discovered in my teens, is a most powerful inducement to acquire a classical education.)

We can also watch writers working to elucidate the intricacies of women's passionate feeling for each other, as in the poetry of Katherine Philips or the restrained prose of Elizabeth Carter, and we can recognise a continuing struggle to create new models of female partnership and shared lives, whether in fictional utopias or the half-century long adventure in living conducted by the Ladies in Llangollen Vale in the second half of the eighteenth century.

Reading is not a passive activity. Many of the writers included in this book engage in conscious dialogue with the earlier authors they have read and with their own contemporaries: Elizabeth Barrett Browning eulogises George Sand; Maria Edgeworth naughtily mocks, by pastiche, high-flown sentiments such as those of Anna Seward who so loved Edgeworth's own stepmother. Amy Levy, Vernon Lee and Mary Robinson, in their poetry, implicitly engage in a three-way conversation, and Amy Lowell tries to engage three earlier literary 'Sisters' in the dialogue she wishes she could have had with them. Suniti Namjoshi questions *Twelfth Night* and its creator — and just about everyone talks at some stage to and through Sappho.

Most of the authors included in this book wrote well before the twentieth century. There are arguments for and against modernising earlier texts. Retaining original conventions of spelling, punctuation and capitalisation may impart a false 'quaintness'. But wholesale modernising also falsifies, by obliterating the fact of difference and distance which separate but need not bar us from the past. To me that obliteration is the greater evil. Consequently, modernisation has been kept to a bare minimum and in most cases avoided entirely. I believe the tiny amount of additional effort occasionally required of the reader will be more than repaid by the richness of the original texts. In two cases, where particular difficulties might be encountered, I have provided accompanying modern versions of the sixteenth-century poems concerned.

No Grand Unified Theory of lesbian sexuality or identity underpins this anthology, although I hope that those seeking to formulate their own will find its contents stimulating. Nor is this an academic book, although, again, I hope that other scholars will find in it material of use and value. My model has been those many splendid anthologies of the inter-war years, such as the Saturday Books, intended for that creature in whom I stubbornly continue to believe: the intelligent, literate and intellectually curious general reader.

I realise that for many academic critics and literary historians working today the very act of using the word lesbian to describe women of earlier centuries is anathema. Although I recognise that words such as 'homosexual' are nineteenth-century coinages, I do not believe that means that the human reality they describe had no existence before that date. Certainly, the various meanings of the word 'lesbian' have for centuries included the emotional and sexual ones it primarily holds today, and versions of the type of woman it connotes are clearly recognisable down the ages, long before the Early Modern period.

I have my own views and theories about lesbian identity, but it has not been my concern here to argue a case. Rather, I have tried to select and arrange material in such a way that voices speak to us, and to each other, across the centuries. I have not done this because I believe in some universal, transhistorical Eternal Lesbian. (Who would dare to, in these days of rigorously enforced pluralities?) Nevertheless, it seems to me that certain patterns of response and action emerge; and that what often unites them is a spirit of Resistance – resistance to the notion that human passions can or should be satisfactorily contained and satisfied within the narrow formula of Man + Woman = Completion.

Resistance in this book takes many forms, inevitably inflected by period, place and culture. Sappho expresses her hope that her most gifted pupil, clearly destined to be a poet, may be spared the marriage which she fears would silence her; Erasmus uses a marriage-resisting virgin as the occasion for one of his best-selling Latin exercises; and a sixteenth-century lady pens a fearsome curse directed against anyone foolish enough to seek to separate her from the woman of her choice. More than one woman in this book takes a wife, rather than becoming one herself; others pay for their servants' dowries but cling firmly to their own unmarried state. Two wives, one fictional, one not, reject their husbands in order to lie in the arms of their maidservants. More than one set of sisters make clear their strong sense that no other human relationship could supplant their sibling bond.

The historical scope of this anthology is wide – from the Book of Ruth to poems written only weeks before going to press – and its modes and tones are many: fiction and fact, prose and verse, the work of friends and foes. The basely scurrilous jostles with the sometimes almost intolerably lofty; and the fictional creations (both vehemently hostile and embarrassingly deferential) of male and heterosexual women authors take their place with 'the real thing' offered to us by lesbian writers. Not all the authors included in this book fit neatly into the categories of hetero- or homosexual, and neither do many of the characters they have created. Passionate debates about the nature and direction of human sexual desire are scarcely unique to our own age, and one period's self-evident truth is another's laughable error. Despite the vagaries of scientific theories and moral dicta, however, some ideas have proved remarkably persistent across the millennia, constantly resurfacing with only the most minor changes in their dress. The notion that souls sometimes end up in bodies of the wrong gender, for example (which goes back at least as far as Aristophanes), and the belief in the essentially androgynous nature of genius clearly had as much to say to the very heterosexual Victorian Elizabeth Barrett Browning as to that proud invert, Radclyffe Hall, more than sixty years later.

So many have struggled for so long to recognise and articulate the mysterious relations between biological gender, sexual desire and personal identity. This anthology provides its own contribution to those debates, but also offers an interval of rest and refreshment from them.

My best advice to you is to find yourself a pillow, make yourself comfortable and enjoy this book.

Title Story
EMMA DONOGHUE

The Little Girls
A Fourth-Form Friendship
The Friendly Young Ladies

On My First Approaches
From a Lady Who Had a Desire to See Her
Write Soon

On the Friendship Betwixt Two Ladies
A Confusion of Feelings
Friendship's Mysteries

The Delicate Fire
On Finding the Garter She Left in My Room
Bliss

Elegy for a Lady in Love With Another Lady
The Death of the Heart
The Getting of Wisdom

Two Serious Ladies
Happy Easter, My Lady
The Anniversary

The Old Beauty
The Silver Locks: Addressed to an Aged Friend
Elegy Written at the Sea-side

[*Written especially for this book: 1999.*]

In the Beginning . . . ?

In this first section we meet the two main prototypes to whom lesbians and their forerunners in the West have returned time and time again — Ruth of the Old Testament, and sixth-century BC Sappho of Lesbos. Sappho's name and example will appear constantly throughout this book, a heroine to some, arch-villain to others.

Accompanying these two women of the ancient world, one pagan, one Biblical, are a variety of early attempts to 'explain' the phenomenon which we, even from this distance, can recognise as lesbianism or its near relation. It's written in the stars; it's written on the body; it was wrathfully ordained by the gods; it's all just a terrible accident caused by a drunken Creator.

from The Book of Ruth

*In this Old Testament story, Naomi, a widow, is further bereaved by the
death of her two sons. She urges her daughters-in-law, Ruth and Orpah, to
make a new life for themselves apart from her, but Ruth refuses. The extract
begins at chapter 1, verse 8 and is given in the Authorized Version, the only
version known to many of the women writers in this volume.*

8. And Naomi said unto her two daughters in law, Go, return each to
her mother's house: the LORD deal kindly with you, as ye have dealt
with the dead, and with me.

9. The LORD grant you that ye may find rest, each of you in the house
of her husband. Then she kissed them; and they lifted up their voice,
and wept.

10. And they said unto her, Surely we will return with thee unto thy
people.

11. And Naomi said, Turn again, my daughters: why will ye go with
me? are there yet any more sons in my womb that they may be your
husbands?

12. Turn again, my daughters, go your way; for I am too old to have
an husband. If I should say, I have hope, if I should have an husband
also to night, and should also bear sons;

13. Would ye tarry for them till they were grown? would ye stay for
them from having husbands? nay, my daughters; for it grieveth me much
for your sakes that the hand of the LORD is gone out against me.

14. And they lifted up their voice, and wept again: and Orpah kissed
her mother in law; but Ruth clave unto her.

15. And she said, Behold, thy sister in law is gone back unto her people,
and unto her gods: return thou after thy sister in law.

16. And Ruth said, Intreat me not to leave thee, or to return from following after thee: for whither thou goest, I will go; and where thou lodgest, I will lodge: thy people shall be my people, and thy God my God:

17. Where thou diest, will I die, and there will I be buried: the LORD do so to me, and more also, if ought but death part thee and me.

18. When she saw that she was stedfastly minded to go with her, then she left speaking unto her.

19. So they two went until they came to Bethlehem. And it came to pass, when they were come to Bethlehem, that all the city was moved about them, and they said, Is this Naomi?

20. And she said unto them, Call me not Naomi, call me Mara: for the Almighty hath dealt very bitterly with me.

21. I went out full, and the LORD hath brought me home again empty: why then call ye me Naomi, seeing the LORD hath testified against me, and the Almighty hath afflicted me?

22. So Naomi returned, and Ruth the Moabitess, her daughter in law, with her, which returned out of the country of Moab: and they came to Bethlehem in the beginning of the barley harvest.

Sappho

For more than two thousand years legends have clustered thickly round the name of Sappho of Lesbos. She has been variously glorified and vilified: in antiquity critics called her 'the tenth muse', whilst ancient comic dramatists made her a grotesque and obscene figure of fun. The controversy over her sexuality began early and has continued long. Some have been particularly anxious to emphasise her love for Phaon, the young man for whom, allegedly, she threw herself from the Leucadian Rocks, despairing because he no longer loved her. She might be a suicide, but at least she was normal! Other commentators have insisted that she was Lesbian in both the geographical and sexual senses. Nineteenth-century textual scholars fought fiercely over her moral reputation, and sometimes amended texts so that they appeared to confirm her supposedly impeccable heterosexuality.

The difficulties entailed in disentangling fact from legend were compounded by the loss of the greater part of her poetic works; only fragments remain, scattered through the works of ancient grammarians, critics and historians who quoted a few lines, sometimes only a word or two, to illustrate a point. Over the past century or so, a few more precious fragments have been discovered, on papyri retrieved by archaeologists from the sands of Egypt. Ironically, the very fragmentedness of Sappho's poems has often proved an inspiration to subsequent writers, offering them the opportunity to fill the gaps and silences in a way which both 'completes' her and expresses themselves.

For the ancients, Sappho was pre-eminently the poet of sexual love. They prized her psychologically acute treatment of its pains and joys, and her keen awareness that pain and pleasure were often two sides of the same coin; the adjective glukupikros, *bitter-sweet, was deemed to be her coinage, difficult though it is for us now to imagine a world without it.*

For lesbian poets in particular, Sappho has long been both an inspiration and an enduring challenge, the supreme model against whom to measure their own poetic achievement.

Maddening though it is for Greekless readers to be told that the full glory of Sappho is lost in translation, it is sadly true. Translators always impose something of their own age upon the works they seek to render. John Addison, Dante Gabriel Rossetti, 'Michael Field' and A. E. Housman will inevitably present us with four different Sapphos, and our own age will come no closer to the original. Not that that should make us stop trying.

The poems which follow illustrate some of Sappho's most characteristic qualities and themes: the physically overwhelming power of sexual desire; the vivid evocation of the beauty of the natural world, made as erotic as the human loves played out within it; sexual loneliness; her power of invective; and her tender love of young women. The translations, drawn from various centuries, demonstrate how different each age's Sappho may be.

Two versions of Sappho's φαινεται μοι
κῆνος

Sapho's Ode out of Longinus (1685)
WILLIAM BOWLES

I

The Gods are not more blest than he,
Who fixing his glad Eyes on thee,
With thy bright Rays his Senses chears
And drinks with ever thirsty ears.
The charming Musick of thy Tongue,
Does ever hear, and ever long;
That sees with more than human Grace,
Sweet smiles adorn thy Angel Face.

II

But when with kinder beams you shine,
And so appear much more divine,
My feeble sense and dazl'd sight,
No more support the glorious light,
And the fierce Torrent of Delight.
Oh! then I feel my Life decay,
My ravish'd Soul then flies away,
Then Faintness does my Limbs suprize,
And Darkness swims before my Eyes.

III

Then my Tongue fails, and from my Brow
The liquid drops in silence flow,
Then wond'ring Fires run through my Blood,
And Cold binds up the stupid Flood,
All pale, and breathless then I lye,
I sigh, I tremble, and I dye.

'Thy fatal shafts unerring move'
TOBIAS SMOLLETT (1721–1771)

This poem appears in Smollett's first novel, Roderick Random *(1748).*
Smollett himself is sometimes claimed to have been homosexual, and it is
interesting that in this version of Sappho's poem, it is Love (with a capital
'L') rather than a specific and gendered beloved who causes the effects it
describes.

Thy fatal shafts unerring move,
I bow before thine altar, Love.
I feel thy soft resistless flame,
Glide swift through all my vital frame.

For while I gaze my bosom glows,
My blood in tides impetuous flows,
Hope, fear, and joy alternate roll,
And floods of transports whelm my soul.

My faltering tongue attempts in vain
In soothing murmurs to complain;
Thy tongue some secret magic ties,
Thy murmurs sink in broken sighs.

Condemned to nurse eternal care,
And ever drop the silent tear,
Unheard I mourn, unknown I sigh,
Unfriended live, unpitied die.

'Cool water gurgles through' (1889)
a version by 'MICHAEL FIELD'

*The first three lines of this poem are a fairly literal translation of three lines
from a fragment of Sappho, found inscribed on a potsherd from the third
century BC. From this beginning 'Michael Field' has gone on to weave a
much longer poem, full of echoes and allusions to other lines and phrases
found elsewhere in Sappho's work.*

*The single name, 'Michael Field', unites the identities of two people,
Katharine Bradley (1846–1914) and Edith Cooper (1862–1913). These two
women were not only aunt and niece but also lovers; their long literary
collaboration is one of the most remarkable in English literary history. To
many people, the gulf between Lesbos of the sixth century BC and England
in the last years of Victoria's reign might seem unbridgeable. Yet ironically
it is in the works of 'the Michaels' that we find poems which come closest to
conveying something of the passionate urgency and vivid sensuousness of their
great original.*

'Αμφι δ'[ὑδωρ] ψυχρον κελαδει υσδων
μαλινων αἰθυσσομενων δε φυλλων
κωμα καταρρει

Cool water gurgles through
The apple-boughs, and sleep
Falls from the flickering leaves,
Where heavy shadows keep
Secluded from man's view
A little cave that cleaves
The rock with fissure deep.

Worshipped with milk and oil
There dwell the Nymphs, and there
They listen to the breeze,
About their dewy hair
The clustered garlands coil,

Or, moving round the trees,
Cherish the roots with care.

There reign delight and health;
There freshness yields the palm
To musical refrain;
For never was such calm,
Such sound of murmuring stealth,
Such solace to the brain,
To weariness such balm.

Even a lover's pains,
Though fiercely they have raged,
Here find at last relief:
The heart by sorrow aged
Divinely youth regains;
Tears steal through parched grief:
All passion is assuaged.

'The moon has set . . .'

Four lines of ancient Greek have for centuries exerted a particular fascination for readers and translators. A literal translation would read: 'It has set now, the moon, the Pleiades too. It is the middle of the night, the hours pass, but I lie here alone.' Until well into the twentieth century, the lines were believed to be by Sappho, although scholars now reject her authorship. For the translators whose work appears below — two eighteenth-century versions and a twentieth-century one — this poem was, nevertheless, indisputably Sappho's. A. E. Housman, himself homosexual and shaping this translation at a time of increasing anti-homosexual hysteria, infuses this ancient lyric with his own characteristic sensibility and imagery ('the land of lost content').

(1)

The Moon has veil'd her Silver Light,
The *Pleiades* have left the Sky;
It's now the Silent Noon of Night,
The Love-sworn Hour is past; yet I
Alone, deserted, pining lie!

John Addison (1735)

(2)

The *Pleiads* now no more are seen,
Nor shines the silver Moon serene,
In dark and dismal Clouds o'ercast;
The love appointed Hour is past:
Midnight usurps her sable Throne,
And yet, alas! I lie alone.

Francis Fawkes (1760)

(3)

The weeping Pleiads wester,
  And the moon is under seas;
From bourne to bourne of midnight
  Far sighs the rainy breeze:

It sighs from a lost country
  To a land I have not known;
The weeping Pleiads wester,
  And I lie down alone.

A. E. Housman (written 1893; published
posthumously, 1936)

Sappho dismisses an uncultured (but possibly rather pretty) woman

Tradition has it that Sappho was not a beauty, judged by the standards of her time and place. Indeed, in one of the fragments she seems to refer to herself as small, dark and ill-favoured.

In this first version of Sappho's retort by Anne Finch, Countess of Winchilsea (1661–1720), the insipid beauty, who is loved for her face alone, is seen off by the female poet whose 'fam'd' verses will continue to dazzle men's eyes (from the page), even after their author's death. Speaking through Sappho, Finch is able to set aside the considerable ambivalence she often expressed about appearing in print.

Melinda on an Insipid Beauty
ANNE FINCH

You, when your body life shall leave,
Must drop entire into the grave;
Unheeded, unregarded, lie,
And all of you together die:
Must hide that fleeting charm, that face in dust,
Or to some painted cloth the slighted image trust;
Whilst my fam'd works shall thro' all times surprise,
My polish'd thoughts, my bright ideas rise,
And to new men be known, still talking to their eyes.

'When Death shall close those Eyes' (1735)
JOHN ADDISON

When Death shall close those Eyes, Imperious Dame!
Silence shall seize on thy inglorious Name.
For thy unletter'd Hand ne'er pluck'd the rose,
Which on *Pieria*'s happy Summit glows.
To *Pluto*'s Realms unhonour'd you shall go,
And herd amongst th'ignobler Ghosts below.
Whilst I on Wings of Fame shall rise elate,
And snatch a bright Eternity from Fate.

Poems for Atthis
'MICHAEL FIELD'

Atthis was one of the dearest of Sappho's beloved women friends. Amongst the most poignant of the Sapphic fragments, is one of just seven words, which may be translated as 'For I loved you once, Atthis, long ago'. The Michael Fields took those last two words and made them the title of one of their own collections, in which they offered translations and reworkings of Sappho. The two poems that follow come from Long Ago. *The angry bitterness of the first poem has its roots in another fragment which reads, 'Atthis, to you the very thought of me is hateful now, and you rush off to Andromeda'.*

XLIV
Οὐ τι μοι ὐμμες
[You are nought to me]

Nought to me! So I choose to say:
We meet, old friends, about the bay;
The golden pulse grows on the shore —
Are not all things as heretofore
Now we have cast our love away?

Sappho. A Study (1862), by Simeon Solomon. A strong, unsentimental vision
drawn by a Jewish artist who was himself homosexual, and who also became
the stuff of a rather different sort of legend. Friend of Swinburne and Pater –
until his arrest for cottaging and his descent into an apparently amiable
alcoholism – Solomon produced works which Wilde counted amongst his
most cherished possessions.

Men throng us; thou art nought to me,
Therefore, indifferent, I can see
Within thine eyes the bright'ning grace
That once thou gavest face to face;
'Tis natural they welcome thee!

Nought to me, like the silver ring,
Thy mislaid, worthless gift. Last spring,
As any careless girl, I lost
The pin, yet, by the tears it cost,
It should have been worth cherishing.

Nought, nought! and yet if thou dost pass
I grow as summer-coloured grass,
And if I wrap my chiton round,
I know thine ear hath caught the sound,
Although thou heedest not, alas!

Nought to me! Wherefore dost thou throw
On me that glittering dance, as though,
Friend, I had ever done thee wrong,
When the crowd asks me for the song,
'Atthis, I loved thee long ago'?

XIV
Το μελημα τουμον
[My darling]

Atthis, my darling, thou did'st stray
A few feet to the rushy bed,
When a great fear and passion shook
My heart lest haply thou wert dead;
It grew so still about the brook,
As if a soul were drawn away,

Anon thy clear eyes, silver-blue,
Shone through the tamarisk-branches fine;
To pluck one iris thou had'st sprung
Through galingale and celandine;
Away, away the flowers I flung
And thee down to my breast I drew.

My darling! Nay, our very breath
Nor light nor darkness shall divide;
Queen Dawn shall find us on one bed,
Nor must thou flutter from my side
An instant, lest I feel the dread,
Atthis, the immanence of death.

And here is Bliss Carman's evocation of Sappho's Atthis.

from *Sappho: One Hundred Lyrics:*
Number XXIII
BLISS CARMAN (1861–1929)

I loved thee, Atthis, in the long ago,
When the great oleanders were in flower,
In the broad herded meadows full of sun.
And we would often at the fall of dusk
Wander together by the silver stream,
When the soft grass-heads were all wet with dew,
And purple-misted in the fading light.
And joy I knew and sorrow at thy voice,
And the superb magnificence of love, –
The loneliness that saddens solitude,
And the sweet speech that makes it durable, –
The bitter longing and the keen desire,
The sweet companionship through quiet days
In the slow ample beauty of the world,
And the unutterable glad release

Within the temple of the holy night.
O Atthis, how I loved thee long ago
In that fair perished summer by the sea!

Sapphics
TOM AITKEN

In this witty jeu d'esprit, Tom Aitken with casual virtuosity explains and demonstrates the metrical form known as 'sapphics'.

Named after Sappho (seventh century BC), who first devised them, Sapphics are usually unrhymed, but can be rhymed: not easy in English.

Sappho, poet, she of the island Lesbos,
Shaped a stanza which eschews rhyme but uses
Pairs of trochees sandwiching one gay dactyl –
    Three times repeated –

Followed by a pithier fourth line, placing
Dactyl, trochee (one of each) riding tandem.
Known afar for loving her girl disciples,
    Was she a lesbian,

Or, from tall Ionian cliff-top falling,
Did she die a hetero, mad for handsome
Boatman Phaon? Scholars reject this twee, too
    Bitter-sweet ending.

Aristophanes explains it all

from Plato's *Symposium*

The comic dramatist Aristophanes appears as a character in Plato's philosophi-
cal dialogue The Symposium *(The Banquet). When it is his turn to speak*
on Love, the subject chosen for the evening's discourse, he offers his own
inimitable History of Sexuality. (Michel Foucault's pales by comparison.)

The translation used here is by Percy Bysshe Shelley, who found some
aspects of Plato's writings on same-sex love unpalatable and shrank from
translating them accurately. He nevertheless produced a version more faithful
to Plato's original than the heavily edited and bowdlerised translation of
The Symposium *which appeared posthumously under his name in 1841; at*
one point during the editing process, Mary Shelley wrote rather plaintively
to her co-editor and keeper of the flame, Leigh Hunt: 'I could not bring
myself to leave out the word love *entirely from a treatise on Love.' One of*
the passages which Mary Shelley and Leigh Hunt censored appears below
(translated in 1818; not published until 1910).

You ought first to know the nature of man, and the adventures he has
gone through; for his nature was anciently far different from that which
it is at present. First, then, human beings were formerly not divided into
two sexes, male and female; there was also a third, common to both the
others, the name of which remains, though the sex itself has disappeared.
The androgynous sex, both in appearance and in name, was common
both to male and female; its name alone remains, which labours under
a reproach.

At the period to which I refer, the form of every human being was
round, the back and the sides being circularly joined, and each had four
arms and as many legs; two faces fixed upon a round neck, exactly like
each other; one head between the two faces; four ears, and two organs
of generation; and everything else as from such proportions it is easy
to conjecture. Man walked upright as now, in whatever direction he
pleased; and when he wished to go fast he made use of all his eight
limbs, and proceeded in a rapid motion by rolling circularly round, –

like tumblers, who, with their legs in the air, tumble round and round. We account for the production of three sexes by supposing that, at the beginning, the male was produced from the Sun, the female from the Earth; and that sex which participated in both sexes, from the Moon, by reason of the androgynous nature of the Moon. They were round, and their mode of proceeding was round, from the similarity which must needs subsist between them and their parent.

They were strong also, and had aspiring thoughts. They it was who levied war against the Gods; and what Homer writes concerning Ephialtus and Otus, that they sought to ascend heaven and dethrone the Gods, in reality relates to this primitive people. Jupiter and the other Gods debated what was to be done in this emergency. For neither could they prevail on themselves to destroy them, as they had the Giants, with thunder, so that the race should be abolished; for in that case they would be deprived of the honours of the sacrifices which they were in the custom of receiving from them; nor could they permit a continuance of their insolence and impiety. Jupiter, with some difficulty having devised a scheme, at length spoke. 'I think,' said he, 'I have contrived a method by which we may, by rendering the human race more feeble, quell the insolence which they exercise, without proceeding to their utter destruction. I will cut each of them in half; and so they will at once be weaker and more useful on account of their numbers. They shall walk upright on two legs. If they show any more insolence, and will not keep quiet, I will cut them up in half again, so they shall go about hopping on one leg.'

So saying, he cut human beings in half, as people cut eggs before they salt them, or as I have seen eggs cut with hairs. He ordered Apollo to take each one as he cut him, and turn his face and half his neck towards the operation, so that by contemplating it he might become more cautious and humble; and then to cure him, Apollo turned the face round, and drawing the skin upon what we now call the belly, like a contracted pouch, and leaving one opening, that which is called the navel, tied it in the middle. He then smoothed many other wrinkles, and moulded the breast with much such an instrument as the leather-cutters use to smooth the skins upon the block. He left only a few wrinkles in the belly, near the navel, to serve as a record of its former adventure.

Immediately after this division, as each desired to possess the other half of himself, these divided people threw their arms around and embraced each other, seeking to grow together; and from this resolution to do nothing without the other half, they died of hunger and weakness: when one half died and the other was left alive, that which was thus left sought the other and folded it to its bosom; whether that half were an entire woman (for we now call it a woman) or a man; and thus they perished. But Jupiter, pitying them, thought of another contrivance, and placed the parts of generation before. Since formerly when these parts were exposed they produced their kind not by the assistance of each other, but like grasshoppers, by engendering upon the earth. In this manner is generation now produced, by the union of male and female; so that from the embrace of a man and woman the race is propagated, but from those of the same sex no such consequence ensues.

From this period, mutual Love has naturally existed in human beings; that reconciler and bond of union of their original nature, which seeks to make two, one, and to heal the divided nature of man. Every one of us is thus the half of what may be properly termed a man, and like a *psetta*[1] cut in two, is the imperfect portion of an entire whole, perpetually necessitated to seek the half belonging to him. Those who are a section of what was formerly one man and woman, are lovers of the female sex, and most of the adulterers, and those women who fall in love with men and intrigue with them, belong to this species. Those women who are a section of what in its unity contained two women, are not much attracted by the male sex, but have their inclinations principally engaged by their own. And the *Hetairistriae*[2] belong to this division.

---

[1] A kind of flat fish.
[2] Female homosexuals.

In vino veritas?

from *Fables*, Book IV, no. 16
by Phaedrus
(*c.* 15 BC–*c.* AD 50)

*The fabulist Phaedrus was a Thracian slave who was eventually given his
freedom and worked in the household of the emperor Augustus.*

Another person asked what cause in nature had produced lesbians [trib-
ades] and effeminate males. The old man explained:
Prometheus, creator of the human race, who made us all out of clay, which
is broken just as soon as it collides with Fortune – Prometheus had been
working all day on shaping as separate pieces the sexual parts that modesty
hides beneath clothing. He was intending soon to fit them on to their
respective bodies, when suddenly he was invited to dinner by Bacchus.
Late at night, he reeled back home having drunk large quantities of nectar.
Then, blundering drunkenly, with his brain fuddled with sleep, he attached
female privates to bodies of the masculine sex, and masculine members to
the females. So now desire finds its satisfaction in perverse pleasures.

Translated by Gillian Spraggs (1999)

Star signs for lesbians

from *Tetrabiblos*, by Ptolemy
(*c.* AD 100–*c.* 178)

*The extract below comes from Ptolemy's chapter on what he calls 'Diseases
of the Soul', amongst which he includes same-sex desire.*

When the sun and the moon are observed in conjunction with Venus
and Mars, but not in conjunction with any of the masculine signs of the

Zodiac, men become hyper-masculine and women also take on masculine characteristics, becoming more forceful and active of soul. But if either or both Mars and Venus is in conjunction with one of the masculine signs, then men become sexually over-active, and are adulterous, insatiable and always ready for shameful and lawless sexual acts, while the women are similarly disposed to unnatural unions, start ogling other women and are what we call *tribades*; for they incline towards females and act the part of men. If Venus only is in conjunction with a masculine sign, they do these things secretly and not openly; but if Mars is too, they do it openly, sometimes even referring to the women they are involved with as their 'wives'.

Betwixt and Between

Over the centuries the notion has persisted that homosexuals, whether male or female, occupy some space between 'real' men and women. We find the idea recurring constantly, across a range of disciplines and expressed in a variety of terms. 'Third sex', 'intermediate sex', 'invert', was the language of the emerging breed of nineteenth-century sexologists, although the concepts their words sought to define were already at least two and a half thousand years old. Here were creatures caught 'in the no-man's land of sex', in Radclyffe Hall's phrase. But this was not necessarily cause for regret, let alone apology. Homosexual apologists in the late nineteenth century drew upon new insights from another emerging discipline — social anthropology — to point to the honoured place which many cultures traditionally accord to their own betwixt-and-betweens: the shamans, seers, healers who often adopted the dress and customs of the opposite sex.

All the women you will encounter in this section are in some way caught betwixt and between. Some experience the gap between their female bodies and their troublingly 'male' desires, as the real Anne Lister and the fictional Mademoiselle de Maupin do. Others feel trapped in time, too late for a previous, more sympathetic historical period, too early for the one they hope will come. That sort of hope prompts one of the women whose case study, from Havelock Ellis's Sexual Inversion, *is reprinted here. Something of that feeling also seems to underlie Elizabeth Barrett Browning's sonnets to George Sand. Some female characters, ranging from the mid-eighteenth-century Miss Barnevelt to the mid-twentieth-century Miss Hampton, positively relish their 'intermediate' status and the freedoms it offers them.*

from *Gallathea* (1585)
JOHN LYLY (?1504–1606)

*Two girls disguised as boys (in order to avoid being sacrificed to Neptune) fall
in love, each believing the other is really male. Only the gods can resolve their
dilemma. Fittingly, it is Venus who proves that Love conquers all, and finds a
way to let it. Venus reminds us that she has already had to resolve a similar
difficulty in the case of two other women, Iphis and Ianthe, whose story is told
in Ovid's* Metamorphoses, *Book IX. Venus's solution is very similar to the
one wished for by Marie Maitland, the sixteenth-century Scottish poet, whose
work may be found in a later section of this book, 'Glimpses'.*

GALLATHEA: Unfortunate Gallathea, if this be Phyllida!

PHYLLIDA: Accursed Phyllida, if that be Gallathea!

GALLATHEA: And was thou all this while enamored of Phyllida, that
sweet Phyllida?

PHYLLIDA: And couldst thou dote upon the face of a maiden, thyself
being one, on the face of fair Gallathea?

NEPTUNE: Do you both, being maidens, love one another?

GALLATHEA: I had thought the habit agreeable with the sex, and so
burned in the fire of mine own fancies.

PHYLLIDA: I had thought that in the attire of a boy there could not
have lodged the body of a virgin, and so was inflamed with a sweet
desire which now I find a sour deceit.

DIANA: Now, things falling out as they do, you must leave these fond,
fond affections. Nature will have it so, necessity must.

GALLATHEA: I will never love any but Phyllida. Her love is engraven
in my heart with her eyes.

PHYLLIDA: Nor I any but Gallathea, whose faith is imprinted in my
thoughts by her words.

NEPTUNE: An idle choice, strange and foolish, for one virgin to dote on another, and to imagine a constant faith where there can be no cause of affection. How like you this, Venus?

VENUS: I like well and allow it. They shall both be possessed of their wishes, for never shall it be said that Nature or Fortune shall overthrow love and faith. Is your loves unspotted, begun with truth, continued with constancy, and not to be altered till death?

GALLATHEA: Die, Gallathea, if thy love be not so.

PHYLLIDA: Accursed be thou, Phyllida, if thy love be not so.

DIANA: Suppose all this, Venus; what then?

VENUS: Then shall it be seen that I can turn one of them to be a man, and that I will.

DIANA: Is it possible?

VENUS: What is to love or the mistress of love unpossible? Was it not Venus that did the like to Iphis and Ianthes? How say ye, are ye agreed, one to be a boy presently?

PHYLLIDA: I am content, so I may embrace Gallathea.

GALLATHEA: I wish it, so I may enjoy Phyllida.

MELEBEUS: Soft, daughter, you must know whether I will have you a son.

TITYRUS: Take me with you, Gallathea. I will keep you as I begat you, a daughter.

MELEBEUS: Tityrus, let yours be a boy, and if you will, mine shall not.

TITYRUS: Nay, mine shall not, for by that means my young son shall lose his inheritance.

MELEBEUS: Why, then get him to be made a maiden, and then there is nothing lost.

TITYRUS: If there be such changing, I would Venus could make my wife a man.

MELEBEUS: Why?

TITYRUS: Because she loves always to play with men.

VENUS: Well, you are both fond, therefore agree to this changing or suffer your daughters to endure hard chance.

MELEBEUS: How say you, Tityrus, shall we refer it to Venus?

TITYRUS: I am content, because she is a goddess.

VENUS: Neptune, you will not dislike it?

NEPTUNE: Not I.

VENUS: Nor you, Diana?

DIANA: Not I.

VENUS: Cupid shall not.

CUPID: I will not.

VENUS: Then let us depart. Neither of them shall know whose lot it shall be till they come to the church door. One shall be; doth it suffice?

PHYLLIDA: And satisfy us both, doth it not, Gallathea?

GALLATHEA: Yes, Phyllida.

from *Arcadia*
SIR PHILIP SIDNEY (1554–1586)

Philoclea, one of the two heroines of Sidney's Arcadia *(1590), has fallen in love with the Amazon, Zelmane, unaware that 'she' is really a prince in disguise. Philoclea's mother, Gynecia, has seen through Zelmane's disguise to the prince beneath. Sidney adds to the confusion by referring to Zelmane as 'she' for much of the narrative. The fixity or fluidity of gender is a recurring preoccupation in Renaissance thought and* Arcadia *is just one of many works of Renaissance literature in which hapless characters fall in and out of love with 'men' or 'women' who are not what they seem.*

For after that Zelmane had a while lived in the lodge with her and that her only being a noble stranger had bred a kind of heedful attention; her coming to that lonely place where she had nobody but her parents, a willingness of conversation, her wit and behaviour, a liking and silent admiration, at length the excellency of her natural gifts joined with the extreme shows she made of most devout honouring Philoclea (carrying thus, in one person, the only two bands of goodwill, loveliness and lovingness) brought forth in her heart a yielding to a most friendly affection; which when it had gotten so full possession of the keys of her mind that it would receive no message from her senses without that affection were the interpreter, then straight grew an exceeding delight still to be with her, with an unmeasurable liking of all that Zelmane did: matters being so turned in her that where at first, liking her manners did breed goodwill, now goodwill became the chief cause of liking her manners, so that within a while Zelmane was not prized for her demeanour but the demeanour was prized because it was Zelmane's.

Then followed that most natural effect of conforming herself to that which she did like, and not only wishing to be herself such another in all things, but to ground an imitation upon so much an esteemed authority; so that the next degree was to mark all Zelmane's doings, speeches, and fashions, and to take them into herself as a pattern of worthy proceeding. Which when once it was enacted not only by the commonalty of passions but agreed unto by her most noble thoughts, and that reason itself (not yet experienced in the issues of such matters) had granted his royal assent, then friendship, a diligent officer, took care to see the statute thoroughly observed. Then grew on that not only she did imitate the soberness of her countenance, the gracefulness of her speech, but even their particular gestures; so that as Zelmane did often eye her, she would often eye Zelmane; and as Zelmane's eyes would deliver a submissive but vehement desire in their look, she, though as yet she had not the desire in her, yet should her eyes answer in like piercing kindness of a look. Zelmane, as much as Gynecia's jealousy would suffer, desired to be near Philoclea; Philoclea, as much as Gynecia's jealousy would suffer, desired to be near Zelmane. If Zelmane took her hand and softly strained it, she also, thinking the knots of friendship ought to be mutual, would with a sweet fastness show she was loth to part from it. And if Zelmane sighed, she should sigh also; when Zelmane was sad, she deemed it wisdom and therefore she would be sad too. Zelmane's languishing countenance, with crossed arms and sometimes cast up eyes, she thought to have an excellent grace, and therefore she also willingly put on the same countenance, till at last, poor soul, ere she were aware, she accepted not only the badge but the service, not only the sign but the passion signified.

For whether it were that her wit in continuance did find that Zelmane's friendship was full of impatient desire having more than ordinary limits, and therefore she was content to second Zelmane though herself knew not the limits, or that in truth true love, well considered, have an infective

power, at last she fell in acquaintance with love's harbinger, wishing.
First she would wish that they two might live all their lives together,
like two of Diana's nymphs. But that wish she thought not sufficient,
because she knew there would be more nymphs besides them who also
would have their part in Zelmane. Then would she wish that she were
her sister, that such a natural band might make her more special to her.
But against that, she considered that, though being her sister, if she
happened to be married she should be robbed of her. Then grown bolder,
she would wish either herself or Zelmane a man, that there might succeed
a blessed marriage betwixt them. But when that wish had once displayed
his ensign in her mind, then followed whole squadrons of longings that
so it might be, with a main battle of mislikings and repinings against
their creation, that so it was not. Then dreams by night began to bring
more unto her than she durst wish by day, whereout waking did make
her know herself the better by the image of those fancies. But as some
diseases, when they are easy to be cured they are hard to be known,
but when they grow easy to be known they are almost impossible to be
cured, so the sweet Philoclea, while she might prevent it, she did not
feel it; now she felt it when it was past preventing, like a river, no
rampires being built against it till already it had overflowed. For now
indeed love pulled off his mask and showed his face unto her, and told
her plainly that she was his prisoner. Then needed she no more paint
her face with passions, for passions shone through her face: then her
rosy colour was often increased with extraordinary blushing, and so
another time, perfect whiteness descended to a degree of paleness; now
hot, then cold, desiring she knew not what, nor how, if she knew what.
[. . .]
At length with a whispering note to herself: 'O me unfortunate wretch,'
said she, 'what poisonous heats be these which thus torment me? How
hath the sight of this strange guest invaded my soul? Alas, what entrance
found this desire, or what strength had it thus to conquer me?' Then a
cloud passing between her sight and the moon, 'O Diana,' said she, 'I
would either the cloud that now hides the light of my virtue would as
easily pass away as you will quickly overcome this let, or else that you
were for ever thus darkened to serve for an excuse of my outrageous
folly.'

Then looking to the stars, which had perfectly as then beautified the clear sky: 'My parents,' said she, 'have told me that in these fair heavenly bodies there are great hidden deities which have their working in the ebbing and flowing of our estates. If it be so, then, O you stars, judge rightly of me, and if I have with wicked intent made myself a prey to fancy, or if by any idle lusts I framed my heart fit for such an impression, then let this plague daily increase in me till my name be made odious to womankind. But if extreme and unresistable violence have oppressed me, who will ever do any of you sacrifice, O you stars, if you do not succour me? No, no, you will not help me. No, no, you cannot help me: sin must be the mother and shame the daughter of my affection. And yet are these but childish objections, simple Philoclea; it is the impossibility that doth torment me: for unlawful desires are punished after the effect of enjoying, but unpossible desires are punished in the desire itself. O then, O ten times unhappy that I am, since where in all other hope kindleth love, in me despair should be the bellows of my affection; and of all despairs the most miserable which is drawn from impossibility. The most covetous man longs not to get riches out of a ground which never can bear anything. Why? Because it is impossible. The most ambitious wight vexeth not his wits to climb into heaven. Why? Because it is impossible. Alas, then, O love, why dost thou in thy beautiful sampler set such a work for my desire to take out, which is as much impossible?

'And yet alas, why do I thus condemn my fortune before I hear what she can say for herself? What do I, silly wench, know what love hath prepared for me? Do I not see my mother as well, at least as furiously as myself, love Zelmane, and should I be wiser than my mother? Either she sees a possibility in that which I think impossible, or else impossible loves need not misbecome me. And do I not see Zelmane (who doth not think a thought which is not first weighed by wisdom and virtue) doth not she vouchsafe to love me with like ardour? I see it; her eyes depose it to be true. What then? And if she can love poor me, shall I think scorn to love such a woman as Zelmane? Away then all vain examinations of why and how. Thou lovest me, excellent Zelmane, and I love thee.' And with that, embracing the very ground whereon she lay, she said to herself (for even to herself she was ashamed to speak it out in words) 'O my Zelmane, govern and direct me, for I am wholly given over unto thee.'

To the fair Clarinda, who made Love to me, imagin'd more than Woman
By Mrs B. [APHRA BEHN] (1640–1689)

Fair lovely Maid, or if that Title be
Too weak, too Feminine for Nobler thee,
Permit a Name that more Approaches Truth:
And let me call thee, Lovely Charming Youth.
This last will justifie my soft complaint,
While that may serve to lessen my constraint;
And without Blushes I the Youth persue,
When so much beauteous Woman is in view.
Against thy Charmes we struggle but in vain
With thy deluding Form thou giv'st us pain,
While the bright Nymph betrays us to the Swain.
In pity to our Sex sure thou wer't sent,
That we might Love, and yet be Innocent:
For sure no Crime with thee we can commit;
Or if we shou'd — thy Form excuses it.
For who, that gathers fairest Flowers believes
A Snake lies hid beneath the Fragrant Leaves.

Thou beauteous Wonder of a different kind,
Soft Cloris with the dear Alexis join'd;
When e'er the Manly part of thee, wou'd plead
Thou tempts us with the Image of the Maid,
While we the noblest Passions do extend
The Love to Hermes, Aphrodite the Friend.

*Anna Howe imagines life as a husband, in a
letter to her dearest friend, Clarissa*

from *Clarissa* (1747–1748)
SAMUEL RICHARDSON (1689–1761)

*In this extract, a female character shows a disquieting ability to imagine
what sort of wife she would want were she a man. No great feat, perhaps,
for a woman created by a male author; but as the next extract from Sarah
Scott's* A Journey Through Every Stage of Life *demonstrates, characters
created by female authors may also imagine, with extraordinary and unnerving vividness, life as a husband.*

I do assure you, my dear, were I a man, and a man who loved my quiet,
I would not have one of these managing wives on any consideration. I
would make it a matter of serious inquiry beforehand, whether my
mistress's qualifications, if I heard she was notable, were *masculine* or
feminine ones.

[...]

Indeed, my dear, I do not think a *man-woman* a pretty character at all:
And, as I said, were I a *man*, I would sooner choose for a dove, tho'
it were fit for nothing, but, as the play says, to go tame about house,
and breed, than a wife that is setting at work (my insignificant self *present*
perhaps) every busy hour my never-resting servants, those of the Stud
not excepted; and who, with a besom in her hand, as I may say, would
be continually filling me with apprehensions, that she wanted to sweep
me out of my own house as useless lumber.

Were indeed the mistress of the family, like the wonderful young
Lady I so *much* and so *justly* admire, to know how to confine herself
within her own respectable rounds of the needle, the pen, the house-
keeper's bills, the dairy for her amusement; to see the poor fed from
superfluities that *would* otherwise be wasted; and exert herself in all the
really useful branches of domestic management; then would she move
in her proper sphere; then would she render herself *amiably* useful, and
respectably necessary; then would she become the *mistress*-wheel of the

family (Whatever you think of your Anna Howe, I would not have her to be the *master*-wheel); and every-body would love her; as every-body did you, before your insolent brother came back, flush'd with his unmerited acquirements, and turn'd all things topsy-turvy.

Leonora imagines life as a husband

from A Journey Through Every Stage of Life (1754)
SARAH SCOTT (1723–1795)

Leonora, disguised as a clergyman, discovers that the Parish she has been offered comes with strings attached, in the shape of the patron's cast-off mistress. For one mad moment she almost thinks it might work . . .

Leonora was now compelled to listen to an Enumeration of all the Profits of the Living, and the Merits of the Lady who was to be tacked to it. The Gentleman expatiated on the Comforts of Matrimony with great Eloquence; and sketched in so lively a manner a snug Parson's Life, that *Leonora* almost saw herself settled in a small House, with more Sash-window than Wall; a little Garden of Ever-greens before it, a Church shadowed with solemn Yews behind, and extended along each Side a Church-yard full of Tombstones, which at the same time shew the Poverty and Vanity of the Relations of the Dead; and a cleanly mincing Wife, with a Multitude of Cherry-cheek'd Children within the House thus properly situated. She excused herself from this delectable State so well drawn out, with all the Civility she could, and left both the Benefices to a better qualified Incumbent.

Harriet Byron encounters Miss Barnevelt

from *Sir Charles Grandison*, Volume I,
Letter X (1754)
SAMUEL RICHARDSON

In his later epistolary novel, Sir Charles Grandison *(one of Jane Austen's favourites), Richardson introduces another, this time one-sided, female passion – that of the 'mannish' Miss Barnevelt for the (usually) horrified heroine, Harriet Byron. It is almost as if in this novel Richardson makes grotesque the depths of female emotion which have made him and Lovelace, his fictional rake, uncomfortable in* Clarissa.

The following extracts chart something of Miss Barnevelt's quixotic progress. The portrait of a 'masculine' woman of the period is interesting in itself, but even more interesting is the ambivalence of Harriet Byron's response. Despite her protestations of embarrassment and shock, Harriet clearly enjoys some aspects of Miss Barnevelt's attentions and also takes a narcissistic pleasure in imagining Miss Barnevelt's description of her own charms. The distinctions between loving oneself and being beloved frequently blur when both parties are women.

Letter X
Miss Byron; In Continuation

Friday Night.

Some amusement, my Lucy, the day has afforded: indeed, more than I could have wished.

[. . .]

Lady Betty received us most politely. She had company with her, to whom she introduced us, and presented me in a very advantageous character.

Shall I tell you how their first appearance struck me, and what I have since heard and observed of them.

The first I shall mention was Miss CANTILLON; very pretty, but visibly proud, affected and conceited.

The second Miss CLEMENTS; plain, but of a fine understanding, improved by reading; and who, having no personal advantages to be vain of, has, by the cultivation of her mind, obtained a preference in every one's opinion over the fair Cantillon.

The third was Miss BARNEVELT, a lady of masculine features, and whose mind belyed not those features; for she has the character of being loud, bold, free, even fierce when opposed; and affects at all times such airs of contempt for her own sex, that one almost wonders at her condescending to wear petticoats.

[. . .]

Nobody, it seems, thinks of a *husband* for Miss Barnevelt. She is sneeringly spoken of rather as a *young fellow* than as a woman; and who will one day look out for a *wife* for herself. One reason, indeed, she every where gives, for being satisfied with being a woman; which is, *that she cannot be married to a* WOMAN.

An odd creature, my dear. But see what women get by going out of character: like the bats in the fable, they are looked upon as mortals of a doubtful species, hardly owned by either, and laughed at by both.

This was the company, and all the company, besides us, that Lady Betty expected. But mutual civilities had hardly passed, when Lady Betty, having been called out, returned, introducing, as a gentleman who would be acceptable to every one, SIR HARGRAVE POLLEXFEN. 'He is,' whispered she to me, as he saluted the rest of the company in a very gallant manner, 'a young baronet of a very large estate; the greatest part of which has lately come to him by the death of a grandmother, and two uncles, all very rich.'

When he was presented to me by name, and I to him – 'I think myself very happy,' said he, 'in being admitted to the presence of a young lady so celebrated for her grace of person and mind.' – 'Much did I hear, when I was at the last Northampton races, of Miss Byron; but little did I expect to find report fall so short of what I see.'

Miss Cantillon bridled, played with her fan, and looked as if she thought herself slighted; a little scorn intermingled with the airs she gave herself.

Miss Clements smiled, and looked pleased, as if she enjoyed good-naturedly, a compliment made to one of the sex which she adorns by the goodness of her heart.

nevelt said she had, from the moment I first entered, beheld
the eye of a lover: and freely taking my hand, squeezed it.
ng creature!' said she; as if addressing a country innocent, and
pe.. ,s expecting me to be covered with blushes and confusion.
[. . .]

Letter XIII
Miss Byron; In Continuation

[*In the midst of a spirited debate about the virtues, or not, of a classical
education, Miss Byron challenges Mr Walden's assertion that he does 'insist
upon it, that without the knowledge of the learned languages, a man cannot
understand his own.'*]

I opposed Shakespeare to this assertion: but wished, on this occasion,
that I had not been a party in this debate; for the baronet was even
noisy in his applauses of what I said; and the applauses of empty
minds always give one suspicion of having *incurred* it by one's own
forwardness.

He drowned the voice of Mr. Walden, who two or three times was
earnest to speak; but not finding himself heard, drew up his mouth as
if to a contemptuous whistle, shrugged his shoulders, and sat collected
in his conscious worthiness: his eyes, however, were often cast upon the
pictures that hung round the room, as much better objects than the living
ones before him.

But what extremely disconcerted me was a freedom of Miss Barnevelt's, taken upon what I last said, and upon Mr. Walden's hesitation,
and Sir Hargrave's applauses: she professd that I was able to bring
her own sex into reputation with her. 'Wisdom, as I call it,' said she,
'notwithstanding what you have modestly alledged to depreciate your
own, when it proceeds through teeth of ivory, and lips of coral, receives
a double grace.' And then clasping one of her mannish arms around me,
she kissed my cheek.

I was surprised, and offended; and with the more reason, as Sir Hargrave,
rising from his seat, declared, that since merit was to be approved in that
manner, he thought himself obliged to follow so good an example.

I stood up, and said – 'Surely, Sir, my compliance with the rest of the company, too much I fear at my own expence, calls rather for civility than freedom from a gentleman. I beg, Sir Hargrave —' There I stopt; and I am sure looked greatly in earnest.

He stood suspended till I had done speaking, and then, bowing, sat down again: but, as Mr. Reeves told me afterwards, he whispered a great oath in his ear, and declared, that he beheld with transport his future wife, and cursed himself if he would ever have another: vowing in the same whisper, that were a thousand men to stand in his way, he would not scruple any means to remove them.

Miss Barnevelt only laughed at the freedom she had taken with me. She is a loud and fearless laugher. She hardly knows *how* to smile: for as soon as anything catches her fancy, her voice immediately bursts her lips, and widens her mouth to it's full extent. – Forgive me, Lucy, I believe I am spiteful.

Just here, Lucy, I laid down my pen, and stept to the glass, to see whether I could not please myself with a wise frown or two; at least with a solemnity of countenance, that, occasionally, I might dash with it my childishness of look; which certainly encouraged this freedom of Miss Barnevelt. But I could not please myself. My muscles have never been used to any thing but smiling: so favoured, so beloved, by every one of my friends; a heart so grateful for all their favours – how can I learn now to frown, or even to look grave!
[. . .]

Letter XV
Miss Byron; In Continuation

Monday, Feb 6.

[*In this letter to her beloved Lucy Selby, Miss Byron has been amusing herself in imagining how Lady Betty, Miss Clements, and Miss Cantillon might describe her when writing to their own friends. And Miss Barnevelt . . . ?*]

Miss Barnevelt would, perhaps, thus write to her Lucy – To *her* Lucy – Upon my word I will not let her have a Lucy – she shall have a brother *man* to write to, not a woman, and he shall have a fierce name.

We will suppose that she also had been describing the rest of the company.

'Well, but my dear Bombardino, I am now to give you a description of Miss Byron. 'Tis the softest, gentlest, smiling rogue of a girl – I protest I could five or six times have kissed her, for what she said, and the manner she spoke in – for she has been used to prate; a favoured child in her own family, one may easily see that. Yet so *prettily* loth to speak till spoken to! – such a blushing little rogue! –'Tis a dear girl! and I wished twenty times, as I sat by her, that I had been a man for her sake. Upon my honour, Bombardino, I believe if I had, I should have caught her up, popt her under one of my arms, and run away with her.'

Some thing like this, my Lucy, did Miss Barnevelt once say.
[. . .]

Belinda encounters Mrs Freke

from *Belinda* (1801)
by MARIA EDGEWORTH (1768–1849)

Even Harriot Freke fails to fluster the calm and practical heroine of Belinda, *a novel by the Anglo-Irish writer, Maria Edgeworth. Mrs Freke spends much of the novel in men's clothes, for one reason or another. Despite her chosen attire, her name and her attempt to elope with Belinda, she is not anything as unambiguous as a lesbian or even a Sapphist.*

Although Mrs Freke is not a feminist, has no sense of female solidarity and is not even basically likeable, there is something disturbing about the viciousness with which her creator punishes her for transgressing against gender norms. Caught in a man-trap set for poachers, she is so badly injured that she will 'never again be able to appear to advantage in men's clothes'.

Belinda was alone, and reading, when Mrs Freke dashed into the room.

'How do, dear creature!' cried she, stepping up to her, and shaking hands with her boisterously, 'How do? Glad to see you, 'faith! Been long here? Tremendously hot to day!'

She flung herself upon the sofa beside Belinda, threw her hat upon the table, and then continued speaking.

'And how d'ye go on here, poor child! 'God! I'm glad you're alone. Expected to find you encompassed by a whole host of the righteous. Give me credit for my courage in coming to deliver you out of their hands. Luttridge and I had such compassion upon you, when we heard you were close prisoner here! I swore to set the distressed damsel free, in spite of all the dragons in Christendom. So let me carry you off in triumph in my unicorn, and leave these good people to stare when they come home from their sober walk, and find you gone. There's nothing I like so much as to make good people stare – I hope you're of my way o'thinking. You don't look as if you were though – but I never mind young ladies' looks – always give the lie to their thoughts. Now we talk o'looks. Never saw you look so well in my life – as handsome as an angel! And so much the better for me. Do you know, I've a bet of twenty guineas on your head – on your face, I mean. There's a young bride at Harrowgate, lady H—, they're all mad about her, the men swear she's the handsomest woman in England, and I swear I know one ten times as handsome. They've dared me to make good my word, and I've pledged myself to produce my beauty at the next ball, and to pit her against their belle for any money. Most votes carry it. I'm willing to double my bet since I've seen you again. Come, had not we best be off? Now don't refuse me and make speeches – you know that's all nonsense – I'll take all the blame upon myself.'

Belinda, who had not been suffered to utter a word whilst Mrs Freke ran on in this strange manner, looked in unfeigned astonishment; but when she found herself seized and dragged towards the door, she drew back with a degree of gentle firmness that astonished Mrs Freke. With a smiling countenance, but a steady tone, she said, that she was sorry Mrs Freke's knight-errantry should not be exerted in a better cause, for that she was neither a prisoner, nor a distressed damsel.

'And will you make me lose my bet?' cried Mrs Freke. 'O, at all events you must come to the ball! I'm down for it. But I'll not press it now, because you're frightened out of your poor little wits, I see, at the

bare thoughts of doing any thing out of rule, by these good people.
Well, well! it shall be managed for you – leave that to me. I'm used to
managing for cowards. Pray tell me, you and lady Delacour are off, I
understand? Give ye joy! She and I were once great friends; that is to
say, I had over her "that power which strong minds have over weak
ones", but she was too weak for me – one of those people that have
neither courage to be good, nor to be bad.'

'The courage to be bad,' said Belinda, 'I believe, indeed, she does
not possess.'

Mrs Freke stared. 'Why, I heard you had quarrelled with her!'

'If I had,' said Belinda, 'I hope that I should still do justice to her
merits. It is said that people are apt to suffer more by their friends than
their enemies. I hope that will never be the case with lady Delacour, as
I confess that I have been one of her friends.'

''Gad, I like your spirit – you don't want courage, I see, to fight
even for your enemies. You are just the kind of girl I admire – I see
you've been prejudiced against me by lady Delacour. But whatever
stories she may have trumped up, the truth of the matter is this;
there's no living with her she's so jealous – so ridiculously jealous – of
that lord of hers, for whom all the time she hasn't the impudence
to pretend to care more than I do for the sole of my boot,' said Mrs
Freke, striking it with her whip, 'but she hasn't the courage to give him
tit for tat. Now this is what I call weakness. Pray, how do she and
Clarence Hervey go on together? Are they out o'the hornbook of pla-
tonics yet?'

'Mr Hervey was not in town when I left it,' said Belinda.

'Was not he? Ho! ho! He's off then! Ay, so I prophesied. She's not
the thing for him. He has some strength of mind – some soul – above
vulgar prejudices. So must a woman be to hold him. He was caught at
first by her grace and beauty, and that sort of stuff; but I knew it could
not last – knew she'd dilly dally with Clary, till he would turn upon
his heel and leave her there.'

'I fancy that you are entirely mistaken both with respect to Mr Hervey
and lady Delacour,' Belinda very seriously began to say, but Mrs Freke
interrupted her, and ran on –

'No! no! no! I'm not mistaken; Clarence has found her out. She's a *very* woman – *that* he could forgive her, and so could I. But she's a *mere* woman – and that he can't forgive – no more can I.'

There was a kind of drollery about Mrs Freke, which, with some people, made the odd things she said pass for wit. Humour she really possessed; and when she chose it, she could be diverting to those who like buffoonery in women. She had set her heart upon winning Belinda over to her party. She began by flattery of her beauty; but as she saw that this had no effect, she next tried what could be done by insinuating that she had a high opinion of her understanding, by talking to her as an *esprit fort*.

'For my part,' said she, 'I own I should like a strong devil better than a weak angel.'

'You forget,' said Belinda, 'that it is not Milton, but Satan, who says, "Fallen spirit, to be weak is to be miserable".'

'You read I see! I did not know you were a reading girl. So did I once! but I never read now. Books only spoil the originality of genius. Very well for those who can't think for themselves – but when one has made up one's opinions, there is no use in reading.'

'But to *make* them up,' replied Belinda, 'may it not be useful?'

'Of no use upon earth to minds of a certain class. You, who can think for yourself, should never read.'

'But I read that I may think for myself.'

'Only ruin your understanding, trust me. Books are full of trash – nonsense. Conversation is worth all the books in the world.'

'And is there never any nonsense in conversation?'

*Miss Lister and Miss Pickford get the
measure of each other*

from the Diaries of Anne Lister
(1791–1840)

*It is rare that we are lucky enough to be able to know as much about the
inner lives of women from earlier historical periods as we know of Anne
Lister. In her voluminous diaries, this Yorkshire heiress left an unusually
frank and self-questioning account of her growing awareness that her own
sexual and emotional life would always be centred on other women. Writing
often in code, she records particular wooings and seductions, affairs and
partings, the ebb and flow of desire. She also provides us with many, often
very entertaining, insights into the practical day-to-day difficulties of living
a lesbian life, not only in her native Yorkshire but also in Europe. We owe
a great deal to the Yorkshire historian Helena Whitbread, who has decoded
and edited two volumes of material from the Diaries,* I Know My Own
Heart *(1988) and* No Priest But Love *(1992). In the passage which follows
we see the beginnings of one particular courtship dance, between Anne Lister
and Miss Pickford (known to her friends as 'Frank'). That redoubtable old
enemy, the fiercely anti-lesbian Roman satirist Juvenal, proves useful here,
as he so often did for women placed as the Misses Lister and Pickford find
themselves.*

Sunday 16 February [Halifax]
Called at the Saltmarshes' . . . I spoke chiefly in favour of Miss Pickford.
They think her blue & masculine. She is called Frank Pickford. She
frightens Emma & seems to enjoy doing so. Miss Pickford is certainly
like a gentle-woman & clever, to neither of which can Emma, or the
people here, lay claim. Miss Pickford's friend, Miss Threlfall, has West
India property. It was 5 or 6, or about 5 hundred a year, but has fallen
to almost nothing.

Monday 17 February [Halifax]

Got to the lecture room at 12.10 by the old church . . . Sat next to Miss Pickford as usual . . . How I can still run after the ladies! She seems sensible & in my present dearth of people to speak [with], I should well enough like to know more of her. I talk a little to her just before & after the lecture &, if she were young & pretty, should certainly scrape acquaintance but, all things considered, I must be cautious. I have no house to ask her to. I must hope for some society in days to come.

Wednesday 19 February [Halifax]

Miss Pickford came up to me in the lecture room . . . I said I should be most happy to call upon her but it was quite out of my power to shew her any civility or attention under present circumstances &, not visiting her sister, there was a delicacy & awkwardness in the thing, but was glad to have met her at the lectures & should always be happy when any casualty gave me the pleasure of seeing her. She said she had often thought I should be congenial with herself. Had moved to me & tried all ways to renew our acquaintance 1st formed 9 or 10 years ago (in 1813) at Bath, but she found it would not do. Thought I had quite forgotten her, did not know her, & she had given up the hope of succeeding. I said I had been asked 2 or 3 times to meet her & had always refused, not wishing to increase my acquaintances at present, but I was glad I had not known what I had lost . . .

Asked Miss Pickford if she should return in a chair. No. Offered to walk back with her. Left her a moment to order the gig, which was waiting for me, to follow. On its beginning to rain a little, said I should ask her to take a seat with me in the gig but I had a young horse, only in the 2nd time. She said she had no fear & we both drove off. Among other things, I noticed Mr W—'s having called the air 'she'. Miss Pickford spoke of the moon being made masculine by some nations, for instance, by the Germans. I smiled & said the moon had tried both sexes, like old Tiresius, but that one could not make such an observation to every one. Of course she remembered the story? She said yes. I am not quite certain, tho, whether she did or not. 'Tis not everyone who would (*vid.* Ovid *Metamorphoses*). This led us to talk of saying just what came uppermost, sure that one's meaning would always be properly taken. She held out her hand to shake hands. I set her down at Mrs Wilcox's gate & we parted very good friends.

Saturday 26 July [Halifax]

At 10¼, went into the stables. The plasterer there (Wm. Eden) painting a darkish drab – quite a wrong colour. Did not sufficiently fill up the worm-eaten holes in the wood. Staid there painting these parts over again myself till 12.40, then called in because Miss Pickford had called . . . She rather fought off on the subject of Miss Threlfall, then allowed, or rather, encour-aged it a little, that I told her she coquetted on this subject, & she did not deny that perhaps she did do so; that my remark was not unjust. We had been talking about being whimmy. I said I believed the people here thought me so. She had heard this, & that I did not go to the Saltmarshes' so often as I used to do. I excused myself that I really had not time. I said I was more whimmy in speech & appearance than reality. We agreed there were some subjects one could not be whimmy upon. Not, for instance, in early-formed close connections. The tie was strong. Said Miss Pickford, 'I could not be so, for I know I could break [Miss] Threlfall's heart.' I took no notice of this but thought to myself, more than ever, what the connection between them must be. Miss Pickford has read the Sixth Satyr [*sic*] of Juvenal. She understands these matters well enough.

Meeting Mademoiselle de Maupin

from *Mademoiselle de Maupin* (1833)
THÉOPHILE GAUTIER (1811–1872)

The following extracts come from one of the most influential novels of the nineteenth century, Théophile Gautier's Mademoiselle de Maupin. *Often called the 'Bible of Decadence', it was one of the first books Oscar Wilde asked to be allowed to have in prison.*

Set in a French château and an Arcadian landscape, the novel looks back to Shakespeare's Forest of Arden and forwards to the perplexities of gender explored and celebrated in Virginia Woolf's Orlando.

Briefly, Mademoiselle de Maupin, masquerading as the mysterious chevalier, Théodore de Serannes, has won the hearts of a pair of siblings — a brother, Alcibiades, and his sister, Rosette: a situation fraught with difficulties, some of which emerge in the first passage below.

She had drunk a few drops of Crème des Barbades, with a glass of Canary, and I about as much. It was certainly not a great deal; but it was sufficient to enliven a couple of women accustomed to drink scarcely anything stronger than water. Rosette leaned backwards, throwing herself across my arm in very amorous fashion. She had cast aside her mantle, and the upper part of her bosom, strained and stretched by this arched position, could be seen; it was enchantingly delicate and transparent in tone, while its shape was one of marvellous daintiness and solidity combined. I contemplated her for some time with indefinable emotion and pleasure, and the reflection occurred to me that men were more favoured in their loves than we, seeing that we gave them possession of the most charming treasures while they had nothing similar to offer us.

What a pleasure it must be to let their lips wander over this smooth fine skin, and these rounded curves which seem to go out to meet the kiss and challenge it! this satin flesh, these undulating and mutually involving lines, this silky hair so soft to the touch; what exhaustless sources of delicate voluptuousness which we do not possess in common with men! Our caresses can scarcely be other than passive, and yet it is a greater pleasure to give than to receive.

These are remarks which undoubtedly I should not have made last year, and I might have seen all the bosoms and shoulders in the world without caring whether their shape was good or bad; but, since I have laid aside the dress belonging to my sex and have lived with young men, a feeling which was unknown to me has developed within me: the feeling of beauty. Women are usually denied it, I know not why, for at first sight they would seem better able to judge of it than men; but as they are the possessors of beauty, and self-knowledge is more difficult than that of any other description, it is not surprising that they know nothing at all about it.

Commonly, if one woman thinks another woman pretty, you may be sure that the latter is very ugly, and that no man will take any notice of her. On the other hand, all women whose beauty and grace are extolled by men are unanimously considered abominable and affected by the whole petticoated tribe; there are cries and clamours without end. If I were what I appear to be, I should be guided in my choice by nothing else, and the disapprobation of women would be a sufficient certificate of beauty for me.

At present I love and know beauty; the dress I wear separates me from my sex, and takes away from me all species of rivalry; I am able to judge it better than another. I am no longer a woman, but I am not yet a man, and desire will not blind me so far as to make me take puppets for idols; I can see coldly without any prejudice for or against, and my position is as perfectly disinterested as it could possibly be.

The length and delicacy of the eyelashes, the transparency of the temples, the limpidity of the crystalline, the curvings of the ear, the tone and quality of the hair, the aristocracy of foot and hand, the more or less slender joints of leg and wrist, a thousand things of which I used to take no heed, but which constitute real beauty and prove purity of race, guide me in my estimates, and scarcely admit of a mistake. I believe that if I had said of a woman: 'Indeed, she is not bad,' you might accept her with your eyes shut.

By a very natural consequence I understand pictures better than I did before, and though I have but a very superficial tincture of the masters, it would be difficult to make me pass a bad work as a good one; I find a deep and singular charm in this study; for, like everything else in the world, beauty, moral or physical, requires to be studied, and cannot be penetrated all at once.

But let us return to Rosette; the transition from this subject to her is not a difficult one, for they are two ideas which are bound up in each other.

As I have said, the fair one had thrown herself back across my arm and her head was resting against my shoulder; emotion shaded her beautiful cheeks with a tender rose-colour which was admirably set off by the deep black of a very coquettishly placed little patch; her teeth gleamed through her smile like raindrops in the depths of a poppy, and the humid splendour of her large eyes was still further heightened by her half-drooping lashes; a ray of light caused a thousand metallic lustres to play on her silky clouded hair, some locks of which had escaped and were rolling in ringlets along her plump round neck, and relieving its warm whiteness; a few little downy hairs, more mutinous than the rest, had got loose from the mass, and were twisting themselves in capricious spirals, gilded with singular reflections, and, traversed by the light, assuming all the shades of the prism: you would have thought that they were such golden threads as surround the heads of the virgins in the old pictures. We both kept silence, and I amused myself with tracing her little azure-blue veins through the nacreous transparency of her temples, and the soft insensible depression of the down at the extremities of her eyebrows.

The fair one seemed to be inwardly meditating and to be lulling herself in dreams of infinite voluptuousness; her arms hung down along her body as undulating and as soft as loosened scarfs; her head bent back more and more as though the muscles supporting it had been cut or were too feeble for their task. She had gathered up her two little feet beneath her petticoat, and had succeeded in crouching down altogether in the corner of the lounge that I was occupying, in such a way that, although it was a very narrow piece of furniture, there was a large empty space on the other side.

Her easy, supple body modelled itself on mine like wax, following its external outline with the greatest possible accuracy: water would not have crept into all the sinuosity of line with more exactness. Clinging thus to my side, she suggested the double stroke which painters give their drawings on the side of the shadow, in order to render them more free and full. Only with a woman in love can there be such undulations and entwinings. Ivy and willow are a long way behind.

The soft warmth of her body penetrated through her garments and mine; a thousand magnetic currents streamed around her; her whole life seemed to have left her altogether and to have entered into me. Every minute she was more languishing, expiring, yielding; a light sweat stood in beads upon her lustrous brow; her eyes grew moist, and two or three times she made as though she would raise her hands to hide them; but half-way her wearied arms fell back upon her knees, and she could not succeed in doing so; — a big tear overflowed from her eyelid and rolled along her burning cheek where it was soon dried.

My situation was becoming very embarrassing and tolerably ridiculous; I felt that I must look enormously stupid, and this provoked me extremely, although no alternative was in my power. Enterprising conduct was forbidden me, and such was the only kind that would have been suitable. I was too sure of meeting with no resistance to risk it, and I was, in fact, at my wit's end. To pay compliments and repeat madrigals would have been excellent at the beginning, but nothing would have appeared more insipid at the stage that we had reached; to get up and go out would have been unmannerly in the extreme; and besides I am not sure that Rosette would not have played the part of Potiphar's wife, and held me by the corner of my cloak.

I could not have assigned any virtuous motive for my resistance; and then, I confess it to my shame, the scene, equivocal as its nature was for me, was not without a charm which detained me more than it should have done; this ardent desire kindled me with its flame, and I was really sorry to be unable to satisfy it. I even wished to be, as I actually appeared to be, a man, that I might crown this love, and I greatly regretted that Rosette was deceived. My breathing became hurried, I felt blushes rising to my face, and I was little less troubled than my poor lover. The idea of our similitude in sex gradually faded away, leaving behind only a vague idea of pleasure; my gaze grew dim, my lips trembled, and, had Rosette been a man instead of what she was, she would assuredly have made a very easy conquest of me.

At last, unable to bear it any longer, she got up abruptly with a sort of spasmodic movement, and began to walk about the room with great activity; then she stopped before the mirror and adjusted some locks of her hair which had lost their folds. During this promenade I cut a poor figure, and scarcely knew how to look.

She stopped before me and appeared to reflect.

She thought that it was only a desperate timidity that restrained me, and that I was more of a schoolboy than she had thought at first. Beside herself and excited to the last degree of amorous exasperation, she would try one supreme effort and stake all on the result at the risk of losing the game.

She came up to me, sat down on my knees more quickly than lightning, passed her arms round my neck, crossed her hands behind my head,

and clung with her lips to mine in a furious embrace; I felt her half-naked
and rebellious bosom bounding against my breast, and her twined fingers
twitching in my hair. A shiver ran through my whole body, and my
heart beat violently.

Rosette did not release my mouth; her lips enveloped mine, her teeth
struck against my teeth, our breaths were mingled. I drew back for an
instant, and turned my head aside two or three times to avoid this kiss;
but a resistless attraction made me again advance, and I returned it with
nearly as much ardour as she had given it. I scarcely know how it would
all have ended had not a loud barking been heard outside the door,
together with the sound of scratching feet. The door yielded, and a
handsome white greyhound came yelping and gambolling into the cot.

Rosette rose up suddenly, and with a bound sprang to the end of the
room. The handsome white greyhound leaped gleefully and joyously
about her, and tried to reach her hands in order to lick them; she was
so much agitated that she found great difficulty in arranging her mantle
upon her shoulders.

This greyhound was her brother Alcibiades's favourite dog; it never
left him, and whenever it appeared, its master to a certainty was not far
off; this is what had so greatly frightened poor Rosette.

In fact Alcibiades himself entered a minute later, booted and spurred,
and whip in hand. 'Ah! there you are,' said he; 'I have been looking for
you for an hour past, and I should certainly not have found you had
not my good greyhound Snug unearthed you in your hiding place.' And
he cast a half-serious, half-playful look upon his sister which made her
blush up to the eyes. 'Apparently you must have had very knotty subjects
to treat of, to retire into such profound solitude? You were no doubt
talking about theology and the twofold nature of the soul?'

'Oh! dear no; our occupation was not nearly so sublime; we were
eating cakes and talking about the fashions — that is all.'

'I don't believe a word of it; you appeared to me to be deep in
some sentimental dissertation; but to divert you from your vaporish
conversation, I think that it would be a good thing if you came and
took a ride with me. I have a new mare that I want to try. You shall
ride her as well, Théodore, and we will see what can be made of her.'

We went out all three together, he giving me his arm, and I giving mine to Rosette. The expressions on our faces were singularly different. Alcibiades looked thoughtful, I quite at ease, and Rosette excessively annoyed.

*　　*　　*

[Yet finally, it seems, Mademoiselle de Maupin satisfies the desire of both brother and sister. Like Shakespeare's Rosalind (a role she has played during the course of the novel), she acts the parts of both man and woman — or does she . . . ?]

Our fair reader would certainly pout at her lover if we revealed to her the formidable total of the lessons imparted by D'Albert's love, assisted by Rosalind's curiosity. Let her recall the best occupied and most charming of her nights, the night when . . . the night which would be remembered a hundred thousand days, did not death come before; let her lay her book aside and compute on the tips of her pretty white fingers how many times she was loved by him who loved her most, and thus fill up the void left by us in this glorious history.

Instead of returning to her own room Rosalind entered Rosette's. What she there said and did I have never been able to ascertain, although I have made the most conscientious researches. Neither in Graciosa's papers, nor those belonging to D'Albert and Silvio have I found anything having relation to this visit. Only, a maid of Rosette's informed me of the following singular circumstance: the bed was disturbed and tossed, and bore the impress of two bodies. Further, she showed me two pearls, exactly similar to those worn in his hair by Théodore when acting the part of Rosalind. She had found them in the bed when making it. I leave this remark to the reader's sagacity, and give him liberty to draw thence any inferences that he likes; for myself, I have made a thousand conjectures about it, each more unreasonable than the rest, and so absurd that I really dare not write them even in the most virtuously periphrastic style.

It was quite noon when Théodore left Rosette's room.

He did not appear at dinner or supper. D'Albert and Rosette did not seem at all surprised at this. He went to bed very early, and the following morning, as soon as it was light, without giving notice to any one, he saddled his page's horse and his own, and left the mansion, telling a footman that they were not to wait dinner for him, and that he might perhaps not return for a few days.

A most unusual creature

from *Lodore* (1835)
MARY SHELLEY (1797–1851)

Fanny Derham is not the heroine of Mary Shelley's Lodore; *she is a woman so unusual for her time that her story cannot yet be told, as the narrator insists in the closing paragraph of the novel. Fanny is independent, determined never to marry, highly educated (she reads Plato in the original Greek), and the nearest thing to a lesbian character Mary Shelley ever created: a woman 'more made to be loved by her own sex than by the opposite one'. The three extracts given here describe the contrast between Fanny's education for independence and the heroine's education for marriage; the results of Fanny's education, as seen in conversation with the heroine, Ethel; and the conclusion of the novel.*

Lodore had formed his ideal of what a woman ought to be, of what he had wished to find his wife, and sought to mould his daughter accordingly. Mr. Derham contemplated the duties and objects befitting an immortal soul, and had educated his child for the performance of them. The one fashioned his offspring to be the wife of a frail human being, and instructed her to be yielding, and to make it her duty to devote herself to his happiness, and to obey his will. The other sought to guard his from all weakness, to make her complete in herself, and to render her independent and self-sufficing. Born to poverty as Fanny was, it was thus only that she could find happiness in rising above her sphere; and, besides, a sense of pride, surviving his sense of injury, caused him to wish that his child should set her heart on higher things, than the distinctions and advantages of riches or rank; so that if ever brought into collision with his own family, she could look down with calm superiority on the 'low ambition' of the wealthy. While Ethel made it her happiness and duty to give herself away with unreserved prodigality to him, whom she thought had every claim to her entire devotion; Fanny zealously guarded her individuality, and would have scorned herself could she have been brought to place the treasures of her soul at the disposal of any power, except those moral laws which it was her earnest endeavour never to transgress. Religion, reason, and justice – these were the landmarks of her life. She was kind-hearted, generous, and true – so also was Ethel; but the one was guided by the tenderness of her heart, while the other consulted her understanding, and would have died rather than have acted contrary to its dictates.

*　　　*　　　*

'And thus you foster sorrow, and waste your life in vain regrets?'

'Pardon me! I do not waste my life,' replied Fanny, with her sunny smile; – 'nor am I unhappy – far otherwise. An ardent thirst for know-ledge, is as the air I breathe; and the acquisition of it, is pure and unalloyed happiness. I aspire to be useful to my fellow-creatures: but that is a consideration for the future, when fortune shall smile on me; now I have but one passion; it swallows up every other; it dwells with my darling books, and is fed by the treasures of beauty and wisdom which they contain.'

Ethel could not understand. Fanny continued: – 'I aspire to be useful; – sometimes I think I am – once I know I was. I was my father's almoner.

'We lived in a district where there was a great deal of distress, and a great deal of oppression. We had no money to give, but I soon found that determination and earnestness will do much. I[t] was my father's lesson, that I should never fear any thing but myself. He taught me to penetrate, to anatomize, to purify my motives; but once assured of my own integrity, to be afraid of nothing. Words have more power than any one can guess; it is by words that the world's great fight, now in these civilized times, is carried on; I never hesitated to use them, when I fought any battle for the miserable and oppressed. People are so afraid to speak, it would seem as if half our fellow-creatures were born with deficient organs; like parrots they can repeat a lesson, but their voice fails them, when that alone is wanting to make the tyrant quail.'

As Fanny spoke, her blue eyes brightened, and a smile irradiated her face; these were all the tokens of enthusiasm she displayed, yet her words moved Ethel strangely, and she looked on her with wonder as a superior being. Her youth gave grace to her sentiments, and were an assurance of their sincerity. She continued: –

'I am becoming flighty, as my mother calls it; but, as I spoke, many scenes of cottage distress passed through my memory, when, holding my father's hand, I witnessed his endeavours to relieve the poor. That is all over now – he is gone, and I have but one consolation – that of endeavouring to render myself worthy to rejoin him in a better world. It is this hope that impels me continually and without any flagging of spirit, to cultivate my understanding and to refine it. O what has this life to give, as worldlings describe it, worth one of those glorious emotions, which raise me from this petty sphere, into the sun-bright regions of mind, which my father inhabits! I am rewarded even here by the elevated feelings which the authors, whom I love so passionately, inspire; while I converse each day with Plato, and Cicero, and Epictetus, the world, as it is, passes from before me like a vain shadow.'

These enthusiastic words were spoken with so calm a manner, and in so equable a voice, that there seemed nothing strange nor exaggerated in them. It is vanity and affectation that shock, or any manifestation of feeling not in accordance with the real character. But while we follow our natural bent, and only speak that which our minds spontaneously inspire, there is a harmony, which, however novel, is never grating. Fanny Derham spoke of things, which, to use her own expression, were to her as the air she breathed, and the simplicity of her manner entirely obviated the wonder which the energy of her expressions might occasion.

Such a woman as Fanny was more made to be loved by her own sex than by the opposite one. Superiority of intellect, joined to acquisitions beyond those usual even to men; and both announced with frankness, though without pretension, forms a kind of anomaly little in accord with masculine taste. Fanny could not be the rival of women, and, therefore, all her merits were appreciated by them. They love to look up to a superior being, to rest on a firmer support than their own minds can afford; and they are glad to find such in one of their own sex, and thus destitute of those dangers which usually attend any services conferred by men.

*   *   *

Thus we have done our duty, in bringing under view, in a brief summary, the little that there is to tell of the personages who formed the drama of this tale. One only remains to be mentioned: but it is not in a few tame lines that we can revert to the varied fate of Fanny Derham. She continued for some time among her beloved friends, innocent and calm as she was beautiful and wise; circumstances at last led her away from them, and she has entered upon life. One who feels so deeply for others, and yet is so stern a censor over herself – at once so sensitive and so rigidly conscientious – so single-minded and upright, and yet open as day to charity and affection, cannot hope to pass from youth to age unharmed. Deceit, and selfishness, and the whole web of human passion must envelope her, and occasion her many sorrows; and the unworthiness of her fellow-creatures inflict infinite pain on her noble heart: still she cannot be contaminated – she will turn neither to the right nor left, but pursue her way unflinching; and, in her lofty idea of the dignity of her nature, in her love of truth and in her integrity, she will find support and reward in her various fortunes. What the events are, that have already diversified her existence, cannot now be recounted; and it would require the gift of prophecy to foretell the conclusion. In after times these may be told, and the life of Fanny Derham be presented as a useful lesson, at once to teach what goodness and genius can achieve in palliating the woes of life, and to encourage those, who would in any way imitate her, by an example of calumny refuted by patience, errors rectified by charity, and the passions of our nature purified and ennobled by an undeviating observance of those moral laws on which all human excellence is founded – a love of truth in ourselves, and a sincere sympathy with our fellow-creatures.

'The Manly Young Lady'

from *Sketches of Young Ladies*, by 'QUIZ'
(? Revd Edward Caswall, sometimes
wrongly attributed to Dickens)
and illustrated by 'Phiz' (1837)

*This vignette from the very first year of Victoria's reign offers a friendly
and rather admiring portrait of a newly emerging type of young woman: this
is a young lady who having begun life as a 'tomboy' has become, to all
intents and purposes, a thoroughly good chap. The irony, of course, is that
the more closely her conduct mirrors that of any well-conducted and well-bred
young gentleman, the more bemused and disconcerted her male contemporaries
become (though, interestingly, their consternation never seems to turn to active
hostility). In the end, she gets married, but it seems unlikely that she will
ever 'dwindle into a wife'.*

There is a sort of young lady rarely met with in these times, whom we
call 'the manly young lady'. This specimen is found most in those
counties where there is good hunting, and prefers the north to the south.
There is one at the present quite perfect within a hundred miles of
Cambridge, and two-and-twenty year old, to use her own expression.

The manly young lady talks a great deal of dogs and horses, distinguishing them by their sex. Thus she feels no repugnance whatever in
signifying to you her favourite female dog by a short monosyllable, and
always says, 'My mare.' She always makes her calls on horseback, dressed
in an old blue riding habit, none the better for wear, with a little ground
ash in her hand, which she has a knack of flourishing about all the time
she is speaking. She is generally seen with her father, the squire, a stout
thick gentleman in tops. She was never known to work with a needle,
but is a capital hand at netting with a large mesh for the fruit-trees.
Once, indeed, she attempted to hem a pocket handkerchief, but after
two weeks' labour desisted in the middle of the work. Her shoes are
always very thick at the sole; none of your weak flimsy ladies' shoes,
but regular solids, and no mistake; made by John Cummings, the village

manufacturer and post-office keeper, under her own express direction.

The manly young lady always wished to be a boy, ever since she was a child in arms. In conversation, she is most particularly positive; and should you sit next to her at dinner, ten to one but she puts you down half a dozen times at least. If you do not ask her to take wine before the fish is removed, she is sure to ask you herself, making you blush, and looking all the time as unconcerned as if she were your father. Mind that on these occasions you fill her glass to the brim, if you wish to escape further confusion. Should you help her, as you do other ladies, no more than half full, she will not stickle at it, but will tell you at once that you don't half please her. One thing be most particularly cautious of, and that is, never to dine at the same table with her after you have been hunting in her company. She will be sure to entertain the party with some anecdote at your expense. Although our acquaintance is very extensive, we have known intimately but one manly young lady in our time, and of her we always felt afraid. It was quite wonderful how she would tell an anecdote making against our reputation as a horseman. Such bangers she would introduce for the sake of giving her stories a zest, that we felt half inclined to challenge her to mortal combat, forgetting altogether that she was a woman.

The favourite accomplishments of the manly young lady, are whistling and playing the flute. In general she changes with the barometer, which she has had hung up by a nail in her own bedroom for her own exclusive use. In fine weather, when she can get out, she is all spirits; in wet weather she sits moping indoors, looking over the Sporting Magazine, or reading Isaac Walton. She was never yet seen by naturalists in the act of reading a novel; and as for love stories, abhors them as trash. She is always certain of a pretty property, so what need is there that she should be falling in love? especially when she is so well able to take care of herself, that she has been known to travel alone, outside the coach, all the way from Manchester to London. We do not hesitate to affirm this, because we are certain that we ourselves once met her. It was about eleven at night, and our coach had stopped to take supper. We ourselves had been sitting inside to be out of the wind. We alighted, and, after two or three minutes' delay in looking after our trunk and bag, walked into the supper room. What was our surprise, to behold a

'The Manly Young Lady' by 'Phiz'

young lady sitting at the head of the table, surrounded by strange gentlemen, and pouring out tea, in the coolest manner imaginable, just as if the strange gentlemen were her own brothers. This, thought we, must be the manly young lady; and so it was, sure enough, as we soon discovered from her conversation, which turned entirely on the new patent drag.

Whether these sorts of accomplishments are admired by the poor, we know not; but certain it is that the manly young lady is invariably beloved by her humble village neighbours. It might be thought that the true reason of this is a mutual vulgarity. But here we beg to state most positively, for once and all, that, however vulgar may be what the manly young lady does, yet she has a way of doing it, and a sort of natural stylishness about her, which precludes the possibility of any one imagining her to be otherwise than a perfect lady in all points. This, indeed, might be expected from her birth; for it is an invariable rule, that the manly young lady has good connexions, and a baronet for her uncle at least, if not for her father. The true cause of her popularity with the poor we take to be this, that she has not got an atom of pride about her, but is both willing and able to talk with them familiarly on their concerns. She knows the proper age for killing a pig, and the best food for fattening him; gives good advice about planting potatoes; finds a buyer for the calf; and calls all the children by their christian names, without confusing Jim with Jack.

We confess to our shame, that, being of a retiring disposition, we had always held in abhorrence the manly young lady, whom we have before mentioned as our acquaintance. She frightened us; and we, in turn, took every opportunity of avoiding both her and her anecdotes. One cold frosty morning, however, we were perfectly cured of our animosity, by meeting her walking through the snow, and carrying in her own hand a basin of broth for sick Betty Gore. Since then, we have always felt an interest for her; and were quite rejoiced when, a year afterwards, she married a young clergyman, and settled down all at once into the most domestic and useful of wives that we ever had the pleasure of numbering among our acquaintance.

Sonnets for George Sand
ELIZABETH BARRETT BROWNING (1806–1861)

'What idea do you have of women, O you who are of the Third Sex?'
Flaubert wrote to George Sand in 1868. For Elizabeth Barrett Browning,
too, the much-admired George Sand could not be securely categorised as
either male or female; she sees Sand as combining elements of both genders
in a way that unsettles the fixity of gender itself. These two terrible and
very mixed-up sonnets reveal all sorts of ambivalences, recognisably of the
period, about the relationship between gender, sexuality and creativity.

George Sand's autobiography, Histoire de ma vie (The Story of my
Life), *published in 1856, had recounted her experiences of 'passing' as a*
man in Paris. Some of them are included in a later section of this book,
'Breeches Parts'.

To George Sand
A Desire

Thou large-brained woman and large-hearted man,
Self-called George Sand! whose soul, amid the lions
Of thy tumultuous senses, moans defiance
And answers roar for roar, as spirits can:
I would some mild miraculous thunder ran
Above the applauded circus, in appliance
Of thine own nobler nature's strength and science,
Drawing two pinions, white as wings of swan,
From thy strong shoulders, to amaze the place
With holier light! that thou to woman's claim
And man's mightest join beside the angel's grace
Of a pure genius sanctified from blame,
Till child and maiden pressed to thine embrace
To kiss upon thy lips a stainless fame.

To George Sand
A Recognition

True genius, but true woman! dost deny
The woman's nature with a manly scorn,
And break away the gauds and armlets worn
By weaker women in captivity?
Ah, vain denial! that revolted cry
Is sobbed in by a woman's voice forlorn, —
Thy woman's hair, my sister, all unshorn
Floats back dishevelled strength in agony,
Disproving thy man's name: and while before
The world thou burnest in a poet-fire,
We see thy woman-heart beat ever more
Through the large flame. Beat purer, heart, and higher,
Till God unsex thee on the heavenly shore
Where unincarnate spirits purely aspire!

Two lesbian case studies
from *Sexual Inversion*
HAVELOCK ELLIS (1859–1939)

For most British homosexual men and women during the first half of the twentieth century, Havelock Ellis was a far more important figure than Freud. Trained in medicine, in love with literature, humble about his own sexual 'inadequacies' and married to a lesbian wife (Edith, an author in her own right), Ellis did much to document and analyse the experience of being homosexual in Victorian and Edwardian Britain. His first significant work on the subject — Sexual Inversion, *written with the homosexual apologist, John Addington Symonds, who died before publication — appeared in 1897 and was quickly and successfully prosecuted for obscenity. In that volume (revised, enlarged and incorporated within* Studies in the Psychology of Sex *over the following decades) were included a number of first-hand accounts by homosexual women. Two of them, which largely disappeared from later volumes, are given here. I acquired my own five volumes of the 1924 American edition of* Studies *when I was an inquisitive ten year old, at the local Scout Jumble Sale for the princely sum of 3d. per volume (the whole set for the equivalent of 7p).*

It was fashionable in the 1970s and 1980s to accuse 'sexologists' such as Ellis (and his Austrian contemporary, Krafft-Ebing) of producing distortedly pathologising versions of homosexual life. It is important, however, to understand that, for many of the men and women who agreed to allow the publication of their case histories, Ellis offered a rare and generous opportunity to let them speak for themselves, to tell their own truths and shape their own narratives. These are not merely victims of other people's falsifying classifications.

A class of women to be first mentioned, a class in which homosexuality, while fairly distinct, is only slightly marked, is formed by the women to whom the actively inverted woman is most attracted. These women differ in the first place from the normal or average woman in that they are not repelled or disgusted by lover-like advances from persons of their own sex. They are not usually attractive to the average man, though to this rule there are many exceptions. Their faces may be plain or ill-made, but not seldom they possess good figures, a point which is apt to carry more weight with the inverted woman than beauty of face. Their sexual impulses are seldom well marked, but they are of strongly affectionate nature. On the whole, they are women who are not very robust and well-developed, physically or nervously, and who are not well adapted for child-bearing, but who still possess many excellent qualities, and they are always womanly. One may perhaps say that they are the pick of the women whom the average man would pass by. No doubt this is often the reason why they are open to homosexual advances, but I do not think it is the sole reason. So far as they may be said to constitute a class, they seem to possess a genuine though not precisely sexual preference for women over men, and it is this coldness rather than lack of charm which often renders men rather indifferent to them.

The actively inverted woman differs from the woman of the class just mentioned in one fairly essential character: a more or less distinct trace of masculinity. She may not be, and frequently is not, what would be called a 'mannish' woman, for the latter may imitate men on grounds of taste and habit unconnected with sexual perversion, while in the inverted woman the masculine traits are part of an organic instinct which she by no means always wishes to accentuate. The inverted woman's masculine element may in the least degree consist only in the fact that she makes advances to the woman to whom she is attracted and treats all men in a cool, direct manner, which may not exclude comradeship, but which excludes every sexual relationship, whether of passion or merely of coquetry. As a rule the inverted woman feels absolute indifference towards men, and not seldom repulsion. And this feeling, as a rule, is instinctively reciprocated by men.

Case XXVIII. – Miss S., age 38, living in a city of the United States of America, a business woman of fine intelligence, prominent in professional and literary circles. Her general health is good, but she belongs to a family in which there is a marked neuropathic element. She is of rather phlegmatic temperament, well poised, always perfectly calm and self-possessed, rather retiring in disposition, with gentle, dignified bearing.

She says she cannot care for men, but that all her life has been 'glorified and made beautiful by friendship with women', whom she loves as a man loves women. Her character is, however, well disciplined, and her friends are not aware of the nature of her affections. She tries not to give all her love to one person, and endeavours (as she herself expresses it) to use this 'gift of loving' as a stepping-stone to high mental and spiritual attainments. She is described by one who has known her for several years as 'having a high nature, and instincts unerringly toward high things'.

Case XXIX. – Miss M., aged 29, the daughter of English parents (both musicians), who were both of what is described as 'intense' temperaments, and there is a neurotic element in the family; she is herself, however, free from nervous disease, though very sensitive in nature. At birth she was very small (? born prematurely). In a portrait taken at the age of 4 the nose, mouth and ears are abnormally large, and she wears a little boy's hat. As a child she did not care for dolls or for pretty clothes, and often wondered why other children found so much pleasure in them.

'As far back as my memory goes', she writes, 'I cannot recall a time when I was not different from other children. I felt bored when other little girls came to play with me, though I was never rough or boisterous in my sports'. Sewing was distasteful to her. Still she cared little more for the pastimes of boys, and found her favourite amusement in reading, especially adventures and fairy tales. She was always quiet, timid and self-conscious. The instinct first made its appearance in the latter part of her eighth or the first part of her ninth year. She was strongly attracted by the face of a teacher who used to appear at a side window on the second floor of the school-building and ring a bell to summon the children to their classes. The teacher's face seemed very beautiful but sad, and she thought about her continually. A year later this teacher was married and left the school, and the impression gradually faded away. The next feelings were experienced when she was about eleven years of age. A young lady came to visit a next-door neighbour, and made so profound an impression on the child that she was ridiculed by her playmates for preferring to sit in a dark corner on the lawn – where she might watch this young lady – rather than to play games. Being a sensitive child, after this experience she was careful not to reveal her feelings to anyone. She felt instinctively that in this she was different from other children. So she did not speak to anyone of her feelings. Her sense of beauty developed early, but there was always an indefinable feeling of melancholy associated with it. The twilight – a dark night when the stars shone brightly – all of these had a very depressing effect upon her but possessed a strong attraction nevertheless, and pictures appealed to her. At the age of twelve, she fell in love with a schoolmate, and wept bitterly because they could not be confirmed at the same time. The face of this friend reminded her of one of Dolce's Madonnas which she loved. Later on she loved an invalid friend very dearly, and devoted herself to her care; and upon the death of this friend, eight years afterwards, she resolved never to let her heart go out to anyone again. She is reticent regarding the details of these relationships, but it is evident that specific physical gratification plays no part in them. 'I love few people', she writes, 'but in these instances when I have permitted my heart to go out to a friend I have always experienced most exalted feelings, and have been made better by them morally, mentally and spiritually. Love is with me a religion. The very nature of my affection for my friends precludes the possibility of any element entering into it which is not absolutely pure and sacred'.

With regard to her attitude towards the other sex, she writes: 'I have never felt a dislike for men, but have good comrades among them. During my childhood I associated with both girls and boys, enjoying them all, but wondering why the girls cared to flirt with boys. Later in life I have had other friendships with men, some of whom cared for me, much to my regret, for, naturally, I do not care to marry'.

She is a musician, and herself attributes her nature in part to her artistic temperament. She is of good intelligence, and always stood well in her classes, but the development of the intellectual faculties is somewhat uneven. While weak in mathematics, she shows remarkable talent for various branches of physical science, to which of late years she has devoted herself, but has always been hampered by this deficiency in mathematics. She is small, though her features are rather large. Medical examination shows a small vagina and orifice, though scarcely, perhaps, abnormally so in proportion to her size. A further more detailed examination has recently been made in connection with the present history (though not at my instance) by an obstetric physician of high standing, and I am indebted to his kindness for the following notes: –

'Anatomically Miss M. is very near being a normal woman. Her pelvic measurements are about normal, being –

Bis-ant. superior spines		9½ in.
Bis-iliac crests		10½ in.
Bi-greater trochanteric		12 in.
External conjugate		7 in.
Height		5 ft. 4 in.
Neck Measurements {	Around its base	13¼ in.
	On level with cricoid cart.	11½ in.
	About the larynx	11½ in.

Sexual Organs – (*a*) Internal: Uterus and ovaries appear normal (*b*) External; Small clitoris, with this irregularity, that the lower folds of the labia minora, instead of uniting one with the other and forming the fraenum, are extended upward along the sides of the clitoris, while the upper folds are poorly developed, furnishing the clitoris with a very scant hood. The labia majora depart from normal conformation in being fuller in their posterior half than in their anterior part, so that when the subject is in the supine position they sag, as it were, presenting a slight resemblance to fleshy sacs, but in substance and structure they feel normal.

'The deviations mentioned are all I am able to note from the strictly normal form and shape of these organs.

'The general conformation of the body is feminine. But with arms, palms up, extended in front of her with inner sides of hands touching, she cannot bring the inner sides of forearms together, as nearly every woman can, showing that the feminine angle of arm is lost. The breasts are of fair size, and the nipples readily respond to titillation. Titillation of the sexual organs receives no response at all. [This does not show that the sexual sense is lost, but proves the absence of any habits of excessive sexual excitement leading to sexual hyperæsthesia.] I am persuaded, however, that Miss M. possesses the sexual sense to a very marked degree.'

She is left-handed and shows a better development throughout on the left side. She is quiet and dignified, but has many boyish tricks of manner and speech which seem to be instinctive; she tries to watch herself continually, however, in order to avoid them, affecting feminine ways and feminine interests, but always being conscious of an effort in so doing.

Miss M. can see nothing wrong in her feelings; and until, a year ago, she came across the translation of Krafft-Ebing's book she had no idea 'that feelings like mine were "under the ban of society" as he puts it, or were considered unnatural and depraved'. She would like to help to bring light on the subject and to lift the shadow from other lives.

An Extraordinary Woman

from *Extraordinary Women*
COMPTON MACKENZIE (1883–1972)

Compton Mackenzie seems to have been the sort of heterosexual man who was so confident in his own sexuality that he could be relaxed about other people's. His 1956 novel, Thin Ice, *was a sympathetic portrait of a male homosexual civil servant struggling to negotiate the farcical but deadly complexities of a legal system which outlawed him. The novel appeared before Sir John Wolfenden published the report which eventually led to the partial decriminalisation, in 1967, of male homosexuality. Mackenzie's novel is often said to have been a factor in that process.*

Extraordinary Women, set largely among the homosexual ex-patriate community of Capri, which Mackenzie knew well, includes many thinly disguised portraits of well-known contemporary lesbians. Rory Fremantle (whose identity Sir Compton gallantly declined, albeit very courteously, to disclose to me when, as a very young research student, I wrote to him thirsting for enlightenment) may in fact be a composite portrait of a genuinely recognisable type. The enthusiasms and pursuits which punctuate her life have their counterparts elsewhere; her passion for an idealised Ancient Greece, for example, is shared by the Michael Fields and Natalie Clifford Barney; she breeds bull-dogs, Radclyffe Hall and Una Troubridge bred dachshunds and a variety of other, in the main rather badly treated, pedigree dogs. Fremantle, like Colette's lover, 'Missie' (the Marquise de Belboeuf), looked so unconvincing when in women's clothes that many assumed she was a man in drag. Extraordinary Women *is a comic novel, and many of its lesbians are highly amusing, but lesbianism itself is not assumed to be ridiculous. Clearly the novel was known to Angela Thirkell: her character, Miss Bent, regards Rory Fremantle as a real-life role model and champion of the lesbian cause. Mackenzie's novel was published in 1928, that year so rich in fictional lesbians.*

Aurora Freemantle was so masculine as almost to convey the uncomfortable impression that she really was a man dressed up in female attire. But she was without doubt an Englishwoman who had lived for over twenty-five years in Paris, where under the pseudonym of Demonassa she had contributed poems to various advanced reviews and under her own name pence to support them. She had begun as a symbolist and was at present an imagist; but through all the mutable fashions of literature she had remained faithful to the breeding of French bulldogs. She was not beautiful, having herself a considerable likeness to the bulldogs she loved. Her prominent chin was as hispid as the leaves of borage. She was indeed, if one may use a botanical family to classify a human being, a boraginacious woman combining in herself the sentimentality of the forget-me-not with the defiance of the bugloss. Like the Demonassa whose name she had borrowed from Lucian she was rich, and like her she could fairly be called a Corinthian inasmuch as she had done more than anybody to promote the sport of boxing among women. She had derived as much pleasure from the protection of likely young feminine feather-weights as in the bewhiskered prime of the Victorian era elderly gentlemen derived from the protection of ballet-dancers. In early days she had had some bitter experiences in the way of empirical love-making; but for many years now, until Rosalba Donsante entered her life, she had always been able to feel that she was the protector with perpetual freedom to dismiss the protected. At present, however, Rosalba eluded her. And to the enslavement of Rosalba Rory set that massive and hispid jaw. One of her practical reasons for coming to Sirene (romantically she could not bear the thought of even the briefest separation) was the hope that she might cut Rosalba off from relying too much upon her grandmother's financial help, which was one of the chief bars to the indisputable protection that she had craved ever since she met Rosalba at a friend's house in Paris last October. Under the pseudonym of Demonassa Rory had expressed very frankly her feminine ideal, and there is no doubt that Rosalba came nearer than anybody so far to realizing it. Poems of hers written before Rosalba came into this world foreshadowed her. She might have met her unborn shade and cried '*Tu Marcellus eris.*' There was published privately in the early 'nineties a slim volume of verse bound in sea-green vellum called *Cydro*, which is still met with in second-hand book catalogues under the heading 'Curious.' Rory Freemantle had not yet assumed the name Demonassa at this period, and the only indication of authorship was a portrait of her at the beginning which in spite of being reproduced from a silver-point, with all the advantages that such an ethereal style of sketching provides, showed a determined young woman quite alien from the Cydro whose beauty and fascination the poems celebrated. This Cydro became in turn Gyrinno, Anactoria, Atthis, Megara, Telesippa, Leaena, Megilla, Gongyla, Ismenodora, or Mnesidice; and she was sometimes a slim anonymous flute-player of Pyrrha or Methymna flitting through the verses of Demonassa as her prototype may have flitted through the olive groves of Mytilene. But whatever her name or occupation she certainly might always have been Rosalba with her upcurving faun's mouth, Rosalba with her long legs and weight of glinting hair. And now when that poetic ideal was incarnate in Rosalba's Greek beauty verse was not sufficient. Rory must take to painting and paint her. She was rich enough to experiment with another art in approaching middle-age, and the fashion of the moment was kind to her lack of technique. She was rich enough to be credited with a freshness of vision, and the portraits she made of Rosalba that first winter had a vogue in her Parisian côterie. They made one feel, her friends assured her, that the war would at last come to an end. Whereupon the Germans nearly broke through again, and the côterie was dispersed. Rory did not allow Rosalba to be dispersed. She had not found the incarnation of her feminine ideal after searching twenty-five years to lose her a few months later. She left her bulldogs and feather-weight female boxers and followed her ideal to Lucerne. Here it was that owing to the restrictions of war-time which made Mytilene a difficult island to reach they planned to spend the late spring and summer in Sirene.

Meetings with Miss Bent and Miss Hampton
ANGELA THIRKELL (1890–1961)

In 1933, Angela Thirkell boldly co-opted Anthony Trollope's fictional county of Barsetshire. From then until her death, she used it as the setting for a series of richly comic novels in which she depicted the changing fortunes of

Miss Radclyffe Hall
From a caricature by Matt

John as seen by *T.P.'s Weekly*, 1926

the landed classes and people 'of the middling sort' who occupied the villages and small towns of one small piece of rural England. Two of her most endearing characters are Miss Hampton, the fearless novelist, and her companion Miss Bent. Both are 'maiden ladies' only in a rather irrelevantly technical sense. Serena Thirkell, the novelist's grand-daughter, told me that Miss Bent and Miss Hampton may have been based on some of her grandmother's friends whom the young Serena met as a child. Certainly, Angela Thirkell was no stranger to 'Vice' (as Miss Hampton always enthusiastically called same-sex loves). Her son, Colin McInnes, who became a distinguished novelist of a rather different sort, was himself homosexual.

The three extracts below come from Cheerfulness Breaks In *(1940)*, Private Enterprise *(1947) and* County Chronicle *(1951).*

At Adelina Cottage Philip rang the bell. The door was opened by a rather handsome woman with short, neatly curled grey hair, not young, in an extremely well-cut black coat and skirt, a gentlemanly white silk shirt with collar and tie, and neat legs in silk stockings and brogues, holding a cigarette in a very long black holder.

'Come in and have a drink,' said Miss Hampton.

'Certainly,' said Philip. 'This is Mr. Bissell, the Headmaster of the Hosiers' Boys Foundation School, who is bringing his staff and boys down here and wants to find a cottage. Brown says you have Maria's key.'

'French or Italian?' said Miss Hampton, who had already three-quarters filled four very large cocktail glasses, or indeed goblets, with gin. 'Bent has just taken Smigly-Rydz out, so I might as well mix hers too. She won't be a moment.'

'Is Smigly-Rydz a new dog?' said Philip. 'It was Benes last winter.'

'Gallant little Czecho-Slovakia!' said Miss Hampton in a perfunctory way. 'But it's gallant little Poland now, so we've changed Schuschnigg's name; Benes's I mean, but one gets a bit mixed, everyone being gallant.'

'And wasn't he Zog at Easter?' said Philip.

'So he was. Gallant little Albania,' said Miss Hampton. 'We bought him after Selassie died. We buried Selassie in the garden. Put it down, Philip, and you too, Mr. Bissell. That's the name, isn't it? I never forget names. So you keep a boys' school; and in London; interesting; much vice?'

Mr. Bissell spilt a good deal of his cocktail and remained tongue-bound.

'Come, come,' said Miss Hampton filling his glass up to the brim again. 'We're all men here and I'm doing a novel on a boys' school, so I might as well know something about it. I'm thinking of calling it "Temptation at St. Anthony's"; good name, don't you think?'

'Excellent,' said Philip.

Mr. Bissell was pretty strong on psychology and had for years been accustomed to explain certain facts to his pupils, drawing his examples first from botany, then from nature study, and later from outspoken serious talks, from which most of his boys had emerged with a very low opinion of their Headmaster's intellect, who could think them such chumps as he evidently did. He had also had many an interesting and intellectual exchange of views with other authorities at conferences, but his soul was extremely innocent and when he thought of exposing Mrs. Bissell to such a woman as Miss Hampton he heartily wished the war had never been invented. But he lacked the social courage to flee, and the strong cocktail was reacting unfavourably on his legs, so he looked at her, fascinated, and said nothing.

'Well, here's fun,' said Miss Hampton, taking a deep drink of what Mr. Bissell saw with terror to be her second cocktail. 'I study vice. Interesting. It's a thing you schoolmasters ought to know about. Prove all things, you know, and stick to what's good. Here comes Bent. She'll tell you about vice.'

The door of the little sitting-room burst open and a black dog came in dragging Miss Bent after him. The dog, presumably Smigly-Rydz-Zog-Benes-Schuschnigg, was one of those very stout little dogs with a black shaggy coat, short in the leg, with a head as large as an elephant's and mournful eyes. Miss Bent, whom he had just taken round the village, was a rather flabby edition of Miss Hampton. Her coat and skirt of an indefinite tartan had obviously been made locally, her figure bulged in a very uncontrolled way, her short hair of a mousy colour looked as if she trimmed it with her nail-scissors, her stockings were cotton and rather wrinkled, her shoes could only be called serviceable, and she wore several necklaces.

'Come along, Bent,' said Miss Hampton, handing the fourth cocktail to her friend. 'Put it down. Here's Mr. Winter come for Maria's key. Mr. Bissell has a boys' school and I'm going to pick his brains for my new novel.'

'Hampton sold one hundred and fifty thousand of her last novel in America,' said Miss Bent, looking very hard at Mr. Bissell. 'That was the one that was the Banned Book of the Month here. But of course one can't hope for that luck again. After all, other people must have their turn. I have a friend on the Banned Book Society Council and he says Esmé Bellenden's *Men of Harlech* will probably be the next choice. Have you read it?'

Mr. Bissell, helpless with confusion and cocktails, said he hadn't, and was Esmé Bellenden a man or a woman.

'I couldn't possibly say,' said Miss Bent, 'and what is more I don't suppose anyone could.'

[. . .]

Miss Hampton said before they went they must just look over Adelina, so the whole party inspected the rest of the cottage, which consisted of a kitchen behind the sitting-room, a narrow breakneck staircase, a bedroom overlooking the street almost entirely filled by a very large square flat divan which made Mr. Bissell back out of the room in terror, a little bedroom behind called the guest room, and a tiled bathroom, all spotlessly clean.

*   *   *

Mrs. Arbuthnot fetched the chairs from the drawing-room and obediently sat down by Miss Bent.

'Have you read Hampton's last book?' said Miss Bent.

Mrs. Arbuthnot said she was very sorry she hadn't and what was it called.

'*Chariots of Desire*,' said Miss Bent reverently. 'It is about the sex life of lorry drivers. All from nature. It sold thirty-three thousand copies here and could have sold three times as many if it weren't for the paper and the printers and the binders. Hampton puts every ounce of herself into her books. She never spares herself,' said Miss Bent, gazing with affectionate concern at her friend, who had mounted the steps, put the rod onto its support, dusted her hands together in a manly way and gone with Miss Arbuthnot into the scullery to continue operations on the window curtain there.

Mrs. Arbuthnot said she had read Miss Hampton's public-school novel, *Temptation at St. Anthony's*, and enjoyed it frightfully.

'People do enjoy it,' said Miss Bent tolerantly. 'But vice goes much deeper than mere enjoyment. It is scientific. She is writing a new book now, about co-educational schools. It will be strong meat, but England can take it. She is going to call it *A Gentle Girl and Boy*. Keats of course.'

Mrs. Arbuthnot said she looked forward to reading it and had often noticed how nice and gentle boys from co-educational schools were, but the girls seemed to stay just the same. Miss Bent congratulated her on her perspicacity and was obviously going to enlarge on the subject when, rather to Mrs. Arbuthnot's relief, her sister-in-law and Miss Hampton came back from the scullery, having hung the curtains and discussed the gas-cooker of which Miss Hampton approved.

'I like your sister-in-law,' she said to Mrs. Arbuthnot, looking with approval upon Miss Arbuthnot's tall, strong figure and her rather masculine face. 'Not one of Ours, but a Good Fellow,' which appeared to be the highest compliment she could pay.

* * *

'Well, here's to literature and lots of clean fun,' said Mr. Wickham, finishing the bottle with a bow to Miss Hampton. 'What's the latest?'

'*I'll* tell them, Hampton,' said Miss Bent. 'Hampton is prostrated with the effort,' she continued. 'She wrote the last words on Friday night. It is the Biggest Thing she has done yet.'

'All right, I'll be the Mug,' said Mr. Wickham. 'What's it about this time?'

'It is an unfaltering exposure of infidelity,' said Miss Bent reverently.

Mr. Wickham was heard to say that Johnny Turk called us infidels.

'No, no; not *that* kind,' said Miss Bent sharply. 'It goes deep, very deep, psychologically and ethically. We haven't decided on the title yet. Hampton thinks "My Lesbia has a roving eye."' She paused for the words to sink in.

'And what do *you* think?' said Mr. Wickham.

'It was difficult, difficult,' said Miss Bent, raising her coral necklaces and letting them clash upon her Mixo-Lydian bosom. 'At first I thought just simply "Sister Helen," but it was not courageous enough. So I said "My Sister, my spouse," which I think gives the tone of Courage which runs through the book. One hundred and eighty thousand words,' said Miss Bent in a low tone, as of one walking in sacred places.

[. . .]

'Fill up,' said Miss Hampton and raising her fifth glass of a great deal of gin and very little vermouth she added, 'To the immortal memory of Charles Dickens.'

The toast was drunk in respectful silence, after which the party was a great success till Mr. Shergold had to tear himself away and go back to his House, so everyone else went round to Maria to hear Mr. Traill's gramophone and then to Louisa to hear Mr. Feeder's wireless and then to Editha to sample some very old brandy imported by the late Mr. Feeder senior.

'Eleven o'clock,' said Miss Bent suddenly. 'Hampton, what about bed?'

'Bent is right,' said Miss Hampton. 'Good-night, all. Come on, Bent. We'll sleep to-night.'

'Hampton does plunge so in bed when she is Writing,' said Miss Bent with a kind of holy awe, 'that it is quite uncomfortable. But now she will be as quiet as a bolster. Come on, Hampton. Where's Amethyst?'

The large-headed dog was dragged by the scruff of its neck from under the sofa and the party dispersed.

'Meeting Angela Thirkell'
ELLEN GALFORD

This enthusiastic response to Angela Thirkell's Barsetshire and its denizens comes from an article which Ellen wrote for me, for an edition of The Women's Press Bookclub Catalogue in 1990.

Her books should carry an ideological health warning. She is – in the offhand manner of her time and social background – appallingly racist, anti-Semitic, and riddled with petty snobberies. Yet, despite her jingoistic anglocentricity, her reactionary opinions and her fawning adoration for the titled county set, I admit myself to be hooked on Angela Thirkell.

What, you may well ask, could a lesbian feminist of Jewish extraction and transatlantic upbringing, with political consciousness presumably in good working order, find to like in a writer parked so firmly on the opposite side of the barricades?

I blame it on my mother. She was a school librarian, a New Jersey-dwelling anglophile, whose idea of the perfect Saturday night was to retire to bed at 8.30 with a dish of chocolate ice cream and the novels of Angela Thirkell. They were, she said, far more soothing than valerian, and funny too.

[. . .]

The women [in Thirkell's novels] have the best tunes: Mrs. Morland, scatty author of romantic thrillers, struggling to support her brood of rambunctious little boys, and to keep her hairpins from falling out; Mrs. Tebben, who applies the intellect that once earned her an Oxbridge First in Economics to the most gruesome forms of domestic thrift, concocting meals of spectacular inedibility; Miss Bunting, formidable old governess who makes mighty Brigadier-Generals quake in their boots – and dozens more, sketched in vivid, and merciless detail.

Men are tolerated rather than celebrated, the butt of some universally understood but unspoken female joke. Thirkell, though loudly proclaiming herself no feminist, was a veteran of two unhappy marriages, and had few illusions about the opposite sex. Nor is this a totally heterosexual milieu. My favourite characters, needless to say, are Miss Hampton and Miss Bent, of Adelina Cottage, Southbridge. The former is a tweedy authoress, specializing in torrid shockers on the sex-lives of long distance lorry drivers ('Strong meat,' says her devoted partner, 'but England can take it!'). The latter, though fond of folk-weave skirts and jangling peasant jewellery, confounds expectations by being the practical one who does all the driving. They are adored by the County for their free-flowing, hard-drinking hospitality, and their ability to shock outsiders: 'Hampton does plunge so in bed, when she's finishing a book!' complains Bent to the puritanical London schoolmaster moving in next door. Others may fall victim to the razor-sharp pen, but Hampton and Bent are treated only with amused affection: Thirkell, for all her bigotry, seems free of anti-lesbian prejudices.

Which is, perhaps, one of the reasons why I retain a soft spot for a writer whose values are, in so many ways, anathema. My mother, who found it difficult to come to terms with my sexuality, encountered her first positive images of lesbians in Angela Thirkell's books. When she visited me in the small house I shared with my partner in North London, she took one look at the incriminatory double bed, then smiled, and said with a wicked glint in her eye, 'Just like Adelina Cottage!'

Who would have thought we'd find our common ground in Barsetshire?

I See You What You Are
from *Feminist Fables* (1981)
SUNITI NAMJOSHI

But suppose that Viola had also been charmed, charmed to the point of a little indiscretion? (And she wasn't indifferent: that praise was genuine.) Suppose she had said, 'I see you what you are, but you, you are deceived,' and Olivia understanding, had understood also that deceived she was not. Would that have been wrong? Would that of necessity be dreadfully wrong? Because Viola does charm. And when was Olivia less than graceful? Foolish, perhaps, – Not foolish enough? – but never wrong.

See *Twelfth Night* I, v.
Viola, disguised as a page, is sent by Orsino to woo Olivia by proxy. Olivia falls in love with her.

In Foreign Parts

'In Foreign Parts' reveals that persistent fascination with 'the exotic', that place in which we find or locate our dreams and nightmares, the things and people who attract and repel us by their difference (and terrify us when they prove not so very different after all). Western Europe's long-lived obsession with 'The East', which sometimes seems to begin at Vienna, is matched only by British writers' traditional suspicion of foreigners and the foreign, which starts at Dover. Other women represented here have rejoiced at the expansion of possibilities which foreign parts may offer (yes, the pun is intentional, and one exploited by Esther Isaac in 'Last Mango in Paris').

Lady Mary visits the Turkish Baths at Adrianopolis

from the Letters of Lady Mary Wortley Montagu (1689–1762)

The European imagination has long been fascinated by the Orient, especially by the sexual mores (whether actual or imagined) of its women. Westerners have dwelt lovingly upon the lubricious possibilities not only afforded but (wistfully believed to be) compulsory for members of the Grand Seraglio of Constantinople and other harems. As the wife of a British Ambassador to Turkey, Lady Mary Wortley Montagu ventured into the all-female world of the Bagnio, the renowned Turkish Baths. Although, as she notes in this letter, ''Tis no less than Death for a Man to be found in one of these places', she nevertheless wickedly wishes for the invisible presence of a male artist, Mr Gervase, to depict the scene. In the nineteenth century, fondly fantasised versions of this spectacle would abound, the most famous, probably, being Ingres's 'Les Bains Turcs'.

To Lady — 1 April 1717

Adrianople, Ap. 1. O.S.

I am now got into a new World where every thing I see appears to me a change of Scene, and I write to your Ladyship with some content of mind, hoping at least that you will find the charm of Novelty in my Letters and no longer reproach me that I tell you nothing extrodinary. I won't trouble you with a Relation of our tedious Journey, but I must not omit what I saw remarkable at Sophia, one of the most beautifull Towns in the Turkish Empire and famous for its Hot Baths that are resorted to both for diversion and health. I stop'd here one day on purpose to see them. Designing to go incognito, I hir'd a Turkish Coach. These Voitures are not at all like ours, but much more convenient for the Country, the heat being so great that Glasses would be very troublesome. They are made a good deal in the manner of the Dutch Coaches, haveing wooden Lattices painted and gilded, the inside being painted with baskets and nosegays of Flowers, entermix'd commonly with little poetical mottos. They are cover'd all over with scarlet cloth, lin'd with silk and very often richly embrodier'd and fring'd. This covering entirely hides the persons in them, but may be thrown back at pleasure and the Ladys peep through the Lattices. They hold 4 people very conveniently, seated on cushions, but not rais'd.

In one of these cover'd Waggons I went to the Bagnio about 10 a clock. It was allready full of Women. It is built of Stone in the shape of a Dome with no Windows but in the Roofe, which gives Light enough. There was 5 of these domes joyn'd together, the outmost being less than the rest and serving only as a hall where the portress stood at the door. Ladys of Quality gennerally give this Woman the value of a crown or 10 shillings, and I did not forget that ceremony. The next room is a very large one, pav'd with Marble, and all round it rais'd 2 Sofas of marble, one above another. There were 4 fountains of cold Water in this room, falling first into marble Basins and then running on the floor in little channels made for that purpose, which carry'd the streams into the next room, something less than this, with the same sort of marble sofas, but so hot with steams of sulphur proceeding from the baths joyning to it, twas impossible to stay there with one's Cloths on. The 2 other domes were the hot baths, one of which had cocks of cold Water turning into it to temper it to what degree of warmth the bathers have a mind to.

I was in my travelling Habit, which is a rideing dress, and certainly appear'd very extrodinary to them, yet there was not one of 'em that shew'd the least surprize or impertinent Curiosity, but receiv'd me with all the obliging civillity possible. I know no European Court where the Ladys would have behav'd them selves in so polite a manner to a stranger. I beleive in the whole there were 200 Women and yet none of those disdainfull smiles or satyric whispers that never fail in our assemblys when any body appears that is not dress'd exactly in fashion. They repeated over and over to me, Uzelle, pek uzelle, which is nothing but, charming, very charming. The first sofas were cover'd with Cushions and rich Carpets, on which sat the Ladys, and on the 2nd their slaves behind 'em, but without any distinction of rank by their dress, all being in the state of nature, that is, in plain English, stark naked, without any Beauty or deffect conceal'd, yet there was not the least wanton smile or immodest Gesture amongst 'em. They Walk'd and mov'd with the same majestic Grace which Milton describes of our General Mother. There were many amongst them as exactly proportion'd as ever any Goddess was drawn by the pencil of Guido or Titian, and most of their skins shineingly white, only adorn'd by their Beautifull Hair divided into many tresses hanging on their shoulders, braided either with pearl or riband, perfectly representing the figures of the Graces. I was here convinc'd of the Truth of a Refflexion that I had often made, that if twas the fashion to go naked, the face would be hardly observ'd. I perceiv'd that the Ladys with the finest skins and most delicate shapes had the greatest share of my admiration, tho their faces were sometimes less beautifull than those of their companions. To tell you the truth, I had wickedness enough to wish secretly that Mr Gervase could have been there invisible. I fancy it would have very much improv'd his art to see so many fine Women naked in different postures, some in conversation, some working, others drinking Coffee or sherbet, and many negligently lying on their Cushions while their slaves (generally pritty Girls of 17 or 18) were employ'd in braiding their hair in several pritty manners. In short, tis the Women's coffee house, where all the news of the Town is told, Scandal invented, etc. They gennerally take this Diversion once a week, and stay there at least for 5 hours without geting cold by immediate coming out of the hot bath into the cool room, which was very surprizing to me. The Lady that seem'd the most considerable amongst them entreated me to sit by her and would fain have undress'd me for the bath. I excus'd my selfe with some difficulty, they being all so earnest in perswading me. I was at last forc'd to open my skirt and shew them my stays, which satisfy'd 'em very well, for I saw they beleiv'd I was so lock'd up in that machine that it was not in my own power to open it, which contrivance they attributed to my Husband. I was charm'd with their Civillity and Beauty and should have been very glad to pass more time with them, but Mr W[ortley] resolving to persue his Journey the next morning early, I was in haste to see the ruins of Justinian's church, which did not afford me so agreable a prospect as I had left, being little more than a heap of stones.

Adeiu, Madam. I am sure I have now entertaind you with an Account of such a sight as you never saw in your Life and what no book of Travels could inform you of. 'Tis no less than Death for a Man to be found in one of these places.

'Of the Game of Flatts'

from *Satan's Harvest Home* (1749)
ANON

What follows is an oft-repeated travellers' tale which seems to have entered English in this version via the 1744 translation of a sixteenth-century Romanian diplomat's account of his travels in Turkey. This extract comes from an anonymous pamphlet of 1749, enticingly called Satan's Harvest Home. *Emma Donoghue suggests that because the publication was available in a wide range of retail outlets – the equivalent of today's corner shop – this anecdote of 'The Turkish Female Husband' was probably unusually well known. The 'W—n of Q—y' probably refers to the Women of Quality: once again vice is safely somewhere else – far away either geographically (Turkey) or socially (among the aristocracy). Even the narrator's obvious hostility fails to obscure the dignity and pathos of what he calls the old woman's 'absurd reply'.*

I am credibly informed, in order to render the Scheme of Iniquity still more extensive amongst us, a new and most abominable Vice has got footing among the W—n of Q—y, by some call'd the Game of Flats; however incredible this may appear to some People, I shall mention a Story from an Author of very great Credit, applicable to the Matter, who, speaking of the *Turks*, says,

'A *Turk* hates bodily Filthiness and Nastiness, worse than Soul-Defilement; and, therefore, they wash very often, and they never ease themselves, by going to Stool, but they carry Water with them for their Posteriors. But ordinarily the Women bathe by themselves, bond and free together; so that you shall many Times see young Maids, exceeding beautiful, gathered from all Parts of the World, exposed naked to the View of other Women, who thereupon fall in Love with them, as young Men do with us, at the Sight of Virgins.

'By this you may guess, what the strict Watch over Females comes to, and that it is not enough to avoid the Company of an adulterous Man, for the *Females* burn in Love, one towards another; and the Panda-resses to such refined Lovers are the Bards; and, therefore, some *Turks* will deny their Wives the Use of their public Baths, but they cannot do it altogether, because their Law allows them. But these Offences happen among the common sort; the richer sort of Persons have Bathes at home, as I told you before.

'It happened one Time that at the public Baths for Women, an old Woman fell in Love with a Girl, the Daughter of a poor Man, a Citizen of *Constantinople*; and, when neither by wooing nor flattering her, she could obtain that of her which her mad Affection aim'd at, she attempted to perform an Exploit almost incredible; she feign'd herself to be a Man, changed her Habit, hired an House near the Maid's Father, and pretended he was one of the *Chiauxes* [*Sergeants*] of the *Grand Seignor*; and thus, by reason of his Neighbourhood, she insinuated herself into the Man's Acquaintaince, and after some Time, acquaints him with the Desire of his Daughter. In short, he being a man in such a prosperous Condition, the Matter was agreed on, a Portion was settled, such as they were able to give, and a Day appointed for the Marriage; when the Ceremonies were over, and this doughty Bridegroom went into the Bride-chamber to his Spouse; after some Discourse, and plucking off her Head-geer, she was found to be a Woman. Whereupon the Maid runs out, and calls up her Parents, who soon found that they had married her not to a *Man*, but a *Woman*; Whereupon they carried the supposed Man, the next Day, to the General of the *Janizaries*, who, in the Absence of the *Grand Seignor*, was Governor of the City. When she was brought before him, he chid her soundly for her beastly Love; what, says he, are you not asham'd, an old Bedlam [*error for Beldame?*] as you are, to attempt so notorious a Bestiality, and so filthy a Fact?

'Away, Sir, says she! You do not know the Force of Love, and God grant you never may. At this absurd Reply, the Governor could scarce forbear Laughter, but commanded her, presently, to be pack'd away and

drown'd in the Deep; such was the unfortunate Issue of her wild Amours.'
See *Busbequin's* Travels into *Turkey*, pp. 146–7.

Two Poems
by 'LAURENCE HOPE'
(ADELA NICOLSON, 1865–1904)

*The Garden of Kama, and Other Love Lyrics from India, by 'Laurence
Hope', was one of the great publishing successes of 1901. Behind the sexually
ambiguous pseudonym lurked an unambiguously female author, Adela Florence Nicolson. The equally ambiguous title blurred the distinction between
translation and original poems (were they in fact Nicolson's own work?).
Initially treated by critics as the work of a male author, the poems were
nevertheless often called 'Sapphic', largely because of the sensuous intensity
with which they described sexual desire. But these lyrics, which so passionately
address and praise ardently desired women, are in fact the product of a
woman's pen – Sapphic, perhaps, in a fuller sense than those first critics
realised. The sensuousness of language was married to that of music when
four of the poems were set, as* The Indian Love Lyrics, *with enormous
success, by the composer Amy Woodforde Finden. They remained in the
repertoire until shortly after the Second World War; in recent years they
have enjoyed something of a revival. Nicolson herself committed suicide
shortly after her husband's death.*

Valgovind's Song in the Spring

> The Temple bells are ringing,
> The young green corn is springing,
>   And the marriage month is drawing very near.
> I lie hidden in the grass,
> And I count the moments pass,
>   For the month of marriages is drawing near.

Soon, ah, soon, the women spread
The appointed bridal bed
    With hibiscus buds and crimson marriage flowers,
Where, when all the songs are done,
And the dear dark night begun,
    I shall hold her in my happy arms for hours.

She is young and very sweet,
From the silver on her feet
    To the silver and the flowers in her hair,
And her beauty makes me swoon,
As the Moghra trees at noon
    Intoxicate the hot and quivering air.

Ah, I would the hours were fleet
As her silver circled feet.
    I am weary of the daytime and the night
I am weary unto death,
Oh my rose with jasmin breath,
    With this longing for your beauty and your light.

The Temple Dancing Girl

You will be mine; those lightly dancing feet,
    Falling as softly on the careless street
As the wind-loosened petals of a flower,
    Will bring you here, at the Appointed Hour.

And all the Temple's little links and laws
    Will not for long protect your loveliness.
I have a stronger force to aid my cause,
    Nature's great Law, to love and to possess!

Throughout those sleepless watches, when I lay
   Wakeful, desiring what I might not see,
I knew, (it helped those hours, from dusk to day,)
   In this one thing, Fate would be kind to me.

You will consent, through all my veins like wine
   This prescience flows; your lips meet mine above,
Your clear soft eyes look upward into mine
   Dim in a silent ecstasy of love.

The clustered softness of your waving hair,
   That curious paleness which enchants me so,
And all your delicate strength and youthful air,
   Destiny will compel you to bestow!

Refuse, withdraw and hesitate awhile
   Your young reluctance does but fan the flame,
My partner, Love, waits, with a tender smile,
   Who play against him play a losing game.

I, strong in nothing else, have strength in this,
   The subtlest, most resistless, force we know
Is aiding me; and you must stoop and kiss,
   The genius of the race will have it so!

Yet, make it not too long, nor too intense
   My thirst; lest I should break beneath the strain.
And the worn nerves, and over-wearied sense,
   Enjoy not what they spent themselves to gain.

Lest, in the hour when you consent to share
   That human passion Beauty makes divine
I, over worn, should find you over fair,
   Lest I should die before I make you mine.

You will consent, those slim, reluctant feet,
　　Falling as lightly on the careless street
　As the white petals of a wind-worn flower,
　　Will bring you here, at the Appointed Hour.

'A Dancing Girl'
from *Rainbows* (1902)
OLIVE CUSTANCE

At first glimpse this may seem to be a companion piece to 'The Temple Dancing Girl', which precedes it – a fascinated and erotic response to the 'exotic' otherness of a woman of a different race. But Custance's dancing girl rapidly acquires a significance that takes her into realms which transcend geography and empire. Although Olive Custance (1874–1944) eventually became the wife of Lord Alfred Douglas (Oscar Wilde's beloved 'Bosie'), she had previously had a number of affairs with women. She was close to Natalie Clifford Barney, the redoubtable ex-patriate American leader of 'Paris-Lesbos', that heady assemblage of French and ex-patriate lesbian writers and artists who lived and worked in Paris during the fin de siècle *and early years of the twentieth century. Another of Barney's lovers, the Anglo-American poet, Pauline Tarn (better known to us as Renée Vivien), incorporated a portrait of Olive, as 'Dagmar', in her 1904 novel,* Une Femme m'apparut *(A Woman appeared to me).*

'A Dancing Girl' is replete with the language, imagery and erotic tropes characteristic of lesbian poetry written during the Decadence. Individual words – 'secret', 'strange', 'haunting', 'pale' – are all but compulsory, as is the wistfully languorous reference to hair. (How much of it is lovingly brushed and stroked in lesbian life and literature of the period.) Equally characteristic are the various forms of 'half-life' to which this woman desired by – and possibly desiring of – other women, is described: fairies, neither human nor fully immortal; mermaids, half woman half fish; dryads, half mortal, half divine. And, inevitably, the poem implicitly juxtaposes the lost but longed for world of the 'pagan' and the sadness of the Christianity which displaced it. It's difficult not to hear, in the last line, an unmistakable echo of the charge Swinburne levelled at Christ: 'the world has grown grey with thy breath'.

Dark daughter of a dancing race
How do you weave your secret spells?
Song cannot show with what strange grace
You lightly lift your frock of lace
Sewn thick with little silver bells.

You hold us with your haunting eyes,
And in your hair so soft and long
Our souls are snared; yet we are wise,
We *know* you through your dark disguise
You are a witch-girl weird and strong.

A pagan creature, with the grace
Of the lost childhood of the world,
And in your pale fantastic face,
And in your smile we seem to trace,
The fairy with its bright wings furled.

A water nymph you may have been
With heavy lilies in your hair,
Or mermaid swinging in the green
Deep sea, or dryad stretched unseen
Among frail leaves and blossoms fair.

Now, from a lighted stage you glance
Smiling, oh, Sorceress unknown,
And we who watch you in a trance
Enchanted by your mystic dance
Forget how sad the world has grown.

Mrs Copperfield goes to pieces

from *Two Serious Ladies* (1943)
JANE BOWLES (1917–1973)

Everyone knows that people on holiday abroad will do things they'd never dream of doing at home. In this extract from Jane Bowles's delightful novel Two Serious Ladies, *two very nice American middle-aged matrons have made a (modest) bid for freedom by going off for an exotic foreign holiday. Then one of them falls for the voluptuous and friendly charms of Pacifica, a young native woman. Time to take stock.*

Early the next morning Mrs. Copperfield and Pacifica were together in Pacifica's bedroom. The sky was beginning to grow light. Mrs. Copperfield had never seen Pacifica this drunk. Her hair was pushed up on her head. It looked now somewhat like a wig which is a little too small for the wearer. Her pupils were very large and slightly filmed. There was a large dark spot on the front of her checked skirt, and her breath smelled very strongly of whisky. She stumbled over to the window and looked out. It was quite dark in the room. Mrs. Copperfield could barely discern the red and purple squares in Pacifica's skirt. She could not see her legs at all, the shadows were so deep, but she knew the heavy yellow silk stockings and the white sneakers well.

'It's so lovely,' said Mrs. Copperfield.

'Beautiful,' said Pacifica, turning around, 'beautiful.' She moved unsteadily around the room. 'Listen,' she said, 'the most wonderful thing to do now is to go to the beach and swim in the water. If you have enough money we can take a taxicab and go. Come on. Will you?'

Mrs. Copperfield was very startled indeed, but Pacifica was already pulling a blanket from the bed. 'Please,' she said. 'You cannot know how much pleasure this would give me. You must take that towel over there.'

The beach was not very far away. When they arrived, Pacifica told the cab-driver to come back in two hours.

The shore was strewn with rocks; this was a disappointment to Mrs.

Copperfield. Although the wind was not very strong, she noticed that the top branches of the palm trees were shaking.

Pacifica took her clothes off and immediately walked into the water. She stood for a time with her legs wide apart, the water scarcely reaching to her shins, while Mrs. Copperfield sat on a rock trying to decide whether or not to remove her own clothes. There was a sudden splash and Pacifica started to swim. She swam first on her back and then on her stomach, and Mrs. Copperfield was certain that she could hear her singing. When at last Pacifica grew tired of splashing about in the water, she stood up and walked towards the beach. She took tremendous strides and her pubic hair hung between her legs sopping wet. Mrs. Copperfield looked a little embarrassed, but Pacifica plopped down beside her and asked her why she did not come in the water.

'I can't swim,' said Mrs. Copperfield.

Pacifica looked up at the sky. She could see now that it was not going to be a completely fair day.

'Why do you sit on that terrible rock?' said Pacifica. 'Come, take your clothes off and we go in the water. I will teach you to swim.'

'I was never able to learn.'

'I will teach you. If you cannot learn I will let you sink. No, this is only a joke. Don't take it serious.'

Mrs. Copperfield undressed. She was very white and thin, and her spine was visible all the way along her back. Pacifica looked at her body without saying a word.

'I know I have an awful figure,' said Mrs. Copperfield.

Pacifica did not answer. 'Come,' she said, getting up and putting her arm around Mrs. Copperfield's waist.

They stood with the water up to their thighs, facing the beach and the palm trees. The trees appeared to be moving behind a mist. The beach was colorless. Behind them the sky was growing lighter very rapidly, but the sea was still almost black. Mrs. Copperfield noticed a red fever sore on Pacifica's lip. Water was dripping from her hair onto her shoulders.

She turned away from the beach and pulled Mrs. Copperfield farther out into the water.

Mrs. Copperfield held onto Pacifica's hand very hard. Soon the water was up to her chin.

'Now lie on your back. I will hold you under your head,' said Pacifica.

Mrs. Copperfield looked around wildly, but she obeyed, and floated on her back with only the support of Pacifica's open hand under her head to keep her from sinking. She could see her own narrow feet floating on top of the water. Pacifica started to swim, dragging Mrs. Copperfield along with her. As she had only the use of one arm, her task was an arduous one and she was soon breathing like a bull. The touch of her hand underneath the head of Mrs. Copperfield was very light – in fact, so light that Mrs. Copperfield feared that she would be left alone from one minute to the next. She looked up. The sky was packed with gray clouds. She wanted to say something to Pacifica, but she did not dare to turn her head.

Pacifica swam a little farther inland. Suddenly she stood up and placed both her hands firmly in the small of Mrs. Copperfield's back. Mrs. Copperfield felt happy and sick at once. She turned her face and in so doing she brushed Pacifica's heavy stomach with her cheek. She held on hard to Pacifica's thigh with the strength of years of sorrow and frustration in her hand.

'Don't leave me,' she called out.

[. . .]

'I'll tell you,' said Mrs. Copperfield, leaning over the table and suddenly looking very tense. 'I am a little worried – not terribly worried, because I shan't allow anything to happen that I don't want to happen – but I am a little worried because Pacifica has met this blond boy who lives way uptown and he has asked her to marry him. He never says anything and he has a very weak character. But I think he has bewitched her because he pays her compliments all the time. I've gone up to his apartment with her, because I won't allow them to be alone, and she has cooked dinner for him twice. He's crazy for Spanish food and eats ravenously of every dish she puts in front of him.'

Mrs. Copperfield leaned back and stared intently into Miss Goering's eyes.

'I am taking her back to Panama as soon as I am able to book passage on a boat.' She ordered another double whisky. 'Well, what do you think of it?' she asked eagerly.

'Perhaps you'd better wait and see whether or not she really wants to marry him.'

'Don't be insane,' said Mrs. Copperfield. 'I can't live without her, not for a minute. I'd go completely to pieces.'

'But you have gone to pieces, or do I misjudge you dreadfully?'

'True enough,' said Mrs. Copperfield, bringing her fist down on the table and looking very mean. 'I *have* gone to pieces, which is a thing I've wanted to do for years. I know I am as guilty as I can be, but I have my happiness, which I guard like a wolf, and I have authority now and a certain amount of daring, which, if you remember correctly, I never had before.'

Last Mango in Paris (1999)
ESTHER ISAAC

poetry surely made this happen

when I asked you why it mattered a fig or even a lemon
(which
stranded here
where there wasn't one sticking its tart head through the window
you never remembered to buy)
you handed me
this speech

aside of course from ravishing beauty
poetry
hebrew poetry
holds in its palm the roots of a culture
which must go on nourishing stems flower-heads and seed-banks
both under glass
and in the wilderness
outlasting manna
and richer than the salt of the earth or sea
(whether lost or promised or newly repossessed)

which was when
I came up with a wandering mango
both flushed and green

As I began to strip its skin
the ripe flesh oozing fluently
over my wrists and fingers
I glimpsed a magical mango fish
whose tones of gold
light a far tropical sea
somewhere off the coast of India
and then crossing my mind's eye
this mango humming bird
flew from Jamaica
in love with the bubbles of honey
sucked hurriedly from scarlet blooms
brushed by a black-winged (mango) butterfly

meanwhile across the sea
performing an act of mango trickery
a skinny genius conjured so tall a tree
out of blank air and steaming Indian earth
that you had to reach and squeeze the fruit
and stroke the bloom
and beside you
out of nowhere
one slight pinched kid
with black astonished eyes
gazed into the branches
and grasping your hand
cried
'man kay . . . man kay'
'tree and fruit
tree and fruit'
needing to keep his grip on both
and be sure you missed out on neither

And I watched you
lying beside me
swallowing these slivers of yellow flesh
roughly sliced on delft
tasting of terebinth

And I saw how quickly poetry becomes a mouth

> *And beguiled we both did eat of this first ripe fruit*
> *And the eyes of us both were opened*
> *And in the heat of the afternoon*
> *both at last lay naked*

two women speechless with mango
savouring the ripening buds of the other's mother tongue

Courts, Courtesans
and Whores

The loves and passions of the women encountered in 'Courts, Courtesans and Whores' reveal sexual desire and activity between a class of women whose morally stigmatised lives nevertheless keep them, and their preferred form of love, safely distanced from the virtuous reader. In ancient Syria, Renaissance Europe and eighteenth-century or Victorian London, we find that women who live by paid sex with men – both eminent courtesans and down-on-their-luck whores – may turn for pleasure to sex with other women. The world of courtly women, to which Miss Hobart belonged and which Delarivier Manley fictionalises, may seem a far cry from the buying and selling of sex, but the difference may simply be one of currency – not money but power changes hands.

Clonarium questions Leaena closely about her new client

from *The Dialogues of the Courtesans*
Lucian (*c*. AD 115–after 180)

This animated conversation comes from The Dialogues of the Courtesans, *by Lucian of Samosata, and was written at some time in the second century AD. For subsequent centuries it was to become one of the most frequently cited sources of information about sex between women — a fact which would probably have astounded both author and characters. Prurient as Clonarium's enquiries may seem, the dialogue as a whole is in fact relaxed about its subject-matter, and there is something deeply appealing about the freshness and vividness of this conversation overheard at a distance of almost two thousand years.*

CLONARIUM: We've been hearing strange things about you, Leaena. They say that Megilla, the rich Lesbian woman, is in love with you just like a man, that you live with each other, and do goodness knows what together. Hullo! Blushing? Tell me if it's true.

LEAENA: Quite true, Clonarium. But I'm ashamed, for it's unnatural.

CLONARIUM: In the name of Mother Aphrodite, what's it all about? What does the woman want? What do you do when you are together? You see, you don't love me, or you wouldn't hide such things from me.

LEAENA: I love you as much as I love any woman, but she's terribly like a man.

CLONARIUM: I don't understand what you mean, unless she's a sort of woman for the ladies. They say there are women like that in Lesbos, with faces like men, and unwilling to consort with men, but only with women, as though they themselves were men.

LEAENA: It's something like that.

CLONARIUM: Well, tell me all about it; tell me how she made her first advances to you, how you were persuaded, and what followed.

LEAENA: She herself and another rich woman, with the same accomplishments, Demonassa from Corinth, were organising a drinking party, and had taken me along to provide them with music. But, when I had finished playing, and it was late and time to turn in and they were drunk, Megilla said, 'Come along Leaena, it's high time we were in bed; you sleep here between us.'

CLONARIUM: And did you? What happened after that?

LEAENA: At first they kissed me like men, not simply bringing their lips to mine, but opening their mouths a little, embracing me, and squeezing my breasts. Demonassa even bit me as she kissed, and I didn't know what to make of it. Eventually Megilla, being now rather heated, pulled off her wig, which was very realistic and fitted very closely, and revealed the skin of her head which was shaved close, just as on the most energetic of athletes. This sight gave me a shock, but she said, 'Leaena, have you ever seen such a good-looking young fellow?' 'I don't see one here, Megilla,' said I. 'Don't make a woman out of me,' said she. 'My name is Megillus, and I've been married to Demonassa here for ever so long; she's my wife.' I laughed at that, Clonarium, and said, 'Then, unknown to us, Megillus, you were a man all the time, just as they say Achilles once hid among the girls, and you have everything that a man has, and can play the part of a man to Demonassa?' 'I haven't got what you mean,' said she, 'I don't need it at all. You'll find I've a much pleasanter method of my own.' 'You're surely not a hermaphrodite,' said I, 'equipped both as a man and a woman, as many people are said to be?'; for I still didn't know, Clonarium, what it was all about. But she said, 'No, Leaena, I'm all man.' 'Well,' I said, 'I've heard the Boeotian flute-girl, Ismenodora, repeating tales she'd heard at home, and telling us how someone at Thebes had turned from woman to man, someone who was also an excellent soothsayer, and was, I think, called Tiresias. That didn't happen to you, did it?' 'No, Leaena,' she said, 'I was born a woman like the rest of you, but I have the mind and the desires and everything else of a man.' 'And do you find these desires enough?' said I. 'If you don't believe me Leaena,' said she, 'just give me a chance, and you'll find I'm as good as any man; I have a substitute of my own. Only give me a chance, and you'll see.'

Well I did, my dear, because she begged so hard, and presented me with a costly necklace, and a very fine linen dress. Then I threw my arms around her as though she were a man, and she went to work, kissing me, and panting, and apparently enjoying herself immensely.

CLONARIUM: What did she do? How? That's what I'm most interested to hear.

LEAENA: Don't enquire too closely into the details; they're not very nice; so, by Aphrodite in heaven, I won't tell you!

On ladies who make love

from *Les Vies des dames galantes*
ABBÉ DE BRANTÔME (?1540–1614)

Like many clerics, Pierre de Bourdeille, the Abbé de Brantôme, had a good nose for gossip. His salacious but affable Vies des dames galantes *was posthumously published between 1665 and 1666 and contains innumerable anecdotes about the sexual and emotional lives of the French aristocracy and royal family during the sixteenth century. In his essay on 'Ladies who make love and their cuckold husbands', Brantôme ponders the meaning and status of sex between women: does it really count? and can it be safely dismissed as just another nasty foreign habit?*

So I shall ask another question, one which I think has been completely unexplored and perhaps not even thought of: whether two women amorously inclined to one another, as one has often seen and often sees these days, sleeping together and doing what we call *donna con donna* (in imitation of the learned Sappho), can commit adultery and between them make their husbands cuckolds.

Certainly, if one believes Martial, in his first book, epigram CXIX, they do commit adultery. Here he introduces and addresses a woman named Bassa, a tribade, attacking her very strongly because one never sees men going into her house, to the point where she was assumed to be a second Lucrece, but she has just been found out, since many women and girls are regularly seen going in, and it has been discovered that she herself served them, acting as a fake man and adulterer, and had sex with them – as Martial puts it, 'geminos committere cunnos'.

[. . .]

I knew a courtesan at Rome, a wily old bird if ever there was one, called Isabella de Luna, a Spanish woman, who had this kind of relationship with a courtesan called Pandora, one of the most beautiful women in Rome at that time, who had just been married to a butler of the Cardinal of Armagnac, but had not given up her former occupation; but this Isabella kept her, and usually slept with her; and, unrestrained and disorderly in her speech as she was, I have often heard her say that she made her more of a whore than ever, and made her cuckold her husband more than all the ruffians she'd ever had sex with. I don't know what she meant by that, unless she was basing it on Martial's epigram.

People say that Sappho of Lesbos was a past-mistress of this practice; indeed, it's said she invented it, and that ever since the Lesbian ladies have imitated her in it, and do so to this day. This is what Lucian says: that such women, who won't let men touch them, but approach other women just as men do, are 'Lesbians'. And such women who enjoy this activity and won't let men come near them, but give themselves sexually to other women as if to men, are called *tribades*, a Greek word derived, as I have been told by Greeks, from τριβω, τριβειν [*tribo, tribein*], which means *fricare*, to rub, or fret, or rub against each other; and tribades are known in French as 'fricatrices', or those who play at *fricarelle* in the manner of *donna con donna*, as one sees today.

[. . .]

[Lucian] tells us that women come together to copulate with each other, copulating like men, with lascivious, strange and monstrous devices, sterile in form; and that the name now rarely applied to these fricatrices, then used freely everywhere for the feminine sex, should be Philaenises, from Philaenis, who imitated some mannish forms of love. However he adds that it is far better for a woman to be lasciviously inclined to play the man, than for a man to become effeminate [. . .] So the woman, in this view, who thus imitates the man, can have the reputation of being more valorous and courageous than another, as indeed I have known some to be, both in body and spirit.

In another place, Lucian introduces two ladies discussing this kind of love; and one asks the other if such and such a woman had been in love with her, and if she had slept with her, and what she had done to her. The other replied frankly: 'First, she kissed me like men do, not just lip to lip but opening her mouth [. . .] and, although she had no male member and seemed just like us other women, she said she had the heart, affections and all other qualities of a man; then I embraced her as if she were a man and she did it to me, kissing me and "going" (I don't understand that word); and apparently finding extreme pleasure in it; and she copulated in a way which was much pleasanter than a man's.' So that's what Lucian says on the subject.

Now, from what I've heard tell, there are many such ladies and Lesbians, in many places and regions, in France, in Italy and in Spain, Turkey, Greece and other places. And where women are recluses and don't have complete freedom of action, this practice thrives especially: for, when such women are physically overheated, they say, they do need to avail themselves of this remedy to refresh themselves a little, or entirely, from their heat.

The Turkish women go to their baths more for this lechery than for anything else, and are much given to it: even the courtesans, who have men at their beck and call at all hours, still indulge in these fricarelles, seek each other out and make love to each other, as I have heard tell some do in Italy and in Spain. In our own France, such women are quite common; and yet people say it hasn't been that long that they've been mixed up in it, and indeed that the fashion for it was imported from Italy by a lady of quality whom I refuse to name.

Lord Rochester 2, Miss Hobart 0

from *Memoirs of the Count de Grammont*
ANTHONY HAMILTON (?1646–1720)

One of the few women who gave Lord Rochester, the libertine poet of Charles II's court, a run for his money in the seduction stakes was Miss Hobart, an intriguing figure (in all senses). That part of her story told here comes from Anthony Hamilton's Memoirs of the Count de Grammont at the Court of Charles II, *originally published in 1713 in French.*

This extract, based on a translation made by a M. Boyer early in the eighteenth century, comes from a revised edition produced by the eighteenth-century novelist Horace Walpole (1717–1797) – particularly appropriate since he was no stranger to passions between women: in later life he became especially close to his niece, Mary Berry, the ardent friend of the renowned sculptress, Anne Damer, who was herself the daughter of one of his closest friends, Henry Conway. Mrs Thrale's intemperate remarks on Mrs Damer may be found elsewhere in this book, under 'Dealings with the Enemy'.

Introducing Miss Hobart

Miss Hobart's character was at that time as uncommon in England, as her person was singular, in a country where, to be young, and not to be in some degree handsome, is a reproach; she had a good shape, rather a bold air, and a great deal of wit, which was well cultivated, without having much discretion. She was likewise possessed of a great deal of vivacity, with an irregular fancy; there was a great deal of fire in her eyes, which, however, produced no effect upon the beholders: and she had a tender heart, whose sensibility some pretended was alone in favor of the fair sex.

Miss Bagot was the first that gained her tenderness and affection, which she returned at first with equal warmth and sincerity; but perceiving that all her friendship was insufficient to repay that of Miss Hobart, she yielded the conquest to the governess's niece, who thought herself as much honored by it as her aunt thought herself obliged by the care she took of the young girl.

It was not long before the report, whether true or false, of this singularity, spread through the whole court, where people, being yet so uncivilized as never to have heard of that kind of refinement in love of ancient Greece, imagined that the illustrious Hobart, who seemed so particularly attached to the fair sex, was in reality something more than she appeared to be.

Satirical ballads soon began to compliment her upon these new attributes; and upon the insinuations that were therein made, her companions began to fear her. The governess, alarmed at these reports, consulted Lord Rochester upon the danger to which her niece was exposed. She could not have applied to a fitter person: he immediately advised her to take her niece out of the hands of Miss Hobart, and contrived matters so well that she fell into his own.

[*Miss Hobart attempts to seduce Miss Temple and to warn her against the men at Court.*]

She had already made all necessary advances to gain possession of her confidence and friendship; and Miss Temple, less suspicious of her than of Lord Rochester, made all imaginable returns. She was greedy of praise, and loved all manner of sweetmeats, as much as a child of nine or ten years old: her taste was gratified in both these respects. Miss Hobart having the superintendence of the duchess's baths, her apartment joined them, in which there was a closet stored with all sorts of sweetmeats and liqueurs: the closet suited Miss Temple's taste, as exactly as it gratified Miss Hobart's inclination, to have something that could allure her.

Summer, being now returned, brought back with it the pleasures and diversions that are its inseparable attendants. One day when the ladies had been taking the air on horseback, Miss Temple, on her return from riding, alighted at Miss Hobart's, in order to recover her fatigue at the expense of the sweetmeats, which she knew were there at her service; but before she began she desired Miss Hobart's permission to undress herself and change her linen in her apartment; which request was immediately complied with: 'I was just going to propose it to you,' said Miss Hobart, 'not but that you are as charming as an angel in your riding habit, but there is nothing so comfortable as a loose dress, and being at one's ease: you cannot imagine, my dear Temple,' continued she, embracing her, 'how much you oblige me by this free, unceremonious conduct; but, above all, I am enchanted with your particular attention to cleanliness: how greatly you differ in this, as in many other things, from that silly creature, Jennings! Have you remarked how all our court fops admire her for her brilliant complexion, which perhaps, after all, is not wholly her own; and for blunders, which are truly original, and which they are such fools as to mistake for wit: I have not conversed with her long enough to perceive in what her wit consists; but of this I am certain, that if it is not better than her feet, it is no great matter. What stories have I heard of her sluttishness! No cat ever dreaded water so much as she does: fie upon her! Never to wash for her own comfort, and only to attend to those parts which must necessarily be seen, such as the neck and hands.'

Miss Temple swallowed all this with even greater pleasure than the sweetmeats; and the officious Hobart, not to lose time, was helping her off with her clothes, while the chambermaid was coming. She made some objections to this at first, being unwilling to occasion that trouble to a person, who, like Miss Hobart, had been advanced to a place of dignity; but she was overruled by her, and assured that it was with the greatest pleasure she showed her that small mark of civility. The collation being finished, and Miss Temple undressed: 'Let us retire,' said Miss Hobart, 'to the bathing-closet, where we may enjoy a little conversation secure from any impertinent visit.' Miss Temple consented, and both of them sitting down on a couch: 'You are too young, my dear Temple,' said she, 'to know the baseness of men in general, and too short a time acquainted with the court to know the character of its inhabitants. I will give you a short sketch of the principal persons, to the best of my knowledge, without injury to any one, for I abominate the trade of scandal.'

[*Lord Rochester, angry that Miss Hobart has made trouble between him and Miss Temple, arranges for Miss Temple to be warned off. His friend Killegrew*

pretends to mistake Miss Temple (who is masked) for Miss Hobart, and
tells the supposed Miss Hobart:]

your passion and inclinations for Miss Temple are known to every one
but herself; for whatever methods you used to impose upon her innocence, the world does her the justice to believe that she would treat you
as Lady Falmouth did, if the poor girl knew the wicked designs you
had upon her: I caution you, therefore, against making any further
advances to a person too modest to listen to them: I advise you likewise
to take back your maid again, in order to silence her scandalous tongue;
for she says everywhere that she is with child, that you are the occasion
of her being in that condition, and accuses you of behaving towards her
with the blackest ingratitude, upon trifling suspicions only: you know
very well, these are no stories of my own invention; but that you may
not entertain any manner of doubt, that I had all this from her own
mouth; she has told me your conversation in the bathing-room; the
characters you there drew of the principal men at court; your artful
malice in applying so improperly a scandalous song to one of the loveliest
women in all England; and in what manner the innocent girl fell into
the snare you had laid for her, in order to do justice to her charms.

[*Killegrew warns 'Miss Hobart' that one man is planning to fight a duel
with her because of her scandalous remarks:*]

Indeed, these invectives are of the blackest and most horrible nature: he
says it is most infamous, that a wretch like yourself should find no other
employment than to blacken the characters of gentlemen to gratify your
jealousy; that if you do not desist from such conduct for the future, he will
immediately complain of you; and that if her Royal Highness will not do
him justice, he is determined to do himself justice, and to run you through
the body with his own sword, though you were even in the arms of Miss
Temple, and that it is most scandalous that all the maids of honor should
get into your hands before they can look around them.

[*Miss Temple panics:*]

as soon as she had regained the free use of her senses, she hastened back to St. James, without answering a single question that the other put to her; and having locked herself up in her chamber, the first thing she did, was immediately to strip off Miss Hobart's clothes, lest she should be contaminated by them; for after what she had been told concerning her, she looked upon her as a monster, dreadful to the innocence of the fair sex, of whatever sex she might be; she blushed at the familiarities she had been drawn into with a creature, whose maid was with child, though she never had been in any other service but hers: she therefore returned her all her clothes, ordered her servant to bring back all her own, and resolved never more to have any connection with her. Miss Hobart, on the other hand, who supposed Killegrew had mistaken Miss Temple for herself, could not comprehend what could induce her to give herself such surprising airs, since that conversation; but being desirous to come to an explanation, she ordered Miss Temple's maid to remain in her apartments, and went to call upon Miss Temple herself, instead of sending back her clothes; and being desirous to give her some proof of friendship before they entered upon expostulations, she slipped softly into her chamber, when she was in the very act of changing her linen, and embraced her. Miss Temple finding herself in her arms before she had taken notice of her, everything that Killegrew had mentioned, appeared to her imagination: she fancied that she saw in her looks the eagerness of a satyr, or, if possible, of some monster still more odious; and disengaging herself with the highest indignation from her arms, she began to shriek and cry in the most terrible manner, calling both heaven and earth to her assistance.

The first whom her cries raised were the governess and her niece. It was near twelve o'clock at night; Miss Temple in her shift, almost frightened to death, was pushing back with horror Miss Hobart, who approached her with no other intent than to know the occasion of these transports. As soon as the governess saw this scene, she began to lecture Miss Hobart with all the eloquence of a real duenna; she demanded of her, whether she thought it was for her that her Royal Highness kept the maids of honor? whether she was not ashamed to come at such an unseasonable time of night into their very apartments to commit such violences? and swore that she would, the very next day, complain to the duchess. All this confirmed Miss Temple in her mistaken notions; and Hobart was obliged to go away at last, without being able to convince or bring to reason creatures, whom she believed to be either distracted or mad. The next day Miss Sarah did not fail to relate this adventure to her lover, telling him how Miss Temple's cries had alarmed the maids of honor's apartment, and how herself and her aunt, running to her assistance, had almost surprised Miss Hobart in the very act.

Two days after, the whole adventure, with the addition of several embellishments, was made public; the governess swore to the truth of it, and related in every company what a narrow escape Miss Temple had experienced, and that Miss Sarah, her niece, had preserved her honor, because, by Lord Rochester's excellent advice, she had forbidden her all manner of connection with so dangerous a person. Miss Temple was afterwards informed, that the song that had so greatly provoked her alluded to Miss Price only: this was confirmed to her by every person, with additional execrations against Miss Hobart, for such a scandalous imposition. Such great coldness after so much familiarity, made many believe, that this adventure was not altogether a fiction.

This had been sufficient to have disgraced Miss Hobart at court, and to have totally ruined her reputation in London, had she not been, upon the present, as well as upon a former occasion, supported by the duchess: her Royal Highness pretended to treat the whole story as romantic and visionary, or as solely arising from private pique: she chid Miss Temple, for her impertinent credulity: turned away the governess and her niece, for the lies with which she pretended they supported the imposture; and did many improper things in order to re-establish Miss Hobart's honor, which, however, she failed in accomplishing.

Inside the Cabal

from *The New Atalantis* (1709–1710)
DELARIVIER MANLEY (1663–1742)

Delarivier Manley's scandalous roman à clef, The New Atalantis, *mixed fantasy and contemporary politics (her treatment of the latter brought Manley temporary imprisonment). Here, Intelligence, the goddess of rumour-mongering and inside information, reveals the dubious activities of a group of aristocratic women whom she calls 'The Cabal'. Ambivalence seems too tame a word to describe the conflicting attitudes the author displays in this passage towards sexual love and intimacy between women.*

Vice or virtue?

But to satisfy your Excellency, these ladies are of the new Cabal, a sect (however innocent in it self) that does not fail from meeting its share of censure from the world. Alas! what can they do? How unfortunate are women? If they seek their diversion out of themselves and include the other sex, they must be criminal? If in themselves (as those of the new Cabal), still they are criminal? Though censurers must carry their imaginations a much greater length than I am able to do mine, to explain this hypothesis with success. They pretend to find in these the vices of old Rome revived and quote you certain detestable authors who (to amuse posterity) have introduced you lasting monuments of vice, which could only subsist in imagination and can, in reality, have no other foundation that what are to be found in the dreams of poets and the ill nature of those censurers, who will have no diversions innocent, but what themselves advance!

Oh how laudable! how extraordinary! how wonderful! is the un-common happiness of the Cabal? They have wisely excluded that rapacious sex who, making a prey of the honour of ladies, find their greatest satisfaction (some few excepted) in boasting of their good for-tune, the very chocolate-house being witnesses of their self-love where, promiscuously among the known and unknown, they expose the letters of the fair, explain the mysterious and refine upon the happy part, in their redundancy of vanity consulting nothing but what may feed the insatiable hydra!

Jealousy

The Cabal run no such dangers, they have all the happiness in themselves! Two beautiful ladies joined in an excess of amity (no word is tender enough to express their new delight) innocently embrace! For how can they be guilty? They vow eternal tenderness, they exclude the men, and condition that they will always do so. What irregularity can there be in this? 'Tis true, some things may be strained a little too far, and that causes reflections to be cast upon the rest. One of the fair could not defend herself from receiving an importunate visit from a person of the troublesome sex. The lady who was her favourite came unexpectedly at the same time upon another. Armida heard her chair set down in the hall and presently knew her voice, enquiring with precipitation who was above? Having observed a common coach at the gate without a livery, the lover became surprised to the last degree to see Armida's. She trembled! she turned pale! she conjured him to pass into her closet and consent to be concealed till the lady was gone! His curiosity made him as obliging as she could desire; he was no sooner withdrawn, but his fair rival entered the chamber enraged, her voice shrill, her tone inquisitive and menacing, the extremes of jealousy in her eyes and air. 'Where is this inconstant – where is this ungrateful girl –? What happy wretch is it upon whom you bestow my rites? To whom do you deliver the possession of my kisses and embraces? Upon whom bestow that heart so invaluable and for which I have paid the equivalent? – Come let us see this monster to whom my happiness is sacrificed – Are you not sufficiently warned by the ruin of so many? Are you also eager to be exposed, to be undone, to be food for vanity, to fill the detestable creatures with vain glory! What recompense? – ah, what satisfaction! – Can there be in any heart of theirs, more than in mine – Have they more tenderness – more endearments – their truth cannot come in comparison! Besides, they find their account in treachery and boasting, their pride is gratified, whilst our interest is in mutual secrecy, in natural justice and in mutual constancy.'

Scandal

Such excursions as these have given occasion to the enemies of the Cabal to refine, as much as they please, upon the mysteries of it. There are, who will not allow of innocency in any intimacies, detestable censurers who, after the manner of the Athenians, will not believe so great a man as Socrates (him whom the oracle delivered to be the wisest of all men) could see every hour the beauty of an Alcibiades without taxing his sensibility. How did they recriminate for his affection, for his cares, his tenderness to the lovely youth? How have they delivered him down to posterity as blameable for too guilty a passion for his beautiful pupil? – Since then it is not in the fate of even so wise a man to avoid the censure of the busy and the bold, care ought to be taken by others (less fortified against occasion of detraction, in declining such unaccountable intimacies) to prevent the ill-natured world's refining upon their mysterious innocence.

Meetings

The persons who passed us in those three coaches were returning from one of their private, I was going to say silent, meetings, but far be it from me to detract from any of the attributes of the sex. The Lady L— and her daughters make four of the cabal. They have taken a little lodging about twelve furlongs from Angela in a place obscure and pleasant with a magazine of good wine and necessary conveniences as to chambers of repose, a tolerable garden and the country in prospect. They wear away the indulgent happy hours according to their own taste. Their coaches and people (of whom they always take as few with them as possible) are left to wait at the convenient distance of a field in length, an easy walk to their bower of bliss. The day and hour of their *rendezvous* is appointed beforehand; they meet, they caress, they swear inviolable secrecy and amity. The glass corroborates their endearments. They momently exclude the men: fortify themselves in the precepts of virtue and chastity against all their detestable undermining arts: arraign without pity or compassion those who have been so unfortunate as to fall into their snare: propagate their principles of exposing them without mercy: give rules to such of the Cabal who are not married how to behave themselves to such who they think fit they should marry, no such weighty affair being to be accomplished without the mutual consent of the society, at the same time lamenting the custom of the world, that has made it convenient (nay, almost indispensable) for all ladies once to marry. To those that have husbands, they have other instructions, in which this is sure to be one: to reserve their heart, their tender amity for their fair friend, an article in this well-bred, wilfully undistinguishing age which the husband seems to be rarely solicitous of.

Bisexuals, keep out

Those who are in their opinion so happy as to be released from the imposing matrimonial fetters are thought the ornament of the Cabal and by all most happy. They claim an ascendant, a right of governing, of admitting or extending; in both they are extremely nice, with particular reserve to the constitution of the novice, they strictly examine her genius, whether it have fitted her for the mysteries of the Cabal, as if she may be rendered insensible on the side of Nature. Nature, who has the trick of making them dote on the opposite improving sex, for if her foible be found directed to what Nature inspires, she is unanimously excluded, and particular injunctions bestowed upon all members of this distinguishing society from admitting her to their bosom, or initiating her in the mysteries of their endearments.

An initiation

from *Fanny Hill*
by JOHN CLELAND (1709–1789)

*An archetypal version of the lesbian frequently encountered in erotic fiction
written by men is that of the older, sexually experienced woman who 'initiates'
a young virgin into the pleasures of sex, and prepares her for The Real
Thing (defloration by a man).*

*Here is the first stage of that process as recounted in one of the most
notorious works in the European canon of erotic literature – John Cleland's*
Memoirs of a Woman of Pleasure *(1748–1749), better known as* Fanny
Hill. *Cleland himself appears to have been homosexual which may offer a
different perspective on the book's glorification of penetrative sex and male
genitalia – not so much a heterosexual male fantasy of self-aggrandisement
as a homosexual one of desire and longing.*

No sooner then was this precious substitute of my mistress's lain down, but
she, who was never out of her way when any occasion of lewdness presented
itself, turned to me, embraced and kissed me with great eagerness.

This was new, this was odd; but imputing it to nothing but pure
kindness, which, for aught I knew, it might be the London way to
express in that matter, I was determined not to be behind-hand with
her, and returned her the kiss and embrace, with all the fervour that
perfect innocence knew.

Encouraged by this, her hands became extremely free, and wandered
over my whole body, with touches, squeezes, pressures, that rather
warmed and surprised me with their novelty, than they either shocked
or alarmed me.

The flattering praises she intermingled with these invasions contributed
also not a little to bribe my passiveness, and knowing no ill, I feared none;
especially from one who had prevented all doubts of her womanhood by
conducting my hands to a pair of breasts that hung loosely down, in a
size and volume that full sufficiently distinguished her sex, to me at least,
who had never made any comparison.

I lay then all tame and passive as she could wish, whilst her freedom raised no other emotion but those of a strange, and, till then, unfelt pleasure. Every part of me was open, and exposed to the licentious courses of her hands, which, like a lambent fire, ran over all my body, and thawed all coldness as they went.

My breasts, if it is not too bold a figure to call so two hard, firm, rising hillocks, that just began to show themselves, or signify anything to the touch, employed and amused her hands awhile, till slipping down lower, over a smooth track, she could just feel the soft silky down that had but a few months before put forth and garnished the mount-pleasant of those parts, and promised to spread a grateful shelter over the sweet seat of the most exquisite sensation, and which had been, till that instant, the seat of the most insensible innocence. Her fingers played and strove to twine in the young tendrils of that moss, which nature has contrived at once for use and ornament.

But not contented with these outer posts, she now attempts the main spot, and began to twitch, to insinuate, and at length to force an introduction of a finger into the quick itself, in such a manner that, had she not proceeded by insensible gradations that inflamed me beyond the power of modesty to oppose its resistance to their progress, I should have jumped out of bed, and cried for help against such strange assaults.

Instead of which, her lascivious touches had lighted up a new fire that wantoned through all my veins, but fixed with violence in that center appointed them by nature, where the first strange hands were now busied in feeling, squeezing, compressing the lips, then opening them again, with a finger between, till an 'Oh!' expressed her hurting me, where the narrowness of the unbroken passage refused its entrance to any depth.

In the meantime the extension of my limbs, languid stretchings, sighs, short heavings, all conspire to assure that experienced wanton that I was more pleased than offended at her proceedings, which she seasoned with repeated kisses and exclamations, such as 'Oh! what a charming creature thou art! ... What a happy man will he be that first makes a woman of you! ... Oh! that I was a man for your sake! ...' with the like broken expressions, interrupted by kisses as fierce and salacious as ever I received from the other sex.

For my part, I was transported, confused, and out of myself; feelings so new were too much for me. My heated and alarmed senses were in a tumult that robbed me of all liberty of thought; tears of pleasure gushed from my eyes, and somewhat assuaged the fire that raged all over me.

Phœbe herself, the hackneyed, thoroughbred Phœbe, to whom all modes and devices of pleasure were known and familiar, found, it seems, in this exercise of her art to break young girls, the gratification of one of those arbitrary tastes, for which there is no accounting. Not that she hated men, or did not even prefer them to her own sex; but when she met with such occasions as this was, a satiety of enjoyments in the common road, perhaps too, a secret bias, inclined her to make the most of pleasure wherever she could find it, without distinction of sexes. In this view, now well assured that she had, by her touches, sufficiently inflamed me for her purpose, she rolled down the bed-clothes gently, and I saw myself naked, my shift being turned up to my neck, whilst I had no power to oppose it. Even my glowing blushes expressed more desire than modesty, whilst the candle left, to be sure not undesignedly, burning, threw a full light on my whole body.

'No!' says Phœbe, 'you must not, my sweet girl, think to hide all these treasures from me. My sight must be feasted as well as my touch ... I must devour with my eyes this springing BOSOM ... Suffer me to kiss it ... I have not seen it enough ... Let me kiss it once more ... What firm, smooth, white flesh is here! ... How delicately shaped! ... Then this delicious down! Oh! let me view the small, dear, tender cleft! ... This is too much, I cannot bear it! ... I must ... I must —' Here she took my hand, and in a transport carried it where you may easily guess; but what a difference in the state of the same thing ... A spreading thicket of bushy curls marked the full-grown, complete woman. Then the cavity to which she guided my hand easily received it; and as soon as she felt it within her, she moved herself to and fro, with so rapid a friction that I presently withdrew it, wet and clammy, when instantly Phœbe grew more composed, after two or three sighs, and heart-fetched Oh's! and giving me a kiss that seemed to exhale her soul through her lips, she replaced the bedclothes over us. What pleasure she had found I will not say; but this I know, that the first sparks of kindling nature, the first ideas of pollution, were caught by me that night; and that the acquaintance and communication with the bad of our sex is often as fatal to innocence as all the seductions of the other.

Discovering the real thing

from *My Secret Life* by 'WALTER' (?1880s–1890s)

One of the most remarkable documents of Victorian England is My Secret Life, *the monumental autobiography of an unidentified man known only as 'Walter'. Its massive volumes document one English gentleman's sexual life, from childhood to early old age, and they contain a mass of fascinating and revealing detail about some of the social realities underlying and underpinning Victorian morality and 'family values'. Historians and critics differ about the reliability of this record – pure fact or self-glorifying fantasy? To me the work has always seemed remarkably convincing, and although much of Walter's life and world repels, there is a basic honesty, mingled with respect and fellow-feeling for the girls and women, so many of whose sexual services he bought during decades of paid sex. As he entered middle age, Walter became increasingly exercised and curious about homosexuality. He came to distrust his own reactions of horror and repulsion, suspecting they were the product of cultural training rather than of any innate or 'natural' aversion. (Eventually, and with an empiricism typical of him, he tested his theory by having sex with another man. But that's another story. . . .)*

In the extracts below, we can trace something of Walter's dawning realisation that the sexual activity between women which he occasionally witnessed in the brothels might not be, as he had always assumed it was, just a fake side-show staged to titillate male clients. Here, he came to realise, were often real desires, real pleasure and real emotions.

The square brackets are Walter's own, the comments added, often years after the events they describe, when he was preparing his memoirs for press.

This form of sexual voluptuousness amongst women now haunted me. I questioned Liz about Sarah's behaviour in bed with her, for she always now slept with her, and no man was ever there. – It was not as formerly when Sarah said, 'You mustn't come for three days,' and so on. I found that Sarah had a letch for frigging herself, and *that* with the young one seemed her solace in the absent pleasure with the male. Her taste for the man it may be was diminishing. She had done this almost from the first day Liz came to London. Then I guessed that Sarah did something more. – I asked questions, and threatening not to see Liz any more if she did not tell me the truth. She disclosed that Sarah pulled the girl on the top of her, and pressing clitoris to clitoris rubbed them together, till Sarah at least had the full enjoyment of that voluptuous friction. – It was flat fucking, tribadism, the amusement of girls at boarding schools and convents, and perhaps harems [and often as I know since, of some harlots].

'Don't tell her,' said Liz. – 'She has made me promise not, and says you'd hate me if you knew of it – you won't hate me will you? I don't like her *thinging* me – I don't like her wet thing *in* mine.' 'Is it not nice?' 'It be a little nice sometimes, but I don't like thinging like that.' – I promised to keep Lizzie's secret.

'You call it thinging, why?' 'Cos her thing be gin my thing,' said the girl laughing, – 'it be like two snails.' I roared with laughter at such an illustrative remark, and never heard flat fucking called *thinging* before or since. [I have since heard a funny term for it tho.]

Then I began to think about flat fucking, and recollected what in my youth Fred had said, and what I had been told by Camille of women rubbing their cunts together, that I had seen two French women doing it (for my amusement, as I thought, and simply to show me how by placing themselves like a man and woman in copulation, they could close their cunts on each other). One woman I recollected had a strongly developed clitoris and I had not liked it. But I did not believe in women having pleasure that way, and the baudy sight had passed from my mind. Nor had any clear idea of the truth even arisen in my mind, when I saw two servants on each other in the bath room at my cousin's school, or Gabrielle on Violette.

I had heard since of women flat fucking, and suddenly recollected a row at a brothel, in which the amusement had been referred to.

*   *   *

I had never given the subject much thought, but now began to think of the way women could bring their organs together for mutual pleasure, and of various tricks that way which I had seen women perform, but the subject never seems to have interested me fully till now. Then I got some medical books and some French books, and under Lesbos, Tribade &c. and some other words, got the key to the full mysteries of Sappho and the Lesbians, which added a mite more to my knowledge and admiration of the wonders of the article called cunt.

My promise of secrecy I kept, but often looked at Sarah and longed to question her on this subject. I began to talk about quim to quim friction – flat fucking – and explained the word *tribadism*, which word Sarah had never heard – I let her know that I thought no harm in women rubbing their cunts together, or gamahuching each other; and Sarah at once, I thought, got more free in her manifestations towards the girl.

Dealings with the Enemy

The early entries in this section should perhaps carry health warnings: the Roman writers, Martial and Juvenal, were capable of vitriolic anti-lesbian sentiments, some of which are reprinted here. Why, you may wonder? One of the answers is that lesbians of earlier periods took their information where they could find it. Not for them the ever-proliferating array of books and magazines, films and websites available to lesbians today. For women who knew they loved and desired other women, it was often the discovery of kindred spirits in literature and history that first brought the confidence to voice their own desires for real flesh and blood women. (Remember how useful the beastly Juvenal was to Anne Lister in the early stages of her acquaintance with Miss Pickford, see 'Betwixt and Between'.)

Sometimes the fiercest foes were once the dearest friends: witness the violent outburst of the Duchess of Marlborough against her erstwhile beloved Queen. And sometimes enemies may be friends in disguise, or vice versa. So, for example, it is not clear which category 'A Sapphick Epistle' falls into, and we don't even know the sex, or sexuality, of the author.

This section contains not only fire from enemy lines but some striking examples of women fighting back: Jane Cheyne's 'The Angry Curs', and C. M. Donald's 'Poor Old Fat Woman' would halt any enemy in its tracks.

Juvenal (c. AD 60–?) and
Martial (c. AD 40–103/4)

Although the eighteenth century much admired aspects of Juvenal – his loathing of hypocrisy, hatred of political corruption, and fierce nostalgia for a simpler, nobler time – his treatment of matters sexual was a problem. His misogyny could be easily accommodated; the obscenity with which he voiced it was the real stumbling block. Martial, an inspired but frequently gross epigrammatist, who took the whole of human sexuality as his target, but reserved some of his keenest shots for women, presented similar problems. When Juvenal, Martial and all classical authors had remained safely locked in 'the decent obscurity of a learned language' (to borrow the inspired phrase of 'Decline and Fall' Gibbon), there was no cause for alarm. But while increasing advances in women's education meant that some women now had access to Juvenal and Martial in the original, there was also a growing readership anxious to sample the fruits of a classical literature which could be available to them only in translation. What to translate and how?

William Gifford, one of Juvenal's most notable early nineteenth-century translators, had to work quite hard to persuade himself that it was actually permissible to bring this scabrous author into the light of the English language. We can see something of his moral wrestlings in this passage from 'An Essay on the Roman Satirists' (1802).

When we consider the unnatural vices at which Juvenal directs his indignation, and reflect, at the same time, on the peculiar qualities of his mind, we shall not find much cause perhaps for wonder in the strength of his expressions. I should resign him in silence to the hatred of mankind, if his aim, like that of too many others whose works are read with delight, had been to render vice amiable, to fling his seducing colours over impurity, and inflame the passions by meretricious hints at what is only innoxious when exposed in native deformity: but when I find that his views are to render depravity loathsome; that everything which can alarm and disgust is directed at her [i.e., depravity], in his terrible page, I forget the grossness of the execution in the excellence of the design; and pay my involuntary homage to that integrity which, fearlessly calling in strong description to the aid of virtue, attempts to purify the passions, at the hazard of wounding our delicacy and offending our taste.

The passages that follow demonstrate what translators are up against.

An extract from Juvenal's notorious Satire VI, his sustained diatribe against the fallen nature of the once noble women of his contemporary Rome, translated by WILLIAM GIFFORD (1802)

Whence shall these prodigies of vice be traced?
From wealth, my friend. Our matrons then were chaste
When days of labour, nights of short repose,
Hands still employed, the Tuscan wool to tose,
Their husbands armed and anxious for the State,
And Hannibal hard by the Colline gate,
Conspired to keep all thoughts of ill aloof,
And banished vice far from their lowly roof.
Now all the evils of long peace are ours;
Luxury, more terrible than hostile powers,
Her baleful influence wide around has hurled
And well avenged the subjugated world.
Since Poverty (our better Genius) fled,
Vice like a deluge o'er the State has spread.
Now, shame to Rome! in every street are found
The essenced Sybarite with roses crowned;
Miletan; Rhodian; and Tarentine
Lewd, petulant, and reeling ripe with wine.

Wealth first, the ready pander to all sin,
Brought foreign manners, foreign vices, in.
Wealth enervates and, with seductive art,
Saps every home-bred virtue of the heart.
Yes, *every* — for what cares the drunken dame
(Take arse or tip, to her 'tis all the same!)
Who at deep midnight on fat oysters sups,
And froths with unguents her Falernian cups;
Who swallows oceans till the tables rise
And double lustres dance before her eyes?

Wonder no more why Tullia, homeward bound,
Sniffs with disgust the putrid air around;
Why Maura whispers to her ill-famed friend
As by Shame's antique shrine their way they wend.
Here stop the litters; here my Ladies 'light:
They piss like fountains in the goddess' sight,
Ride one another, and then make for home
While Luna sails high o'er the streets of Rome.

All know by now, my friend, the secret rites
Of the Good Goodness. When the dance excites
The boiling blood; when, to distraction wound,
By wine and music's stimulating sound,
The Maenads of Priapus with wild air
Howl horribly and toss their flowing hair;
Then, how the wine at every pore o'erflows!
How the eye sparkles! How the bosom glows!
How the cheek burns; and, as the passions rise,
How the strong feeling bursts in eager cries!
Saufeia now springs forth and tries a fall
With the town prostitutes and throws them all,
But yields, herself, to Medullina, known
For parts and powers superior to her own.

Maids, mistresses, alike the contest share,
And, sure, 'tis always birth that triumphs there.
Nothing is feigned in this accursèd game;
'Tis genuine all, and such as would inflame
The aged blood of Priam, or inspire
The frozen veins of Nestor with desire.
Impatient Nature cracks: a hollow groan
Of lust breaks forth; the sex, the sex is shown,
And one loud yell re-echoes through the den:
'Now, now 'tis lawful; now admit the men.'

Two versions of Martial's epigram
'Ad Bassam tribadem'
(To Bassa, the Tribade)

The first is translated by Sir Charles Sedley (?1639–1701).

That I ne'er saw thee in a coach with man
Nor thy chaste name in wanton satire met;
That from thy sex thy liking never ran,
So as to suffer a male servant yet;
I thought thee the Lucretia of our time:
But, Bassa, thou the while a fucker wert,
And clashing cunts with a prodigious crime
Didst act of man th'inimitable part.
What Oedipus this riddle can untie?
Without a male there was adultery.

Here is an earlier translation by R. Fletcher, in his Ex Otio Negotium, *or* Martiall his Epigrams Translated, *published in 1656. To modern ears there is something endearingly familiar about the 'outing' in line 6.*

Cause amongst males thou nere was seen to be
Nor as unchast no fable feigned thee,
But all thy offices discharged were
By thine own sex, no man intruding there,
I grant thou seem'dst *Lucretia* to our eye,
But (o mistake!) *Bassa* th'art out ont, fie.
Two Twatts commit the fact, and dare it can,
Whiles a prodigious lust supplies the man,
Th'st made a riddle worth the *Thebane* guile,
Where no man is, adultery bred the while.

Two more epigrams by Martial

Book VII, Epigram LXVII

Philaenis the bulldyke buggers boys
and hornier than a married man
she screws eleven girls a day.
Tucking her skirt up, she will play
at handball; smear herself with grit
and wrestle; with the bum-boys swing
the dumb-bells round; grow foul with sweat,
and even let the trainer's whip
correct her; next, she sinks her booze,
and pukes it up, in time for dinner;
wolfs a share of training rations
sixteen times over; then she swills.
After all this, it's time to fuck.
Pricks she won't suck; she thinks it's sissy,
but gobbles up the cracks of girls.
Philaenis, may the gods bestow
what you think butch — a cunt to lick.

Book VII, Epigram LXX

A real dyke's dyke, Philaenis: quite correctly
she whom you fuck you speak of as your 'girlfriend'.

Translated by Gillian Spraggs (1999)

The Angry Curs
JANE CHEYNE, née Lady Jane Cavendish
(1621–1669)

This exhilaratingly furious piece comes down the centuries still fresh and vigorous. Woe to those who come between the poet and her beloved Sister Brackley! They deserve everything they'll get.

Jane Cheyne was the daughter of the Duke of Newcastle by his first wife, Elizabeth (née Bassett), and stepdaughter of Margaret, Duchess of Newcastle ('Mad Madge' to her less-admiring contemporaries, and author of The New Blazing World *and other writings). Devoted to her sister Elizabeth, Jane wrote with her at least one play,* The Concealed Fanseys, *composed while their father's castle was under siege during the Civil War; the castle eventually fell to the enemy and the sisters were taken prisoner. Cheyne Walk, the Chelsea street, takes its name from Jane's husband, Sir Charles Cheyne, later Viscount Newhaven.*

Who is't that darr tell mee they'l have away
My Sister Brackley, who's my true lifes day
For in hir absence I will be a Nunn
And speak then nothinge, but when will she come
The Plotters of this damned ugley plott
Let Curs of Egipp ever prove their lott
For meate I'de have then all things truely want
But fleas, lice, those plenty and not scant
An for their Beare I'd have it steeped soote
Or as the best stamped Henbane ugley roote

So far their mind I wish it never pleased
But always troubled with a high disease
For Company, Rats squeaking their discourse
And then Catts howleing should be their Carous
Their Clothes in Winter stiff Buckeram thinn
In Summer Pollcat fur lyned all with in
This I would have Ill natures justly payd
And when they trust I'd have them sure betray'd
Now all good people that have gallant minds
Shun this foule creature, as the worst of kinds
From Plague or Pestilence is our lettany
But from ill natures God deliver mee.

A modern version

Who dares to tell me that they'll take my Sister Brackley from me?
She's my true life's day. In her absence I'll live as a nun and say nothing
until she returns. Let the Curses of Egypt befall the people who've
hatched this damnable, ugly plot. If I had my way they'd have nothing
but fleas and lice for meat – they'd have plenty of those, no shortage
there. As for their beer, I'd have it be soot and water or, better still,
full of Henbane, a poisonous plant. And I hope they have no peace of
mind, but are always anxious and troubled. Let them have squeaking
rats for company and conversation, and howling cats to carouse with.
Their clothes in winter should be made of thin, stiff buckram, and in
summer they'd be lined inside with polecat fur. That's the proper way
to repay ill natures, and whenever they trust in people, I'd like to see
them thoroughly betrayed. Now all you nobly minded good people,
shun this foul creature [the plotter], the worst kind of all. We regularly
pray to be delivered from plague or pestilence, but my prayer is may
God deliver me from ill-natured people.

Queen Anne and Abigal Masham:
a letter and a lampoon

In periods of intense intrigue and power-broking, when much is at stake and the pickings are rich, allegations of homosexuality are often a routine element of the in-fighting. Sometimes, however, there is fire as well as smoke. It is clear that Queen Anne (1665–1714), from her earliest adolescence, was part of a friendship circle of physically loving girls and young women. Once Anne became Queen, however, her close friendships with particular women became a source of political anxiety: accusations of undue influence, intriguing and caballing posed as moral concern. When Sarah, Duchess of Marlborough, once Queen Anne's inseparable companion, found herself ousted by her younger cousin, Abigail Masham, the gloves were off. On 26 July 1708 she wrote a letter to the Queen in which she denounced Anne's 'unaccountable' passion for Abigail Masham, and others; a little later, in a spirit of doubtful helpfulness, she also showed the Queen the lampoon which is reprinted below. We do not know for certain the identity of the author, but it seems likely to have been a member of the pro-Marlborough faction.

A letter from a very unruly subject:
Sarah, Duchess of Marlborough breathlessly
denounces Queen Anne

[. . .] and tho your Majesty was pleased to desire me not to speak any more of her [Abigail Masham], which I know to bee her own request & what would bee of great advantage to all her designs if she could obtain it, yet I must humbly beg pardon if I cannot obay that command, the rather because I remember you said att the same time of all things in this world, you valued most your reputation, which I confess surpris'd me very much, that your Majesty should so soon mention that word after having discover'd so great a passion for such a woman, for sure there can bee noe no great reputation in a thing so strange & unaccountable, to say noe more of it, *nor can I think the having noe inclenation for any but of one's own sex is enough to maintain such a charecter as I wish may still bee yours.*

Friend made foe: traditionally believed to be a portrait of Abigail Masham

A New Ballad to the Tune of
Fair Rosamond
(probably written by MAYNWARING)

The lampoon against Queen Anne and
Abigail Masham, who had replaced Sarah
Jennings, the Duchess of Marlborough, in
Queen Anne's affections

When as Queen Anne of great Renown
Great Britain's Scepter sway'd,
Besides the Church, she dearly lov'd
A Dirty Chamber-Maid.

O! Abigail, that was her Name,
She stitch'd and starch'd full well,
But how she pierc'd this Royal Heart,
No Mortal Man can tell.

However, for sweet Service done
And Causes of great Weight,
Her Royal Mistress made her, Oh!
A Minister of State.

Her Secretary she was not
Because she could not write
But had the Conduct and the Care
Of some dark Deeds at Night.

from 'An Ode to *Myra*. In Imitation of *Horace*'s Ode to *Canidia*'
WILLIAM KING
(Printed with King's *The Toast, an Epic Poem in Four Books*
(Dublin, 1732), pp. 82–6)

There is no doubt in this author's mind what some of the meanings of 'exalted Friendship' between women might be. The target here, as Emma Donoghue notes in Passions Between Women: British Lesbian Culture, 1668–1801, *is Lady Frances Brudenell, Duchess of Newburgh, and her circle of Irish 'tribades'. 'Frow' means 'Dutchwoman', which Donoghue suggests is a nickname for the Duchess's lover, probably Lady Allen.*

> Then I'll falsify Report,
> Standing jest of Viceroy's Court;
> Fabled in the Comic Play,
> Tattled over Cards and Tea;
> Always whisper'd with a Sneer,
> When the Frow and thou art near.
> What if *Sappho* was so naught?
> I'll deny, that thou art taught
> How to pair the Female Doves,
> How to practise *Lesbian* Loves:
> But when little *A—n's* spread
> In her Grove or on thy Bed,
> I will swear, 'tis Nature's Call,
> 'Tis exalted Friendship all.

from *Satan's Harvest Home*
ANON. (1749)

This anonymous adversary bites hardest when he seems to fawn: Turkey and Twickenham are linked not only by alliteration but also, possibly, by Mary

Wortley Montagu who visited the former and settled in the latter. (See 'In Foreign Parts', both for Montagu, and for 'A Game of Flatts'.)

Sappho, as she was one of the wittiest Women that ever the World bred, so she thought with Reason, it would be expected she should make some additions to the Science in which Womankind had been so successful: what does she do then? Not content with our Sex, begins *Amours* with her own, and teaches the Female World a new Sort of Sin call'd the *Flats*, that was follow'd not only in *Lucian's* Time, but is practis'd frequently in *Turkey, as well as at* Twickenham at this Day.

from 'A Sapphick Epistle'
'JACK CAVENDISH' (1771)

Whether we're dealing with an enemy or a friend is not always clear in the following work. 'Jack Cavendish', the supposed author of A Sapphick Epistle, *professes to be a great admirer both of Sappho and her latterday counterpart, 'the Honourable and most beautiful Mrs D****' – it's fairly clear that the asterisks pretend to conceal the name of Anne Damer, the sculptress, who was often the subject of gossip and speculation because of her cross-dressing and her relationships with women. Damer was already separated from her husband, who later committed suicide. She was very close to Horace Walpole's niece, Mary Berry, and she inherited Walpole's Twickenham house, Strawberry Hill, when he died in 1797. In the context of the poem, it becomes obvious that 'Jack Cavendish' must be female. Rictor Norton suggests that the name may be intended to refer to Elizabeth Cavendish, another frequent visitor to Strawberry Hill at this time. The text which follows is slightly abridged, since many of its references to contemporary sexual scandals (mainly heterosexual ones) are so obscure as to be untraceable; the footnotes are the author's own.*

from
Jack Cavendish
to the
Honourable and most beautiful Mrs D****

Was there a Maid of Lesbos¹ Isle,
That ever did refuse to smile,
    When Sappho deign'd to woo?
And yet she left their rosy cheeks,
And all their little modest freaks,
    For Phaon – most untrue.

Ah! hapless woman, to confide
In man, and sign to be the bride;
    A vessel full of care:
Would you the wiser Sappho learn,
You might your happiness discern,
    And shun a sharp despair.

When Sappho, the fair Lesbian belle,
Had gain'd the knack to read and spell;
    She woo'd the Graces all:

¹ Lesbos, an Isle of the Ægean Sea, famous for the birth of Miss Sappho, who was the
first young classic maid that bestowed her affections on her own sex: She wrote better
poesy than either Mrs. Montague, Mrs. Greville, Miss Carter, or Miss Aikin, but yet
her verses failed when she came to address the cold Phaon. So when an old maid, and
unfit for man's love, she pursued the young girls of Mytelene, and seduced many. She
was the first Tommy [lesbian] the world has upon record; but to do her justice, though
there hath been many Tommies since, yet we never had but one Sappho.

No more the Lesbian dames my passion move,
Once the dear objects of my guilty love.

Mr. Pope and Mr. Publius Naso Ovid, the first a waspish English Poet, the latter
the most accomplished Roman Gentleman in the reign of Augustus, have given evidence to this heterogeneous passion of Sappho.

No wench of Mytelene's Town,
Or black, or fair, or olive brown,
   Refus'd her amorous call.

By Penny-post she sent her odes,
To matrons, widows, whores and bawds,
   And won them to her will:
For who, Ah tell me cou'd refuse,
The pow'r of such a pleading muse,
   The language of her quill?

Thus happy Sappho past her time,
In making love, and making rhime,
   To all the Lesbian maids:
Who were more constant and more kind,
More pure in soul, more firm of mind,
   Than all the Lesbian blades.

Thrice sensible, discerning dame,
That first pursued the hallow'd flame,
   Of chastity and joy:
That left the brutal clasp of man,
Jove's trite, dull, delegated plan,
   And e'en his Gany-boy.

When this pure scheme the dame pursued,
There was no sin in being lewd,
   It brought no mean disgrace:
'Twas chaste platonick love and law,
As taught in France by Jacques Rousseau,[1]
   That wonder of his race.

[1] Jean Jacques Rousseau, a singular wit and philosopher, the author of the new Eloisa, wherein, to prove the excellence and elegance of his pen, he attempts to unite all contrarities, to make drunkenness amiable, and vice, virtue. He came to England to see the celebrated Scots Hume, (a great philosopher in another way) he lodged at a little Chandler's Shop in Chiswick, under the pretence of learning the manners of the

[. . .]

But now my muse hath ta'en a dance,
And led me off, full frisk to France,
   Which was not my intention;
To Lesbos Isle I meant to stick,
To praise, and visit every nick,
   By help of some invention.

Ah tell me Lady (for you can)
What little joy there is in Man,
   The rough, unweidly [*sic*] bear:
Ah Sappho! I adore thy name,
That did the vulgar Wretch disclaim,
   For the more lovely Fair.

O! think how Phaon us'd the dame,
Curse on his impious heart and name,
   Curse on his cold disdain:
A cruelty, like his, would prove
To me a perfect cure for love,
   Of ev'ry vig'rous swain.

But thank my stars, I have no cause,
To rail at man, or human laws,
   To me they're kind and true:
But I detest the jealous race,
I'd rather see Almeria's face.
   Or gaze on pretty C[rew].

---

people, and the English Language; he always appeared in the Armenian dress, and his
fellow traveller and companion, was, a Pomeranian cur dog. He quarreled with the
sensible Hume, and returned to Paris, w[h]ere he now copies music, prefering that
stile of poverty and independance to elegant retreat.

Oh wou'd the sex pursue my plan,
And turn upon the monster man,
　　What would they not escape:
A thousand woes, a thousand pains,
Swellings, distortions, cramps and strains,
　　The ruin of each shape.

Tell me, for you are vers'd in love,
Did you from man sweet transports prove,
　　To counterpoise the pain?
Can one so slender and so mild,
Support the torments of a child,
　　Nor reprobate the chain.

The marriage chain, Oh hell on earth!
The iron shackle of all mirth,
　　Life's purgatory here:
For woman had been gay, if free,
Nor curs'd to raise up pedigree,
　　To peasant and to peer.

Dear Lady, such is woman's state,
With Charlotte, or with Russia's Kate,
　　Or Moll, or Peg, or Nan:
All sigh, as soon as fledg'd, to have
Some mere, male creature for a slave,
　　To prime their little pan.

Small's then the touch-hole, not being old,
The colour lead, or carrot gold,
　　Or brown, or white or black:
But think, what a fair maid must bear,
When some rough marksman to a hair,
　　Shoots at the little crack.

[. . .]

Ah! Kitty, Kitty, buxom wench,
To let this creature make a trench,
   Where Heav'n but made a slit:
'Tis martyrdom shall wits declare,
To torture such a beauteous fair,
   On such a monstrous spit.

To decency they've no pretence,
The want of that, is want of sense;
   For say, that woman shou'd,
In such a case devote her life,
'Tis worse than stabbing with a knife,
   To rip up flesh and blood.

But delicacy's fled the land,
They'll any thing now take in hand,
   If they can shut their eyes:
Tho' it might make the dumb to speak,
It cannot even make them squeak,
   So well they manage size.

Ah! were the gentle sex like you,
Joy wou'd be rational and true,
   And women might have fame:
You are a pattern of a wife,
That could resign a husband's life,
   To raise a Sapphick name.

[. . .]

Curse on my stars, that I was born,
In such an age of lust and scorn.
  Oh, Sappho, had'st thou been
Alive in these rude, filthy days,
Thy verses had been all in praise
  Of me and beauty's queen.

Oh! had it been my wretched fate,
That Phaon had made me his hate,
  What then had been my case?
Like D[amer] I had scorn'd the youth,
Kiss'd every female's lovely mouth,
  And follow'd ev'ry face.

Look on that mountain of delight,
Where grace and beauty doth unite,
  Where wreathed smiles must thrive;
While Strawberry-hill at once doth prove,
Taste, elegance, and Sapphick love,
  In gentle Kitty ***** [i.e. Clive].

[...]

Ye Sapphick Saints, how ye must scorn
The dames with vulgar notions born,
  Who prostitute to man:
Who toil and sweat the tedious night,
And call the male embrace delight,
  The filthy marriage plan.

[...]

May I not hope — dear, lovely Fair,
Of you to have some little share?
   For if report is right,
The maids of warm Italia's Land,
Have felt the pressure of your hand,
   The pressure of delight.

Nor, D—, let me plead in vain,
Thee fairest of the sister-train,
   With purest, sweetest charms:
No more, dear Dame, my suit resist,
Jack Cavendish cannot exist,
   A moment from your arms.

[1]"Say lovely Dame, that do'st command,
Jack Cavendish's heart and hand,
   And elegies of woe;
Ask not the cause why she doth chuse,
The sounding lute and lyric muse,
   Love taught her tears to flow.

'I burn, I burn,' like Portsmouth Dock,
I have no heart as hard as rock,
   I now consume with flame:
Not Ætna's fires, or pitch or tar,
Or hostile ships engag'd in war,
   Blaze like thy burning dame.

'Thou'rt all my care, and my delight,
My sigh by day, my dream by night,
   Round thee in wreaths I twine:
A thousand tender words I speak,

---

[1] Something of this sort was Miss Sappho's address to the scornful Phaon, who very properly judged, that she was not a proper object of love to him, who had seduced most of the pretty girls of Mytelene.

A thousand melting kisses take,
And feel thee all divine.

'Pride of the age, and of thy race,
Come, come and melt in this embrace,
And all my vows receive:
But if obdurate you will prove,
Deaf to the language of my love,
Take *that* you cannot give.'

FINIS.

from *'The Adulteress'*
a version of Juvenal's Sixth Satire,
published by S. Bladon, London (1773)

Women and Men, in these unnat'ral Times,
Are guilty equal of unnat'ral Crimes:
Woman wirth Woman act the Manly Part,
And kiss and press each other to the heart.

Unnat'ral Crimes like these my Satire vex;
I know a thousand *Tommies* 'mongst the Sex:
And if they don't relinquish such a Crime,
I'll give their Names to be the scoff of Time.

['Tommies' *is eighteenth-century slang for women who have sex with other women (how this may be related to 'tomboy' is not entirely clear, though life teaches us that many a lesbian begins life as a tomboy . . .)*]

Mrs Thrale waxes variously apocalyptic

Hester Thrale (1741–1821), the often much tried but mainly faithful friend of Dr Johnson, had strong opinions about everything, especially female 'vice', as these diary entries show.

1 April 1789
Nature does get strangely out of Fashion sure enough: One hears of Things now, fit for the Pens of Petronius only, or Juvenal to record and satyrize: The Queen of France is at the Head of a Set of Monsters call'd by each other *Sapphists*, who boast her Example; and deserve to be thrown with the *He* Demons that haunt each other likewise, into Mount Vesuvius.

17 June 1790
There is a strange Propensity now in England for these unspeakable Sins. Mrs *Damor*[,] a Lady much suspected for liking her own Sex in a criminal Way, had Miss Farren the fine comic Actress often about her last Year; and Mrs Siddons's Husband made the following Verses on them.

> Her little Stock of private Fame
> Will fall a Wreck to public Clamour,
> If Farren leagues with one whose Name
> Comes near – Aye very near – to *Damn her.*

[*Mrs Thrale was delighted to have her views endorsed from the pulpit, as the following account of one particular sermon shows. She liked the epigram against Mrs Damer well enough to be repeating it still, five years later, with variations.*]

9 Dec. 1795

The Advent Sermon at St Asaph was very good today – very good *indeed*: Mr Butler Clough of Eriviatte[,] one of the Canons preached it – he is an excellent man they say, and I doubt it not: he said how Christianity had mended the World in general; & how the Vices of the Ancients were *unknown* to Modern Times excepting as they are preserved by Poets & Historians. – poor Dear Man!! I read Juvenal's Satires when I came home, and found that *Insatiability* was the worst thing he could urge against the Roman Ladies – except their unnatural Passion for Eunuchs; – of those two Brutal and detestable Vices I'll swear Christianity has not cured them – Witness Cæcilia Tron, & Principessa Belmonste – and hundreds, *hundreds* more: while French and English Women are now publicly said to practise Atrocities of which He – Juvenal was ignorant, for he says in his Sature against Men's horrible Propensity for their own Sex – 'that even Women are more virtuous than they' because tho' Flavia does hire herself out to Fellows – 'She goes home to Bed at last, and lies chastly by the Side of Catulla'. Whereas 'tis now grown common to suspect Impossibilities such I think 'em – whenever two Ladies live too much together; the Queen of France was all along accused, so was Raucoux the famous Actress on the Paris Stage; & 'tis a Joke in London now to say such a one visits *M^s Damer*. Lord Derby certainly insisted on Miss Farren's keeping her at a Distance & there was a droll but bitter Epigram made while they used to see one another often –

> Her little Stock of private Fame
>   Will fall a Wreck to public Clamour,
> If Farren herds with her whose name
>   Approaches very near to *Damn her.*

When every Offence tow'rds God & Reason, & Religion & Nature has been committed, that *can* be committed, I suppose the World will burn; as it drowned 4000 Years ago. In the Emperor Tiberius's Time it was become so sinful that only Christ's Blood could wash it clean, he told us expressly 'twas the last effort; & that he would return to Judge that Earth he died to redeem – he said too that *that* Generation (meaning the next 2000 Years I trust) should not pass away before all should be accomplished — *those 2000 Years are now near gone.*

[*Today, of course, those two thousand years have been completed! Mrs Thrale continued to inveigh against French Sapphic vice. Rumours of a passionate attachment between Marie Antoinette and the Princesse de Lamballe everywhere abounded. Both women eventually went to the scaffold, and some contemporary accounts of the Princesse de Lamballe's execution say that the executioner cut her pubic hair from her body and draped it over his upper lip, symbolically taking back or reclaiming the masculinity her alleged lesbianism stole from him and all men, Mrs Thrale remained obdurate in her opposition.*]

15 January 1796
France — spiritually called Sodom & Egypt — (most justly;) teems with Monsters: — & the Blood drops warmly from the Guillotine.

[*One of her marginal notes to a diary entry rather alarmingly depicts Bath as a new Sapphic Sodom: can this be that same Bath in which Sarah Scott and Lady Bab passed so many happy years? Almost certainly, and probably with Mrs Thrale's whole-hearted admiration. Despite her near-obsessive strictures against the Sapphists, she held the Ladies of Llangollen in the highest esteem. One of life's many little ironies.*]

Its odd that ye Roman Women did not borrow that horrible Vice from Greece — it has a Greek name now & is call'd Sapphism, but I never did hear of it in Italy where the Ladies are today exactly what Juvenal described them in his Time — neither better nor worse as I can find. Mrs Siddons has told me that her Sister was in personal Danger once from a female Fiend of this Sort; & I have no Reason to disbelieve the Assertion. Bath is a cage of these unclean Birds I have a Notion, and London is a Sink for every Sin.

Two Poems
by C. M. DONALD

Here, as so often, the battle-hardened C. M. Donald provides an excellent example of how to deal with the enemy.

'Poor old fat woman'

Poor old fat woman, whither bound?
Home to my hearth, kind sir, she said.
Poor old fat woman, living alone!
I live with a woman who loves me, she said.
No husband for you, poor old fat woman, eh!
I've never wanted one, sir, she said.
Poor old fat woman, what do you want?
Nothing that you can give, sir, she said,
    And you're wasting your time
    And you're wasting mine
So push off and do something useful instead.

'I expect you think this huge dark coat'

I expect you think this huge dark coat
conceals in its capacious folds
some unsavoury old knitted cardigans,
a worn-through pair of trousers and,
inside all that, one sweaty fat woman.
You think I'm hiding in here to protect myself,
that I'm trying to make my bulk inconspicuous.
You be careful, do not attempt to thwart me.
Inside this black coat
    I am
      Sir Despard Murgatroyd.

The Example
from *Feminist Fables* (1981)
SUNITI NAMJOSHI

And the sparrows' children needed a tutor, so they hired a wren. The wren did her job conscientiously and diligently, but the sparrow parents criticized her colour, her modest exterior, and made fun of her sometimes because she wasn't married. And the sparrows' children were like any other children, wily and wilful, simple and gentle, and sometimes very kind and sometimes mean. Then, one day, there was a tremendous scandal. The birds had discovered that the wren's sexuality was not what it should be. They feared for their children. What if the wren should corrupt them morally? They summoned the wren and demanded an explanation. And the wren said, 'What is private is private, and what is public is public.' 'Oh no,' said the parents, 'We understand, you know, that you are not only a lesbian, but also a feminist, and feminists maintain that the public and private are not distinct.' 'But I don't teach sex,' said the wren 'I teach reading and writing and simple arithmetic.' 'Ah, but what you are, after all, is something that our very own children might turn out to be. And what you are is dreadful and horrid.' 'I am not dreadful and I am not horrid,' said the wren indignantly. 'That makes it worse. You set an example,' said the parents sternly. 'So do you,' said the wren. 'Well, you're fired,' was the parents' verdict. And so the sparrows' children grew up anyhow and some were horrid, and some resisted it.

Breeches Parts

'Breeches Parts' introduces us to a remarkable gallery of women for whom lives lived in male attire may bring both dangers and rewards, short-term solutions and unforeseen complications. Catherine Vizzani, for example, whose cross-dressed life is evidently bound up with her sexuality, is variously seen by her contemporaries as a medical monstrosity and a saint. Women who adopt male attire out of necessity, rather than erotic preference, may nevertheless find that the mistaken desires of other women for them disrupt their lives. But such desires are not always or necessarily a product of delusion or deception: the heterosexual Vesta Tilley, whose enormously successful music-hall act as a male impersonator was meant to be 'seen through', found that it still evoked desire in lesbian breasts (something about which she had very mixed feelings). Wearing the trousers is, as C. M. Donald's poem reveals, a very much more complicated matter than it may at first appear.

A true virgin

from *The True History and Adventures of*
Catherine Vizzani

Insights into the lives of earlier lesbians may come from unexpected sources.
In 1743, Giovanni Bianchi, an Italian anatomist, was called in when other
doctors realised that the 'young man' they were dissecting was in fact a young
woman. Bianchi's subsequent researches uncovered a fascinating story of one
young Italian woman's multiple acts of resistance against the sexual and
occupational limitations imposed upon women in her time and place. His
original Italian account was quickly translated into English in two different
versions (1751 and 1755). The text used here comes from the latter edition,
and starts with the title-page of 1751.

Dissertation on the Case of Catherine Vizzani
containing
The Adventures of a young Woman, born at *Rome*,
who for eight years passed in the Habit of a Man, was
killed for an Amour with a young Lady; and being
found, on Dissection, a true Virgin, narrowly escaped
being treated as a Saint by the Popular

§ with some Curious and Anatomical REMARKS on the
Nature and *Existence* of the HYMEN

---

by GIOVANNI BIANCHI
Professor of Anatomy at *Siena*, the Surgeon
who dissected her.

To which are added certain useful REMARKS by the
English Editor

What odd fantastic Things, we Women do!
Ep. to Cato
LONDON
Printed for W. MEYER in *M   's Buildings* near
St. Martin's Lane: MDCCLI [Price 1s.]

[The account begins with general remarks about the celebrated power of love, such]

as to send the Persons thus infatuated a wandering, from one Country to another, in Quest of the desir'd Object; or that others have preferred the Gratification of their Love to Duty and Decency, to Tranquillity and Reputation. The Subject before me is an Instance, that the Wantonness of Fancy, and the Depravity of Nature, are at as great a Height as ever; and that our Times afford a Girl, who, so far from being inferior to Sappho, or any of the *Lesbian* Nymphs, in an Attachment for those of her own sex, has greatly surpassed them in Fatigues, Dangers, and Distress, which terminated in a violent Death. This the following Narrative will manifest, which is a pregnant Example of the shocking Ebullition of human Passions, yet, at the same Time, of a most firm Constancy and Daringness in a young Creature, tho' with a sad Alloy of Guilt and Precipitancy.

[Catherine Vizzani was born in Rome. Her father was a carpenter.]

When she came to her fourteenth year, the Age of love in our forward Climate, she was reserved and shy towards young Men, but would be continually romping with her own Sex, and some she caressed with all the Eagerness and Transport of a male Lover; but, above all, she was passionately enamoured of one *Margaret*, whose Company she used to court, under Pretence of learning Embroidery; and, not satisfied with these Interviews by Day, scarce a Night passed, but she appeared in Man's Cloaths, under her Charmer's Window, though, in all Appearances, her Pleasure must be limited to the viewing Margaret's captivating Charms, and saying soft Things to her. This whimsical Amour went on very quietly for above two Years, but at last *Catherine* being surprized by *Margaret*'s Father, just when her Heart was overflowing with fervid Expressions of Love to his Daughter, he rated her severely, and threatened that the Governor of the City shoud hear of her Pranks.

[This so frightened her that she left the city, went to Viterbo, adopted male attire and took the name of Giovanni Bordoni. She ran out of money, thought

the trouble had blown over, returned to Rome, as a man, and took sanctuary in the Church of Santa Maria in Transtavero. A Canon Giuseppe Lancifi thought 'him' skulking suspiciously, and challenged 'him'. 'He' said it was]

only to avoid the Revenge which had been vowed against her for a little Fault on account of a sweetheart,

[which was true as far as it went. The Canon was so taken with 'Giovanni's' 'modest deportment', that he offered 'him' the sanctuary of the House. A visiting Perugian gentleman engaged 'Giovanni', 'a genteel young Fellow'. (The author at this point bombards us with confused pronouns, and seems to be enjoying it.) The gentleman]

wanting a servant, and seeing Giovanni a genteel young Fellow, made her good Offers, which she was very ready to embrace[.]

[Catherine rapidly became bored by service and asked the Canon to use his good offices with his military brother (in Arezzo, where, for some undisclosed reason, she was passionate to go) to obtain service for her there. Her mother vouched for her offspring, without revealing her gender, but seemingly not actively suppressing the details. (This is all very curious, and not the only curious aspects of Catherine's parents' conduct in all this.) Catherine eventually went to be the 'Body-Footman' to a Signor Francis Maria Pucci of Monte Pulciano, Governor of Angiari (also called Vicar).]

Never was Gentleman better fitted with a Servant than the Vicar with Giovanni; for beside Reading, making Chocolate, and Cookery, she was very dextrous at Pen, Comb and Razor; in a word, she was a thorough Proficient in all the Branches of her Employment.

[But the Vicar-Governor who]

made no Allowance for the Impulses of Nature, or the Fervor of Youth, was used not to spare her, for incessantly following the Wenches, and being so barefaced, and insatiable in her Amours. She had Recourse to several delusive Impudicities, not only to establish the certainty, but raise the Reputation of her Manhood.[1]

[Giovanni instructed 'his' laundress not to tell anyone about his little medical difficulties, telling her]

that she should not betray his Confidence by dropping the least Hint, in any Place, either of his Abilities or Distempers. Her Fetches succeeded far beyond her Desert, that is, to the very Height of her Expectation; so that, within a short Time, it was whispered about that *Giovanni* was the best Woman's Man, and the most addicted to that alluring Sex of all the Men in that Part of the Country.

[When Giovanni was wounded (infected) by sexual loves, the Vicar-Governor reproached his brother, the Canon, for sending such a whoremaster to him. The Canon summoned Peter Vizzani, Catherine-Giovanni's father, to inform him and rebuke him about the conduct of his 'son'.

*   Peter Vizzani]*

---

[1] *English Editor's note to the translation*: The Doctor enters into a nauseous Detail of her Impostures, which is the more inexcusable, they not being essential to the main Scope of the Narrative. These, if agreeable to the *Italian Gout*, would shock the delicacy of our Nation, with whom I hope the following lines will ever be in full Force, as the Standard of Criticism:

> *Immodest Words admit of no Defence;*
> *And Want of Decency is want of Sense.*

Though a Veil be drawn over such Ordures, yet as Giovanni's Activities cannot be one and all concealed, without an Infraction of the Laws of History; and would, besides, occasion too great a Chasm in a Translation; I return to the Original, with saying, that she was two several Times with a Surgeon in that District, to buy Medicaments for the Removal of Disorders, which she pretended to have contracted from infectious Women, being but a raw Soldier in the Wars of Venus.

[NB The translator/editor disclaims indecency and firmly establishes the English *reader's greater fastidiousness, then goes into quite some detail about 'Giovanni's' 'fetches' to spread belief in her masculinity. 'Pretended' in the above passage probably still has the meaning of 'laid claim' rather than 'dishonestly asserting'.]*

who could hardly keep his Countenance during a Remonstrance delivered with a dictatorial Solemnity, calmly answered, that, to his and his dear Wife's inexpressible Grief, their Son was a prodigy of Nature, and that, in his very Childhood they had observed some astonishing Motions of Lust, which had unhappily gathered Vehemence with the Growth of his Body.

[*Having teased the Canon, sufficiently, perhaps, Peter Vizzani then revealed the truth about his offspring's sex. But the Canon didn't reveal it to his brother, and Catherine-Giovanni remained in the employ of the Vicar-General for a further three or four years. The eventual reason for leaving him is not clear.*

After a brief period with another master, Giovanni returned to the service of the Vicar-General.

On various journeys, he had a male bedfellow (fellow servant) who was 'an Adonis', but never made any advances to him (note the author's assumption that 'he', being really 'she', should have done). Giovanni overstepped the mark by courting a young gentlewoman and persuading her to elope with him to Rome, where they would marry. (The date given for this is 'very early one Morning about the Middle of June, in the year One Thousand, Seven Hundred, and Forty Three'.) Rather inconveniently, the younger sister of the gentlewoman decided to come, too!

The runaways were pursued, and their pursuers caught up with their coach. Giovanni pulled a pistol on the chaplain, then began to think a little]

'till *Giovanni*, considering that her true sex would secure her from any very bad Consequence of this Affair, and that one Girl's running away with two others might, in a Court of Justice, if it should go to that Length, be slightly passed over as a Frolick, rather than severely animadverted upon as a Crime, thought it advisable to surrender.

[*But the Chaplain ordered a servant to shoot Giovanni (also, incidentally, killing a fine pointer and fracturing the leg of a twelve-year-old boy who had stopped to watch; the boy also later died). The luckless trio were taken back and the uncle of the two young gentlewomen 'initiated them into a Conservatory of recluse Ladies' at Lucca.*

'Giovanni' woos the young gentlewoman

The wounded Giovanni was taken off to the hospital wing of a nunnery
where (on 16 June 1743) he was]

laid in the seventieth Bed, being entered in the Register of the Patients,
from his own Mouth, by the name of *Giovanni*, Son of *Francisco Bordoni*,
Freeman of *Rome*, and aged Twenty-four Years.

[Giovanni's wound did not heal, pus kept forming; his death was expected]

in this Extremity, a leathern Contrivance, of a cilindrical figure, which
was fastened below the Abdomen, and had been the chief Instrument of
her detestable Imposture, became so troublesome, that she loosened it,
and laid it under her Pillow; and now, brought to a Sense of the Heinous-
ness of her Courses, she disclosed her Secret to the charitable *Maria de
Colomba*, who suffered not a day to pass without bringing or sending
her some Cordials. She told her that she was not only a Female but a
Virgin, conjuring her, at the same Time, to let no Person whatever
know it till her Death, and then to declare it publickly, that she might
be buried in a Woman's Habit, and with the Garland on her Head, an
honary Ceremony observed among us in the burial of Virgins. She
breathed her last, a few Days after this Confidence, in her twenty-fifth
Year. Such was the End of this young Woman after a Disguise of above
eight Years, during which she lived, undiscovered, as a Man Servant,
in different Families; it is indeed, a Proof of singular Address and
Self-Government, that in such a length of Time, she should preserve
her secret from Detection, and be Proof against any Inclination or Love
for a Man, though living continuously in the utmost Freedom with them,
and often lying in the same Bed; a Passion universally natural to young
Women, and so vehement in it's Actings, as to violate the Institutes of
a Cloister, or elope from the Coercion of Parents; but, on the other Hand,
here was Effrontery and Folly in the Abstract, to fall in Love with those
of her own Sex; to amuse them with passionate Addresses; to kindle in
them Desires, without the Power of Gratification; to mind neither Dangers
nor Fatigues, and at last to lose her Life in these fantastical Pursuits. The
leathern Machine which was hid under the Pillow, fell into the Hands of
the Surgeon's Mates in the Hospital, who immediately were for ripping it

up, concluding that it contained Money, or something else of Value, but they found it stuffed only with old Rags: The servants first suspected *Giovanni*'s Sex by her prominent Breasts, when they came to remove her Body from the Bed on which she died: and, making this known to the chief Mates they not only discovered her to be a Woman, but also a Virgin, the Hymen being entire without the least laceration.

[*(Note the happy insistence that there can have been no gratification possible for Giovanni's women partners.) Bianchi's servant – perhaps a young medical trainee? – came to tell him 'with a blush', about this troubling corpse. Catherine was laid out as a virgin (i.e., with the appropriate gown and garland), so they did not disturb the body at that point. Other medics had made incisions in the body already, to see if she was pregnant (before the discovery that she was a virgin).*

The body was buried although the burial was initially opposed]

by the Multitudes, which flocked, from all Parts of the City, to get a sight of her, the Corpse was brought back, though chiefly in Deference to some Religious, who would have her to be nothing less than a Saint, having preserved her Chastity inviolate, amidst the strongest Temptations; some of them also asserting that she might be the Daughter of a *Venetian* Nobleman; and accordingly, an epistolary Account of her, dated at *Siena*, the fifth of *July*, and printed at *Florence*, places her in this honourable Light.

[*(Note the delightfully flawed nature of the reasoning used by those of the religious who wished to confer Saintly status on her. How could any woman, other than a Saint, sleep so often with men without succumbing?)*]

These Reverend Gentlemen certainly took the Matter by a wrong Handle, a Woman's Sanctity not consisting only in having preserved her Chastity inviolate, but in an uniform Purity of Manners, in which how far Catherine excelled, is manifest from every preceding Line; accordingly, I urged that her making Love, and with uncommon Protervity, to women, wherever she came, and her seducing at least two young Women to run away from their Uncle, were flagrant Instances of a libidinous Dispo-

sition; Proceedings incompatible with any virtuous Principle, or so much
as Decency.

*[Thereafter we have Bianchi's remarks on his Dissection of Catherine. He
paid particular attention to the hymen because some anatomists of the period
denied that any such thing existed in the human female.]*

The clitoris of this young Woman was not pendulous, nor of any extraordinary Size, as the Account from *Rome* made it, and as is said, to be
that of all those Females who, among the Greeks, were called *Tribades*,
or who followed the Practices of *Sappho*; on the contrary, her's was so
far from any unusual Magnitude, that it was not to be ranked among
the middle-sized, but the smaller.

*[Bianchi also noted that the left Fallopian tube was three times bigger than
the right. (This concern with physical conformation as an indicator or cause
of 'deviant' sexuality would go on being addressed well into the late nineteenth
and early twentieth centuries: think of Krafft-Ebing, and of Havelock Ellis,
who included such meticulous anatomical measurements in the case history
which appeared earlier, in 'Betwixt and Between'.)]*

Remarks upon the foregoing dissertation by the English editor of *The True History and Adventures of Catherine Vizzani*

These remarks follow upon the 1755 translation of The History and Adventures of Catherine Vizzani. *They were added by the English editor and
translator who, according to the scholar and critic Roger Lonsdale, may well
have been John Cleland, the author of the notoriously pornographic* Fanny
Hill *and* Memoirs of a Coxcomb. *The self-righteous editorial comments
about avoiding vicious books, indecent prints and pictures, and lewd conversation perhaps look rather different in that light.*

*As so often with English commentators on foreign ways, there is an
insistence on the lewdness of other countries and the comparative innocency*

of ours, whether passing scathing judgements on the Italian medical profession, or vilifying the luckless female protagonist of the anecdote incorporated in the 'Remarks'.

For the narrator, this is primarily a story about a greedy wife who robs her own husband; from a lesbian perspective it might more accurately be a story about a woman who steals in order to be able to finance the life she actually wants – one in which she finds and woos a woman of her desire, in the habiliments and power of the only sex which is allowed to woo women. There is greed in this story, though – exercized by the young gentlewoman's relations, who are so keen to co-opt the 'young man's' wealth that they happily urge their young kinswoman into a marriage she very much does not want.

The strictures against women in men's clothes, even if worn only 'for fun', gain extra resonance in the light of the cross-dressing life Charlotte Charke was leading at the same time these 'Remarks' appeared.

The Wits, and even the learned Men of *Italy*, have been long distinguished for their Inclination to Discourses of this Nature, which are frequently interpreted in such a Manner as to do no great Honour to their Abilities, and still less to their Morals. But it may be they are, in this Respect, a little hardly treated; since, in a warm Country like theirs, where Impurities of all Sorts are but too frequent, it may very well happen that such strange Accidents may, from Time to Time, arise as highly to excite both their Wonder and their Attention, rather from their Skill in Anatomy, and their Acquaintance with human Nature, than from any bad Habits or vitiated Inclinations in themselves.

As for the Case of this young Woman, it is certainly very extraordinary, and may therefore justify, at least in some Measure, the Pains which this learned and industrious Man has taken about her. But it does not appear that he has assigned any Cause whatever, or so much as advanced any probable conjecture on this extravagant Turn of her Lewdness, notwithstanding it surprized him so much. Yet this we might reasonably have expected from a Treatise written by one of the Faculty, and one who, without any Scruple, professes that it had taken up so much of his Thoughts.

It should seem, that this irregular and violent Inclination, by which this Woman render'd herself infamous, must either proceed from some Error in Nature, or from some Disorder or Perversion in the Imagination. As to the first of these, the Author seems to have removed all Doubt; since, from the Account he gives of the Dissection of the Body, it is very evident that there was nothing amiss; and we have good Reason to believe, that he meant to insinuate so much at least to his Readers, by insisting so long upon a particular Circumstance. We ought, therefore, to acquit Nature of any Fault in this strange Creature, and to look at the Source of so odious and so unnatural a Vice, only in her Mind; and there, indeed, if closely attended to, it will be found that more monstrous Productions are to be met with than have exercised the Pens of such as have addicted themselves to write of strange births, and such like Prodigies.

It seems therefore most likely that this unfortunate and scandalous Creature had her Imagination corrupted early in her Youth, either by obscene Tales that were voluntarily told in her Hearing, or by privately listening to the Discourses of the Women, who are too generally corrupt in that Country. Her Head thus filled with vicious Inclinations, perhaps before she received any Incitements from her Constitution, might prompt her to those vile Practices, which being begun in Folly, were continued through Wickedness; nor is it at all unreasonable to believe, that, by Degrees, this might occasion a preternatural Change in the animal Spirits, and a kind of veneral Fury, very remote, and even repugnant to that of her Sex.

Something of the like Kind is reported to have happened many Years ago to a very vicious Woman, in a Country that it is not necessary to name. This Woman was the Wife of an Apothecary, very dissolute in her Manners, and, as some thought, a little distracted in her Head. Her Husband bore with her a long Time, out of Respect to her Family, and for the Sake of the Fortune he had with her. But at length she took a Freak of this Kind into her Head, which had very fatal Consequences to an innocent and deserving Person, and which also brought upon the Offender herself a Part at least of that Shame and Punishment which she deserved.

This vile Woman, knowing that her Husband had received a very large Sum of Money, took the Advantage of his Absence, broke open the Place where he kept it, and having got it into her Possession, procured Men's Cloaths, in which she made her Escape. As soon as she found herself in a Place of Security, she provided an Equipage, and assumed the Name of a young Gentleman who was her Relation, by which, without any Suspicion, she introduced herself into the best Companies, and by a suitable Behaviour, maintained the Cheat for some Time perfectly well; a Thing so much more practicable, as her's was an Imposture absolutely new and strange.

It fell out, at some Place of public Diversion, that she heard a Gentlewoman, the most famous of her Time for the Sweetness of her Voice, and her admirable Skill in Music, perform a Canata, accompanied with a Lute. Upon this, it came into her Head to make Love to her, which she did with all the exterior Marks of the warmest Passion. But the Gentlewoman, tho' the Person of this Creature was far from being Disagreeable, had a natural Aversion to her, and could never be brought to have any Liking for her, tho' neither she, nor any Body else, had the least Suspicion of the Imposture.

Her friends, however, who looked upon this as a very extraordinary Match, pressed her to lay hold of so favourable an Opportunity of settling herself handsomely in the World, and becoming the Wife of a Person who was able to maintain her in Splendor, and who, from the Name thus impudently assumed, was generally believed to have a great Estate. All the Excuses she could make could not divert her Relations from the Prosecution of this Design; and at last, tho' with much Reluctance, they so far vanquished her Distaste, as to engage her to accept of this Husband; and that too in a shorter Time than ought to have been taken in a Matter of such Importance. But they were so afraid that the Family of the young Gentleman, for whom this Woman was taken, should hear of the Matter, and prevent the Marriage, that they hurried it on with an indiscreet Zeal, which they very soon repented.

It was at length, therefore, publickly celebrated, and with great Magnificence; which is, perhaps, one of the highest Marks of Impudence with which the World was every acquainted. But, as may be easily believed, the villainous Secret was soon discovered, and the execrable Offender secured. The Noise that this Story made, brought the Apothecary to the first Knowledge of what was become of his Wife; who, after she had undergone such an Examination, as was necessary to render her pretended Marriage, in the Course of a judicial Proceeding, absolutely null and void, was put into his Power, with so much of the Money as remained unsquandered in this wild Adventure.

As for the unfortunate Gentlewoman, who was the Victim of her Friends good Wishes, whose character was perfectly unspotted, and who was esteemed for her Beauty, and admired for her Virtue, as much as for the Excellency of her Voice, and delicate hand upon the Lute, she was so deeply affected with the Shame that attended this Affair, which however, brought not the least Imputation upon her, that it threw her into a violent Disorder of Mind, from which a hectic Fever arose, that killed her in a short Time.

As for the Monster who had been the Author of this Misfortune, her Husband very prudently caused her to be confined as a Lunatic; and in that Condition she some Years after breathed her last, to the great Satisfaction of her Spouse, and of her own Family, who thought themselves, in some Measure, dishonoured by her Infamy.

This shews, as well as the Case which occasioned the mentioning of it, that there is an amazing Violence in these vicious Irregularities, which has this happy Consequence, that they are quickly betrayed, and in most Countries chastized with that Severity which they deserve; and without Doubt, the only Reason that can justify the making Things of this Sort public, is to facilitate their Discovery, and thereby prevent their ill Consequences, which indeed can scarce be prevented any other Way.

[*This is all very reminiscent, in a curious way, of the deliberations of the House of Lords in 1921, when it debated whether or not to extend the workings of the 1885 Criminal Law Amendment Act so that lesbian acts, like male homosexual ones, would become criminal offences. Their Lordships eventually decided it would be better* not *to make 'things of this sort' public.*]

It is therefore very expedient, whenever a Treatise of this Kind is committed to the Press, that it should be accompanied with such Reflections as may render it manifest, that it comes abroad with a good Intent, and with a real View of correcting, not a latent Design of corrupting the Morals of Youth; and, for this Reason, it may not be improper to hint at a few Particulars that are extremely worthy of Notice.

The first is, that it behoves People to be highly cautious, as to that Kind of Discourse which they hold in the Presence of very young People of either Sex; since, tho' it is very easy to foresee that lewd or lax Conversation must have bad effects, yet it is not altogether so easy to comprehend what very bad Effects may follow from it; of which this Discourse, and these Remarks, afford sufficient Instances.

In the next Place, it affords (if that were at all necessary) a new Argument for suppressing those scandalous and flagitious Books, that are not only privately but publickly handed about for the worst Purposes, as well as Prints and Pictures calculated to inflame the Passions, to banish all Sense of Shame, and to make the World, if possible, more corrupt and profligate than it is already. We are very certain that all Things of this Sort must have a very bad Tendency; but surely it must lay some Kind of Restraint, even upon those who are most forward in these Things, if they considered, that they knew not what might be the Consequences, and that they may become inconsiderately the Instruments of much greater Wickedness than they design.

We may add to all this, that from hence may be borrowed a very just Reason for punishing more severely, or at least not making so light of a Practice not altogether uncommon, which is that of Women appearing in public Places in Men's Cloaths; a Thing that manifests an extreme Assurance, and which may have many ill Consequences, and those too of very different kinds. This, by the *Mosaic* Law, is considered as a capital Offence, which deserves so much the more Reflection, as it will be found, upon a strict Enquiry, that most of the Laws in that Code, are founded upon the most perfect Knowledge of human Nature. It is also looked upon as a great Crime by our Law, as well for political as moral Reasons; and therefore it is very strange, that merely to indulge an idle Whim, or a foolish Humour, the best, or at least the most innocent Reasons that can be suggested for it, this should be looked on with an Eye of Indifference, and rather as a species of Levity than of Guilt.

To dispense with Laws from Necessity, or for the sake of some public Convenience, may be excusable, and even reasonable; but to suffer such

Laws as our Ancestors instituted from the wisest Motives, and for the most salutary Purposes, to fall into Dissuetude, and even Contempt, to gratify the Lovers of Diversions; in Favour of which, even their best Advocate is able to say no more, than that they are *silly* Diversons, is not a little strange and surprising, and must give a singular Idea of those Alterations in our Policy and Manners, which have arisen from our Politeness, and our Desire to copy Foreigners in every Thing, not excepting those Follies, of which the wisest People amongst them profess themselves ashamed.

FINIS.

So pretty a fellow

from *A Journey Through Every Stage of Life* (1754)
SARAH SCOTT (1723–1795)

Leonora, the highly intelligent heroine of 'The History of Leonora and Louisa', the first of the many stories which make up Scott's novel, has run away from home with her cousin Louisa, to escape the persecution of her wicked stepmother. For safety they decide that one of them should disguise herself as a man; Leonora's learning and her height make her the obvious choice, but she can only reconcile herself to what Scott calls 'this Metamorphosis of her Sex' by adopting the dress of a clergyman ('which left her Petticoats, though it took from her her Sex'). Her problems begin here . . .

Leonora's beauty charms many of the young Ladies; she soon found by the forward Advances of the Coquets, and the sly glances of the Prudes, that an effeminate Delicacy in a Man is not disagreeable to a Sex to whom it should more peculiarly belong. The Widows indeed, and some of the more experienced Matrons, looked with a Mixture of Scorn upon her; the ancient Ladies especially, to whose Chins Age had given an Ornament that even *Leonora*'s Manhood could not boast, proud of their

hoary Honours would frequently ridicule her want of Beard, and elated
with their Abundance, despise her Poverty. She would have been glad
if she could have borrowed what they might so well have spared; but
as that could not be, she was obliged to bear the Jests which were half
whispered among them, with the best Assurance she could summon, and
had at the same time the Gratification of over-hearing very different
Observations made by the younger Part of the Company; one would
praise her Features, another her Complexion, a third sigh out, as smooth
as *Hebe*'s unrazored Lips; those who had studied Romances compared
her to *Pyrocles*, and in short to all the imaginary Heroes who had been
celebrated for effeminate Beauty, declaring the Description of each was
exactly her Picture. But all lamented the want of a laced Coat and
Bag-Wig, and grieved that so pretty a Fellow should be disgraced by
an odious canonical Habit.

[. . .]

Many Ladies sought *Louisa*'s Friendship for the sake of her Brother, but
none with so much Success as a very pretty young Girl, who was so
very amiable, that *Leonora* grieved at finding her Heart so thrown away.
Lætitia (for that was her Name) endeavoured by all the Arts of Reserve
and Modesty, to hide her Passion from all Eyes, and most of all from
Leonora's; but it is very difficult for Woman to conceal from Woman
the Situation of her Heart [. . .]

   Leonora in pity of so misplaced a Passion took every Opportunity to
inform *Lætitia* of the Insensibility of her Heart, and that Friendship was
the warmest Affection it was capable of feeling. This made little Alter-
ation in the tender *Lætitia*, she was contented in finding *Leonora* would
not be her Lover, as long as she could hope for her as Friend. To those
whose Passions seemed less sincere, *Leonora* was as gallant as they could
reasonably desire, and was as true a Coquet as themselves.

Strange mad pranks?

from *A Narrative of the Life of Mrs Charlotte Charke* (1755)
CHARLOTTE CHARKE (1713–1760)

The life of Charlotte Charke and her Narrative *of it suggest a variety of reasons why women might adopt men's clothing. In the first extract here the four-year-old Charlotte joyfully imitates her father despite some obvious setbacks (being far too small and wearing girls' shoes). Father (Colley Cibber, the playwright, actor and later Poet Laureate) was not amused. Later in Charke's life, male drag seems to have been a matter of necessity; she never tells us what her 'very substantial reasons' are for adopting male attire though one obvious result was the opening up to her of a wide range of paid occupations. One lucrative role she denies having played is that of highwayman. The second and third extracts present an apparently unexpected side-effect of her cross-dressing; on at least two occasions – one close to tragedy, the other close to farce – a woman falls in love with her, believing her to be a man.*

As I have promis'd to conceal nothing that might raise a Laugh, I shall begin with a small Specimen of my former Madness, when I was but four Years of Age. Having, even then, a passionate Fondness for a Perriwig, I crawl'd out of Bed one Summer's Morning at *Twickenham*, where my Father had Part of a House and Gardens for the Season, and, taking it into my small Pate, that by Dint of a Wig and a Waistcoat, I should be the perfect Representative of my Sire, I crept softly into the Servants-Hall, where I had the Night before espied all Things in Order, to perpetrate the happy Design I had framed for the next Morning's Expedition. Accordingly I paddled down Stairs, taking with me my Shoes, Stockings, and little Dimity Coat; which I artfully contrived to pin up, as well as I could, to supply the Want of a Pair of Breeches. By the Help of a long Broom, I took down a Waistcoat of my Brother's, and an enormous bushy Tie-wig of my Father's, which entirely enclos'd my Head and Body, with the Knots of the Ties thumping my little Heels as I march'd along, with slow and solemn Pace. The Covert of Hair in which I was conceal'd, with the Weight of a monstrous Belt and large Silver-hilted Sword, that I could scarce drag along, was a vast Impediment in my Procession: And, what still added to the other Inconveniencies I labour'd under, was whelming myself under one of my Father's large Beaver-hats, laden with Lace, as thick and as broad as a Brickbat.

Being thus accoutred, I began to consider that 'twould be impossible for me to pass for Mr. *Cibber* in Girl's Shoes, therefore took an Opportunity to slip out of Doors after the Gardener, who went to his Work, and roll'd myself into a dry Ditch, which was as deep as I was high; and, in this Grotesque Pigmy-State, walk'd up and down the Ditch bowing to all who came by me. But, behold, the Oddity of my Appearance soon assembled a Croud about me; which yielded me no small Joy, as I conceiv'd their Risibility on this Occasion to be Marks of Approbation, and walk'd myself into a Fever, in the happy Thought of being taken for the 'Squire.

When the Family arose, 'till which Time I had employ'd myself in this regular March in my Ditch, I was the first Thing enquir'd after, and miss'd; 'till Mrs. *Heron*, the Mother of the late celebrated Actress of that Name, happily espied me, and directly call'd forth the whole Family to be Witness of my State and Dignity.

The Drollery of my Figure render'd it impossible, assisted by the Fondness of both Father and Mother, to be angry with me; but, alas! I was borne off on the Footman's Shoulders, to my Shame and Disgrace, and forc'd into my proper Habiliments.

[. . .]

Were I to insert one quarter Part of the strange, mad Pranks I play'd, even in Infancy, I might venture to affirm, I could swell my Account of 'em to a Folio, and perhaps my whimsical Head may compile such a Work; but I own I should be loth, upon Reflection, to publish it, lest the Contagion should spread itself, and make other young Folks as ridiculous and mischievous as myself.

*　　　*　　　*

I appeared as Mr. *Brown*, (A NAME MOST HATEFUL TO ME NOW, FOR REASONS THE TOWN SHALL HAVE SHORTLY LEAVE TO GUESS AT) in

Charlotte Charke, demonstrating, even at the tender age of four, her
'passionate Fondness for a Perriwig'

a very genteel Manner; and, not making the least Discovery of my Sex by my Behaviour, ever endeavouring to keep up to the well-bred Gentleman, I became, as I may most properly term it, the unhappy Object of Love in a young Lady, whose Fortune was beyond all earthly Power to deprive her of, had it been possible for me to have been, what she designed me, nothing less than her Husband. She was an Orphan Heiress, and under Age; but so near it, that, at the Expiration of eight Months, her Guardian resigned his Trust, and I might have been at once possessed of the Lady, and forty thousand Pounds in the Bank of *England*: Besides Effects in the *Indies*, that were worth about twenty Thousand more.

This was a most horrible Disappointment on both Sides; the Lady of the Husband, and I of the Money; which would have been thought an excellent Remedy for Ills, by those less surrounded with Misery than I was. I, who was the Principal in this Tragedy, was the last acquainted with it: But it got Wind from the Servants, to some of the Players; who, as *Hamlet* says, *Can't keep a Secret*, and they immediately communicated it to me.

Contrary to their Expectation, I received the Information with infinite Concern; not more in regard to myself, than from the poor Lady's Misfortune, in placing her Affection on an improper Object; and whom, by Letters I afterwards received, confirmed me, '*She was too fond of her mistaken Bargain*'.

The Means by which I came by her Letters, was through the Perswasion of her Maid; who, like most Persons of her Function, are too often ready to carry on Intrigues. 'Twas no difficult Matter to perswade an amorous Heart to follow its own Inclination; and accordingly a Letter came to invite me to drink Tea, at a Place a little distant from the House where she lived.

The Reason given for this Interview was, the Desire some young Ladies of her Acquaintance had to hear me sing; and, as they never went to Plays in the Country, 'twould be a great Obligation to her if I would oblige her Friends, by complying with her Request.

The Maid who brought this Epistle, inform'd of the real Occasion of its being wrote; and told me, if I pleased, I might be happiest Man in the Kingdom, before I was eight and forty Hours older. This frank

Declaration from the Servant, gave me but an odd Opinion of the Mistress; and I sometimes conceived, being conscious how unfit I was to embrace so favourable an Opportunity, that it was all a joke.

However, be it as it might, I resolved to go and know the Reality. The Maid too insisted that I should, and protested her Lady had suffered much on my Account, from the first Hour she saw me; and, but for her, the Secret had never been disclosed. She farther added, I was the first Person who had ever made that Impression on her Mind. I own I felt a tender Concern, and resolved within myself to wait on her; and, by honestly confessing who I was, kill or cure her Hopes of me for ever.

In Obedience to the Lady's Command I waited on her, and found her with two more much of her own Age, who were her Confidents, and entrusted to contrive a Method to bring this Business to an End, by a private Marriage. When I went into the Rom I made a general Bow to all, and was for seating myself nearest the Door; but was soon lugg'd out of my Chair by a young Mad-cap of Fashion; and, to both the Lady's Confusion and mine, aukwardly seated by her.

We were exactly in the Condition of Lord *Hardy* and Lady *Charlotte*, in *The Funeral*; and I sat with as much Fear in my Countenance, as if I had stole her Watch from her Side. She, on her Part, often attempted to speak; but had such a Tremor on her Voice, she ended only in broken Sentences. 'Tis true, I have undergone the dreadful Apprehensions of a Bomb-Bailiff; but I should have thought one at that Time a seasonable Relief, and without repining have gone with him.

The before-mention'd Mad-cap, after putting us more out of Countenance by bursting into a violent Fit of Laughing, took the other by the Sleeve and withdrew, as she thought, to give me a favourable Opportunity of paying my Addresses; but she was deceived, for, when we were alone, I was ten thousand Times in worst Plight than before: And what added to my Confusion was, seeing the poor Soul dissolve into Tears, which she endeavoured to conceal.

This gave me Freedom of Speech, by a gentle Enquiry into the Cause; and, by tenderly trying to sooth her into a Calm, I unhappily encreased, rather than asswaged the dreadful Conflict of Love and Shame which labour'd in her Bosom.

With much Difficulty, I mustered up Courage sufficient to open a

Discourse, by which I began to make a discovery of my Name and Family, which struck the poor Creature into Astonishment; but how much greater was her Surprize, when I positively assured her that I was actually the youngest Daughter of Mr. *Cibber*, and not the Person she conceived me! She was absolutely struck speechless for some little Time; but, when she regained the Power of Utterance, entreated me not to urge a Falshood of that Nature, which she looked upon only as an Evasion, occasioned, she supposed, through a Dislike of her Person: Adding, that her Maid had plainly told her I was no Stranger to her miserable Fate, as she was pleased to term it; and, indeed, as I really thought it.

I still insisted on the Truth of my Assertion; and desired her to consider, whether 'twas likely an indigent young Fellow must not have thought it an unbounded Happiness, to possess at once so agreeable a Lady and immense a Fortune, both which many a Nobleman in this Kingdom would have thought it worth while to take Pains to atchieve.

Notwithstanding all my Arguments, she was hard to be brought into a Belief of what I told her; and conceived that I had taken a Dislike to her, from her too readily consenting to her Servant's making that Declaration of her Passion for me; and, for that Reason, she supposed I had but a light Opinion of her. I assured her of the contrary, and that I was sorry for us both, that Providence had not ordained me to be the happy Person she designed me; that I was much obliged for the Honour she conferr'd on me, and sincerely grieved it was not in my Power to make a suitable Return.

With many Sighs and Tears on her Side, we took a melancholy Leave; and, in a few Days, the Lady retir'd into the Country, where I have never heard from, or of her since; but hope she is made happy in some worthy Husband, that might deserve her.

She was not the most Beautiful I have beheld, but quite the Agreeable; sung finely, and play'd the Harpsichord as well; understood Languages, and was a Woman of real good Sense: But she was, poor Thing! an Instance, in regard to me, *that the Wisest may sometimes err.*

On my Return Home, the Itinerant-Troop all assembled round me, to hear what had passed between the Lady and me – when we were to celebrate the Nuptials? – Besides many other impertinent, stupid Ques-

tions; some offering, agreeable to their villainous Dispositions, as the
Marriage they suppos'd would be a Secret, to supply my Place in the
Dark, to conceal the Fraud: Upon which I look'd at them very sternly,
and, with the Contempt they deserved, demanded to know what Action
of my Life had been so very monstrous, to excite them to think me
capable of one so cruel and infamous?

For the Lady's sake, whose Name I would not for the Universe have
had banded about by the Mouths of low Scurrility, I not only told them
I had revealed to her who I was, but made it no longer a Secret in the
Town; that, in Case it was spoke of, it might be regarded as an Impossibility, or, at worst, a trump'd-up Tale by some ridiculous Blockhead, who
was fond of hearing himself prate, as there are indeed too many such:
Of which, in Regard to my own Character, I have been often a melancholly Proof; and, as it just now occurs to my Memory, will inform the
Reader.

As Misfortunes are ever the mortifying Parents of each other, so mine
were teeming, and each new Day produced fresh Sorrow: But as if the
very Fiends of Destruction were employed to perpetrate mine, and that
my real Miseries were not sufficient to crush me with their Weight,
a poor, beggarly Fellow, who had been sometimes Supernumerary in
Drury-Lane Theatre, and Part-writer, forged a most villainous Lye; by
saying, I hired a very fine Bay Gelding, and borrowed a Pair of Pistols,
to encounter my Father upon *Epping-Forest*; where, I solemnly protest,
I don't know I ever saw my Father in my Life: That I stopp'd the
Chariot, presented a Pistol to his Breast, and used such Terms as I am
ashamed to insert; threaten'd to blow his Brains out that Moment, if he
did not deliver — Upbraiding him for his Cruelty in abandoning me to
those Distresses he knew I underwent, when he had it so amply in his
Power to relieve me: That since he would not use that Power, I would
force him to a Compliance, and was directly going to discharge upon
him; but his Tears prevented me, and, asking my Pardon for his ill
Usage of me, gave me his Purse with threescore Guineas, and a Promise
to restore me to his Family and Love; on which I thank'd him, and rode
off.

A likely Story, that my Father and his Servants were all so intimidated,
had it been true, as not to have been able to withstand a single stout

Highwayman, much more a Female, and his own Daughter to! However, the Story soon reached my Ear, which did not more enrage me on my own Account, than the impudent, ridiculous Picture the Scoundrel had drawn of my Father, in this supposed horrid Scene. The Recital threw me into such an agonizing Rage, I did not recover it for a Month; but, the next Evening, I had the Satisfaction of being designedly placed where this Villain was to be, and, concealed behind a Screen, heard the Lye re-told from his own Mouth.

He had no sooner ended, than I rushed from my Covert, and, being armed with a thick oaken Plant, knocked him down, without speaking a Word to him; and, had I not been happily prevented should, without the least Remorse, have killed him on the Spot. I had not Breath enough to enquire into the Cause of his barbarous Falshood, but others, who were less concerned than myself, did it for me; and the only Reason he assigned for his saying it, was, *He meant it as a Joke*, which considerably added to the Vehemence of my Rage: But I had the Joy of seeing him well caned, and obliged to ask my Pardon on his Knees – Poor Satisfaction for so manifest an Injury!

*   *   *

One Day, as I was setting some *Windsor* Beans, the Maid came to me, and told me she had a very great Secret to unfold, but that I must promise never to tell that she had discovered it. As I had no extraordinary Opinion of her Understanding, or her Honesty, I was not over anxious to hear this mighty Secret, lest it should draw me into some Premunire; but she insisted upon disclosing it, assuring me 'twas something that might turn to my Advantage, if I would make a proper Use of it. This last Assertion raised in me a little Curiosity, and I began to grow more attentive to her Discourse; which ended in assuring me, to her certain Knowledge, I might marry her Mistress's Kinswoman, if I would pay my Addresses; and that she should like me for a Master extreamly, advising me to it by all Means.

I asked her what Grounds she had for such a Supposition? To which she answer'd, she had Reasons sufficient for what she had said, and I was the greatest Fool in the World if I did not follow her Advice. I positively assured her I would not, for I would not put it in the Power of a Mother-in-Law to use my Child ill; and that I had so much Regard, as I pretended, to the Memory of her Mother, I resolved never to enter into Matrimony a second Time.

Whatever was the Motive, I am entirely ignorant of, but this insensible Mortal had told the young Woman, that I intended to make Love to her; which, had I really been a Man, would have never entered in my Imagination, for she had no one Qualification to recommend her to the Regard of any Thing beyond a Porter or a Hackney-Coachman. Whether she was angry at what I said to the Wench, in regard to my Resolution against marrying, or whether it was a Forgery of the Maid's, of and to us both, I cannot positively say; but a Strangeness ensued, and I began to grow sick of my Place, and stay'd but a few Days after.

In the Interim Somebody happened to come, who hinted that I was a Woman; upon which, Madam, to my great Surprize, attacked me with insolently presuming to say she was in Love with me, which I assured her I never had the least Conception of. *No, truly; I believe*, said she, *I should hardly be 'namoured* WITH ONE OF MY OWN *Sect*: Upon which I burst into a Laugh, and took the Liberty to ask her, if she understood what she said? This threw the offended Fair into an absolute Rage, and our Controversy lasted for some Time; but, in the End, I brought in Vindication of my own Innocence, the Maid to Disgrace, who had uncalled for trumped up so ridiculous a Story.

Mrs. *Dorr* still remained incredulous, in regard to my being a Female; and though she afterwards paid me a Visit, with my worthy Friend (at my House in *Drury-Lane*) who brought my unsuccessful Letter back from my Father, she was not to be convinced, I happening that Day to be in the Male-Habit, on Account of playing a Part for a poor Man, and obliged to find my own Cloaths.

She told me, she wished she had known me better when I lived with her, she would, on no Terms, have parted with her Man *Charles*, as she had been informed I was capable of being Master of the Ceremonies, in managing and conducting the Musical Gardens; for she had a very fine Spot of Ground, calculated entirely for that Purpose, and would have trusted the Care of it to my Government.

George Sand gets back into breeches

from *Histoire de ma vie* (1854)
GEORGE SAND (1804–1876)

Aurore Dudevant (née Dupin), better known to the world as George Sand, was among the most highly regarded novelists of the nineteenth century, and judged by many to be superior to Dickens and Hugo. It is difficult to know whether the notoriety of her private life hindered or helped her literary reputation. This cigar-smoking socialist, whose many lovers included the poet Alfred de Musset and the Polish composer Frédéric Chopin, also dressed as a man and had passionate involvements with other women, notably the actress Marie Dorval. Many at the time and since have called these attachments lesbian although some critics and biographers contest that labelling, resenting what they see as a deliberate, and politically motivated, slur on the character of a woman of genius. What is not contestable is the extent to which other writers of the period, both male and female, treat Sand as belonging to 'a third sex', seeing her as a precursor of a stage of human evolution yet to come – a Creature who both combines and transcends the genders.

In the passage that follows Sand describes the reasons for and some of the consequences of adopting male attire in her late twenties.

Until then, that is to say until my daughter was with me in Paris, I had lived in a less easy way, indeed in a very odd way, but one which nevertheless led very directly to my goal.

I would *not* go over my budget, I would *not* borrow anything; my debt of 500 francs, the only debt of my life, had worried me so much! And what if M. Dudevant had refused to pay it! He did pay it, willingly; but I only dared to tell him about it when I was very ill and fearing to die *insolvent*. I went out looking for work but found none. I'll say later on how my literary fortunes were faring. I had a little portrait *on show* in the café at Quai Saint-Michel, in the house itself, but custom did not come. I had made a mess of my concierge's likeness; that would do me a power of no good in the neighbourhood.

I would have liked to read, but I didn't have the books or the money.

And then it was winter, and it's not economical to stay in your room when you have to count every stick of firewood. I tried to use the Bibliothèque Mazarin, but I think I'd have been better off trying to work on the towers of Notre-Dame, it was so cold there. I couldn't stand it – I feel the cold more than anyone else I know. There were some old *swots* working away there, well dug in at a table, motionless, contented, mummified, apparently unaware that their blue noses were becoming crystallized. I envied their state of petrifaction: I would watch them sit down and stand up as if worked by springs, to make sure that they weren't made of wood.

And then moreover I was eager to de-provincialize myself and to get up to date with the ideas and forms of my time. I felt the necessity of them, and I was curious about them; apart from the most outstanding works, I knew nothing of the contemporary arts; I craved the theatre above all.

I knew well that a poor woman could not allow herself such extravagances. Balzac used to say 'You can't be a woman in Paris on an income of under 25,000 francs.' And this paradox of elegance became a reality for the woman who wanted to be an artist.

Yet I saw my young male friends from Berry, companions of my childhood, living in Paris on just as little as me and keeping up with everything that interests intelligent young people. Literary and political events, the excitements of theatres and art galleries, of the clubs and of the streets – they saw everything, they went everywhere. I had legs as strong as theirs and good little feet from Berry which had learnt to walk on bad roads, balancing on my great sabots. But on the pavements of Paris, I was like a boat on the ice. My fine shoes split in a couple of days, my pattens made me fall over, I never picked up my skirts properly. I was muddy, tired, streaming with cold, and I saw my shoes and clothes, never mind the little velvet hats regularly 'watered' by the drainpipes, going to rack and ruin with terrifying speed.

I had already noticed and experienced those things before I had even thought of setting up house in Paris, and I had put the problem to my mother, who lived there in great elegance and ease on 3500 francs: how could I keep up the most modest outfit in that dreadful climate, unless by staying mewed up in my rooms seven days out of eight? She replied: 'It's quite possible at my age and with my habits; but when I was young and your father wasn't in funds, he had the idea of dressing me as a boy. My sister did the same, and we went everywhere with our husbands, to the theatre, just everywhere. It saved us half our household expenses.'

This idea seemed amusing to me at first, and then highly ingenious. Having been dressed as a boy in my childhood, and then having hunted in shirt and knee-breeches with Deschartres, I was not at all shocked to resume a mode of dress which was nothing new to me. At that time, the fashion was extraordinarily helpful for my disguise. Men wore long, square-cut greatcoats, a style called '*propriétaire*' which came down right to the heels and revealed so little of their figures that my brother, putting on his coat at Nohant, had once said, laughing, to me: 'Nice, isn't it? It's the fashion, and it's not at all uncomfortable. The tailor measures up a sentry-box and it fits up the whole regiment brilliantly!'

So I had myself made a *sentry-box coat* in heavy grey cloth, with trousers and waistcoat to match. With a grey hat and a thick woollen tie, I was the picture of a little first-year student. I can't tell you what pleasure my boots gave me: I'd willingly have slept in them, as my brother did in his early youth when he got his first pair. With those little steep-tipped heels, I was solid on the pavement. I zipped about from one end of Paris to the other. I felt I could have gone round the world. And then, my clothes would stand up to anything. I went out in all weathers, came home at all hours, sat in the stalls at all the theatres. Nobody gave me a second look or suspected my disguise. Apart from the fact that I was obviously at ease in it, the absence of coquetry in my costume and in my expression warded off all suspicion. I was too badly dressed, and looked too simple (my usual expression, absent-minded and ready to go into a daze) to attract or fix attention. Women aren't much good at disguising themselves, even on stage. They don't want to give up the elegance of their figures, the grace of their move-ments, the dazzling glances of their eyes; and yet giving up all that, especially their expressive glances, is the only way to avoid being easily found out. There's a way of slipping quietly everywhere you go without anyone turning to look at you, and of speaking in low, muted tones which don't ring like a flute in the ears of anyone who hears you. Moreover, in order not to be noticed as a *man*, you must already have the habit of not being noticed as a *woman*.

The Girls in the Gallery

from *Recollections of Vesta Tilley* (1923)

Female performers who impersonated men were among the most popular of late Victorian and Edwardian music-hall acts, and their undisputed 'King' was Vesta Tilley (1864–1952). Toffs, tramps, soldiers, sailors, lowly clerks masquerading as gentlemen of private means during their week's holiday at the seaside – she played them all, with meticulous attention to gesture, movement and dress. Such was the perfection of her attire in her gentlemanly roles that fashionable young men thronged the theatres where she performed, to pick up hints about the niceties of collars and cuffs, hats and canes: at the height of her career, she set male fashions. Her audiences included many women – stage-door Jills, rather than the customary stage-door Johnnies – and when she took into her repertoire a song which ended with her scattering coins upon the stage (pennies pretending to be sovereigns), it cost her pounds a week because each coin was eagerly claimed by ardent young women, seeking a souvenir of their favourite performer. Later, in 1934, when Tilley had become Lady de Frece and wrote her Recollections, *she recalled that army of female admirers. Her tone hovers, as you will see, between the serenely gracious and the really rather uncomfortable.*

At one time the stage door was besieged by young men waiting for a favourite actress, with a hansom cab standing by, the masher hoping that the object of his admiration would, immediately he had approached her, join him in a midnight supper, or a moonlight drive, solely on the strength of his immaculate 'get up' and colossal cheek. But gradually the female enthusiast appeared, and the male stage door 'lizard' was less often seen. The girls were more energetic than the men, but were satisfied with a smile of recognition, an autograph, a parting word, and, until another idol arose on their horizon, paid regular visits to the stage door.

It may be because I generally appeared on the stage as a young man that the big percentage of my admirers were women. Girls of all ages would wait in crowds to see me enter or leave the theatre, and each post brought piles of letters, varying from an impassioned declaration of undying love to a request for an autograph, or a photograph, or a simple flower, or a piece of ribbon I had worn. To illustrate the impression I made upon at least one of my girl admirers, I have in my possession now a complete diary of a young girl, covering a period of some ten years, in which she records the first time she saw me, her journeys to see me in the various towns at which I appeared, her opinions of the many new songs I had introduced during the time, all punctuated with expressions of lasting love and devotion. *A Diary of my most loved Artiste Miss Vesta Tilley* is the title.

This diary was sent to me by the writer in 1920. It is now 1933, and even to-day I receive frequent letters from my now grown-up admirer, and I see her often when I go to England. Clearly it is not a case of girlish infatuation, and I hope I have not offended her by mentioning the diary in my book. In any case none but herself and myself know her identity.

There were times, however, when such hero-worship became a little embarrassing, and this happened to me particularly on one occasion in America. The Americans have a very beautiful habit of sending to those whom they admire magnificent 'set-pieces' of flowers, – musical instruments or anything else made up entirely of flowers. When I have been leaving America, my stateroom has been completely filled with these wonderful floral tributes, each one a perfect work of art.

During one of my tours I received masses of most beautiful flowers from a girl who apparently followed me from town to town during the whole trip. Every night, when I appeared on the stage, I invariably saw the same girl in a box, gazing down at me, until at last it began to get slightly on my nerves. As she had made repeated requests to be received in my dressing-room, I at last said she might come and visit me. I took off my wig, undid all my little plaits and left my hair in a fuzzy bush without even bothering to put a comb through it, partially removed my make-up, and smothered my face with cream. As anyone who has ever worked behind the scenes knows full well, an artiste is not at her best when removing grease-paint! I then threw round me the wrapper which I kept or making up only, and said she could come in. She entered, stood still and gazed at me. I let her have a good look and then said: 'There, now you see what you have been following round for so long. Perhaps that will cure you!' But she only said: 'Oh no! I know you have only made yourself look like that on purpose, and I love the real you more than ever!' Now, what can you do with people like that?

But this excessive affection for me was not by any means confined to what I might call the 'flapper' type, and sometimes took a much more practical form. I still have a letter which I received from a middle-aged woman who was a cook, in which she told me how very much she admired me, and what a dear little boy I made, and proceeded to assure me that it would give her the very greatest happiness to serve me. If ever I were ill and wanted special nursing, or wanted someone to look after me, I had only to let her know, and she would leave no matter what situation to come to me and do everything possible. I have never needed her assistance, but am quite sure that had I called on her to help me, I should have had the most devoted slave one could possibly have.

Following in Father's Footsteps (1892)
E. W. ROGERS (1863–1913)

One of Vesta Tilley's best-known songs, 'Following in Father's Footsteps' enabled her to make common cause with many different sections of her audience: her apparent 'maleness' aligned her to other young rips of sons and occasionally erring dads; her actual femaleness made it possible to share a complicit mockery of dads and sons with the wives and mothers in her audience. And the travesti *added a sexual frisson both for heterosexual men, and for women able to respond erotically to the ambiguity she enacted.*

I

To follow in your father's footsteps is
A motto for each boy,
And following in father's footsteps is
A thing I much enjoy.
My mother caught me out one evening up
The West End on the spree,
She said 'Where are you going?'
But I answered, 'Don't ask *me!*'

CHORUS

'I'm following in father's footsteps; I'm following the dear old dad.
    He's just in front with a fine big gal,
    So I thought I'd have one as well.
I don't know where he's going, but when he gets there I'll be
glad!
I'm following in father's footsteps, – yes, I'm following the dear old
dad!'

2

    Pa said that to the North of England he
    On business had to go;
    To Charing-Cross he went, and where he booked
    I booked first-class, also.
    I found myself that night in Paris – to
    The clergyman next door
    I answered, when he said, 'What are
    You in this gay place for?',

'I'm following in father's footsteps; I'm following the dear old dad.
    He's trav'lling now for his firm, you see,
    In fancy goods, it seems to me.
I don't know where he's going, but when he gets there I'll be glad!
I'm following in father's footsteps, – yes, I'm following the dear old
dad!'

3

    At Margate with papa I toddled out
    To have a good old swim;
    I didn't know the proper place to bathe
    So left it all to him.
    I found myself amongst some ladies, and
    Enjoyed it, so did pa!
    Till ma yelled, 'Percy, fie for shame!'
    Said I, it's all right, ma!

'I'm following in father's footsteps; I'm following the dear old dad.
    He's just out there with the fair Miss Jupp,
    To show me how to hold girls up.
I'm going to hold her next, Ma, so when he drops her I'll be glad!
I'm following in father's footsteps, – yes, I'm following the dear old
dad!'

4

    To dinner up in town last night I went.
    And pa went there as well;
    How many Pommerys we had – my word!
    I really couldn't tell.
    At 2 A.M. pa started off for home
    Like *this*, and so did I!
    Father said, 'Mind where you're going! but
    I simply made reply –

'I'm following in father's footsteps; I'm following the dear old dad.
    He's wobbling on in the front, you see,
    And, 'pon my word, he's worse than me.
I don't know where he's going, but when he gets there I'll be glad!
I'm following in father's footsteps, – yes, I'm following the dear old
dad!'

'Father and I went for a walk'
C. M. DONALD

Father and I went for a walk.
'Look, chum,' he said,
'she's very bossy and so are you.
I think it's better if just one
person wears the trousers,' he added
a mite wistfully.

FOLLOWING IN FATHER'S FOOTSTEPS.
Written and Composed by E. W. ROGERS.
Sung by VESTA TILLEY.

Marriage Lines and
Family Matters

Something of women's enormously complex and often contradictory experience of and within marriage is revealed in this section. Here are 'marriage resisters' from the ancient world and the Renaissance, eighteenth-century social engineers trying to phase marriage out and New Women lamenting that so many promising young girls should be lost to it. But there are also women recognising, and demanding recognition of the fact, that their own life-long partnerships can match the most ideal conventional marriages in love, fidelity and sheer stamina.

For lesbian couples, motherhood or the unfulfilled desire for children can be areas fraught with difficult and painful emotions; but some lesbians eagerly embrace the challenge to create new ways of 'doing family', new notions of kinship.

Γελλως παιδοφιλωτερα
("Fonder of children than Gello") (1889)
'MICHAEL FIELD', after Sappho

The Michael Fields here take two Greek words (all that remain from one of Sappho's poems) and weave a new work from it. The Greek means 'fonder of children than Gello', and one of the ancient grammarians tells us, 'Gello was a girl and since she died prematurely the people of Lesbos say her ghost haunts little children and they attribute premature deaths to her.' Marriage, too, may be a form of death. Even though Sappho herself wrote epithalamia (marriage hymns), we know, from other of her fragments, that she also mourned the loss to marriage of the young women she loved best. From the tiny two-word fragment and the grammarian's gloss, the Michaels have created a work which simultaneously celebrates girlhood on the threshold of marriage and voices for Sappho her plea that 'the little thing from Telos', who has the makings of a true poet within her, should be spared 'Hymen's portals'.

Not Gello's self loves more than I
The virgin train, my company.
No thought of Eros doth appal
Their cheeks; their strong, clear eyes let fall
No tears; they dream their days will be
All laughter, love, serenity,
And violet-weaving at my knee —

Subtle Mnasidica in shape
As firm as the unripened grape,
Dica with meeting eyebrows sleek,
And Gorgo of the apple-cheek,

With that young dove-eyed creature come
From Telos, whose soft lips are dumb;
The golden bees about them hum.

Dica put forth her hand to reach
The blue sea-holly on the beach
Last night. I drew the child away;
She knew not where the love-charm lay,
And from the fatal fibre let
Her hand relax; but by his net
One stood she never can forget.

Ah me, and Gorgo too is pale!
Fell Cypris, if thou must prevail,
Mingle no madness in love's wine,
That these should e'en as Sappho pine,
Goddess forbid! The little thing
From Telos must be taught to sing;
The rest to Hymen's portals bring!

The virgin who hates the thought of marriage

from *Colloquia Familiara*
ERASMUS (?1466–1536)

The Colloquia Familiara *(Familiar Colloquies) of the great Dutch humanist Erasmus started life as a modest text-book of twenty little exercises designed to help schoolboys improve their skills in Latin composition. Over the years it expanded to become an international best seller, valued not only for its paedogogic usefulness but also for the shrewd wit and engaging freshness of the social vignettes it contained. This extract comes from a dialogue Erasmus added in 1523, 'Virgo* μισογαμος*' ('The marriage-hating virgin'). Catherine wants to become a nun; Eubulus is trying to persuade her against it . . .*

CATHERINE: There are so many dinner parties in my father's house, it annoys me; and the conversation between the married people isn't always decent. Sometimes, too, it's not possible to say no to a kiss.

EUBULUS: Someone who is determined to avoid everything that annoys them had better give up living. The ears are entirely used to hearing everything, but unless it's worthwhile, they don't pass it on to the mind. Your parents, I imagine, allow you a bedroom of your own?

CATHERINE: Oh yes.

EUBULUS: You can retreat there, if a party grows too uproarious, and while they are drinking and cracking jokes, you will be able to talk to your bridegroom, Christ. I suggest that you pray, sing psalms, give thanks. Your father's home will not corrupt you, but you will make it a purer place.

CATHERINE: But all the same, it would be safer in a community of virgins.

EUBULUS: I don't disapprove of a community that practises chaste behaviour, but I wouldn't want you to deceive yourself with false ideas. When the time comes that you have been in there for a while, when you have given it a closer inspection, it's possible that it won't all shine quite so brightly as it seemed to do before. And believe me, not all who wear a nun's veil are virgins.

CATHERINE: Do say some good words about them.

EUBULUS: By all means; good words are those that are true. But maybe the expression 'Virgin Mother', that until now we have reckoned to be appropriate to one person only, is to be applied to many, so that they too may be said to be virgins after they have given birth.

CATHERINE: Heaven forbid.

EUBULUS: Yes, and furthermore, there are other respects in which not everything about those virgins is strictly virginal.

CATHERINE: No? In what way, may I ask?

EUBULUS: Because more are to be met with who copy Sappho's practices than who reproduce her genius.

CATHERINE: I don't completely follow what you're saying.

EUBULUS: And that, my dear Catherine, is why I'm telling you this, so that the time doesn't come when you do understand it.

Translated by Gillian Spraggs (1999)

An unhappy wife

from Memoirs of the Verney Family

This fragment of family history depicts a household in crisis during one intense three-week period. We cannot know the underlying causes of Mary Verney's deeply troubled and often violent behaviour or why she clings so desperately to her maid, Jane, who 'is more to her than all the world'. It is some consolation to know that in later years Mary knew periods of calm and happiness, although her husband needed to engage a gentlewoman to act as companion to her and to oversee the household when she was unable to do so herself.

This account was written in dialect, phonetically spelt; very regretfully I have decided to modernise it, sacrificing something of its original savour to make it fully accessible to today's readers.

[*Lady Hobart writes to Sir Ralph Verney about his daughter-in-law, Mary, who is suffering from depression.*]

23 March 1664

Tuesday our cousin [*Mary*] was very ill all day, and highly discontented. At night they had no way but to give her a sleeping-pill, and she slept all night and till ten in this morning, and waked very tame but sullen [. . . *She*] wishes she had never come to London, but stayed with dear mother, for nobody does love her but she and poor Jane [*her maid*].

March 1664

As the weather is windy and stormy abroad, we have had our share with my cousin within. She has been very ill-humoured, by fits I may tell you mad. She has cried and screamed [*? and sung*] and railed on us, and poor doctor too. [. . .] she says [. . .] there is no one but her maid Jane, who does not long for her death. She says such things as flesh and blood never heard. Two days I kept away from her, only morning and night looked in to see how her two maids were looking after her. I believe if she had all her estate in her power, Jane should have it before all the world.

I fear your son will not have much comfort in this woman, for indeed she grows worse than ever. She grows very malicious in her tongue to us all. She has set us all out [*i.e., reviled us*] to Sir Robert Wiseman in a base manner. However, I will bear with her, and do all I can till her husband comes, which I hope will not be long, for she is not to be without him; she is afraid to do twenty things when he is here that she does now. Still she is fond of Jane, and if I may say between you and I, she is more to her than all the world; she now lies with [*i.e., shares a bed with*] her.

[. . .]

Truly she is stark mad [. . .] Sir Robert Wiseman says it were fit she should be removed [. . .] for his part he would not have her for a hundred pounds in his house. They say he gave her very good counsel, and did chide her mightily. [. . .] I fear she will be worse; she eats one bit and feeds Jane with another, and drinks to her, and they lie in one another's arms; so much dearness I never saw.

[. . .]

7 April 1664

Yesterday Dr Bates saw her in a worse fit than ever he did, and he said he would come no more. At night she beat her maid Jane out of her bed, and was raving all night. I am fain to hire one to watch, for the maids are afraid. She sent this day for Dr Colladon; she has sent often, but he came not till today. She hates us and the doctor to death. She struck at me, but I am careful not to come too near her – I keep knives and shears from her. Ah how I pity poor cousin Mun [*Edmund Verney, Mary's husband*], that must bear this heavy cross.

[Edmund writes to his father.]

8 April 1664

I arrived here yesterday, and found a wife [. . .] in a very ill humour, saying she was happy to see me before she dies. [. . .] This morning she tried to throw herself out of the window, and took a pin and tried to swallow it, saying she must go to Hell; certainly her mind is greatly troubled, she has such a will that she refuses everything one asks her to do.

14 April 1664

My wife grows worse in body and mind, and I fear she may grow worse
still in spirit, for she is so headstrong that she will not eat anything, or
do what one begs her to do, such a Devil of a will she has, and such
deep melancholy and suspicion. But why am I angry? I blame myself
very much for that, for alas the poor girl is completely mad, and wouldn't
know what to do, and I am so afflicted by it that I don't know what to
do or which way to turn.

The Unaccountable Wife

from *A Patch-Work Screen for the Ladies* (1723)
JANE BARKER (*c.* 1652–1727)

Jane Barker's A Patch-Work Screen for the Ladies *is a loosely knit mixture
of stories, poems, songs (and the occasioned recipe), held together by the
narrator, Galesia. In the remarkable tale reprinted here, the old and familiar
story of an unfaithful husband and a wronged wife gives way to a disturbing
account of the wife's obsessive love for her rival – a love adhered to despite
all reason and self-interest.*

*It is, perhaps, the prerogative of fiction to make coherent and give shape
to situations which life leaves fragmented and unresolved, as in the case of
the unfortunate Mary and Edmund Verney whom we have just met in this
section.*

This Gentleman, said *Galesia*, had married a young Gentlewoman of
Distinction, against the Consent of her Friends; which she accomplish'd
by the Help of her Mother's Maid-Servant. To say the Truth, though
her Birth was very considerable, yet her Person was not at all agreeable;
and her Fortune but indifferent: her Parents, I suppose, thinking, that
more than just enough to support her, would but betray her to an
unhappy Marriage. In short, married she was to the foresaid young Man,
whose Person was truly handsome; and with Part of her Fortune he

plac'd him-self in the Army, bestow'd another Part in furnishing her a House, and so liv'd very decently; and notwithstanding her indifferent Person, he had Children by her, though they did not live long. Thus they made a pretty handsome Shift in the World, 'till a vile Wretch, her Servant, overturn'd all; as follows. This Servant, whether she was a Creature of her Master's before she came to her Mistress, is not known; but she became very fruitful, and had every Year a Child; pretending that she was privately married to an Apprentice. Whether the Wife knew the whole of the Matter, or was impos'd upon, is uncertain; but which way soever it was, she was extremely kind to this Woman, to a Degree unheard-of; became a perfect Slave to her, and, as if she was the Servant, instead of the Mistress, did all the Household-Work, made the Bed, clean'd the House, wash'd the Dishes; nay, farther than so, got up in the Morning, scour'd the Irons, made the Fire, &c. leaving this vile Strumpet in Bed with her Husband; for they lay all Three together every Night. All this her Friends knew, or at least suspected; but thought it Complaisance, not Choice in her; and that she consider'd her own Imperfections, and Deformity; and therefore, was willing to take no Notice of her Husband's Fancy in the Embraces of this Woman her Servant. But the Sequel opens quite another Scene: And now I come to that Part of the Story, where he came to my Mother. His Business was, to desire her to come to his Wife, and endeavour to persuade her to part with this Woman; For, said he, she has already Three Children living, and God knows how many more she may have: Which indeed, Madam, said he, is a Charge my little Substance is not able to sustain; and I have been using all Endeavours to persuade my Wife to part with her, but cannot prevail: Wherefore I beg you, as a Friend, Relation, and her Senior in Years, to come, and lay before her the Reasonableness of what I desire, and the Ridiculousness of her proceeding. Good Heaven! said my Mother, can you think thus to bore my Nose with a Cushion? Can you imagine me so stupid, as to believe your Wife can persist in such a Contradiction of Nature? It is impossible a Wife should oppose her Husband's Desire in parting with such a Woman. Madam, reply'd he, I beg you once more to be so good as to come to my Wife, and then condemn me if I have advanc'd a Falsehood. Well, reply'd my Mother, I will come; though I doubt not but upon due Inspection, the whole, will prove a Farce compos'd amongst you, in which your Wife is to act her Part just as you between you think fit to teach her; which she, out of Fear, or some other Delusion, is to perform. But he averr'd again and again, that, without Fraud or Trick, the Thing was as he said. In short, my Mother went; and there she found the Servant sitting in a handsome Velvet Chair, dress'd up in very good lac'd Linnen, having clean Gloves on her Hands, and the Wife washing the Dishes. This Sight put my Mother into such a violent Passion, that she had much ado to refrain from laying Hands on her. However, she most vehemently chid the Mistress; telling her, That she offended God, disgrac'd her Family, scandaliz'd her Neighbours, and was a Shame to Woman-kind. All which she return'd with virulent Words; amongst other Things, she stood Buff in Favour of that Woman; saying, That she had been not only a faithful Servant, but the best of Friends, and those that desir'd to remove such a Friend from her, deserved not the Name of Friends, neither did she desire they should come into her House: All which she utter'd with such an Air of Vehemency, that there was no Room left to doubt of the Sincerity of her Words; but that all proceeded from an Interiour thoroughly degenerated. All which my Mother related to me with great Amazement: But withal, told me, that she would have me go to her on the Morrow; and with calm and friendly Words, endeavour to persuade her to Reason; for, said she, I was in a Passion at the disagreeable View; but you, who have naturally more Patience than my-self, pray put on the best Resolutions you can to keep your Temper, whatsoever Provocations shall occur. Thus instructed, thus resolved, I went next Day, hoping that a Night's Repose would calm the Storm my Mother's Anger might have rais'd. But when I came, I found it all the same: Though I took her apart, and with the utmost Mildness, persuaded her, and us'd the best Reasons I could think on to inforce those Persuasions, yet all was in vain; and she said, We all join'd with her Husband to make her miserable, by removing from her, the only Friend she had in the World; and passionately swore by Him that made her, that if we combin'd to send the Woman away, she would go with her. I would try that, reply'd I, were I in your Husband's Place: At which her Passion redoubled; and she, with violent Oaths, repeated her Resolution; desiring, that her Friends would meddle with their own Business, and let her alone, to remain in Quiet in her House, and not come to give her Disturbance. After these uncouth Compliments, I left her, carrying with me the greatest Amazement possible. After this, the Husband came to us, and ask'd, If we did not find true what he had told us? Indeed, replied I, true, and doubly true; such a Truth as I believe never was in the World before, nor never will be again. In this Case, said he, What would you counsel me to do? Truly, said my Mother, it is hard to advise; for to let the Woman live there still, is not proper; nor can your Circumstances undergo the Charge: And if your Wife should do as she says, and go with her; I should in some Degree be accessary to the parting Man and Wife. I would venture, said I, for when it comes to the Push, I warrant her she will not go. Hereupon the Man said he would try; and accordingly, hired a Place in a Waggon to carry the Creature into her own Country; hoping, as I suppose, that his Wife would have rested herself contented with him, when the Woman had been gone; but instead thereof, she acted as she said, and went along with her.

This Transaction was so extraordinary, that every-body was amazed at it; and when they had been gone some time, there arose a Murmuring, amongst Friends, Neighbours and Acquaintance, as if he had made his Wife away; and when he told them the Manner of her Departure, they would not believe him, the thing in itself being so incredible.

But we will leave him to make his Party good, as well as he can, amidst the Censure of his Neighbours, the Threats of her Friends, and the Ridicule of his Acquaintance; and follow the Travellers, into the Country whither they were gone.

They arrived safe at the Woman's Father's, where they found as kind a Reception as a poor Cottage could afford; and a very poor one it was, there being no Light but what came in at the Door, no Food but from the Hands of Charity, nor Fewel but what they pilfer'd from their Neighbours Hedges.

Now what this unaccountable Creature thought of this kind of Being, is unknown, or what Measures she and her Companion thought to take, or what Schemes they form'd to themselves, is not conceivable: But whatever they were, the discreet Neighbourhood put a Period to their Projects; for they got a Warrant to have them before a Justice, in order to prevent a Parish Charge; there being two Children there already, which they had sent some time before; and now two helpless Women being come, they knew not where the Charge might light, and therefore proceeded as aforesaid. It happen'd as the Constable was conducting them to the Justice, with a Mob at their Heels, that they pass'd by the House of a Lady of Quality, who looking out of her Window, saw in the midst of this Throng, this unfortunate Wife, whom she immediately knew to be the Daughter of her Friend; knew to be the Child of an honourable Family. It is impossible to describe what Amazement seiz'd her: She call'd out to the Constable and other Neighbours there, bidding them bring that Gentlewoman to her, which they immediately did. This good Lady, out of Respect to her old Friends, a worthy Family, bid them discharge her, telling them, That her-self would be bound that she should be no Parish Charge; so took her into her House, treated her kindly, and offer'd her all she could do on such an Occasion: For all which she return'd the Lady but cold Thanks, and begg'd her Ladyship's Assistance to convey her to *London* along with the other Woman, who, she said, was the truest Friend in the World. The Lady knowing nothing of her Story, with much Goodness provided for her Departure, together with her Companion. In this manner, loaden with Disgrace, they came back to *London*, to her Husband, from whom, no doubt, she found Reproaches suitable to her Folly.

Long it was not, e'er Death made a true and substantial Separation, by carrying the Husband into the other World. Now was the Time to make manifest, whether Promises, Flatteries or Threatnings had made her act the foresaid Scene: But it appear'd all voluntary; for when he was dead, her Friends and Relations invited and persuaded her to leave that Creature and her Children, and come to live with them, suitable to her Birth and Education. But all in vain; she absolutely adher'd to this Woman and her Children, to the last Degree of Folly; insomuch, that being reduc'd to Poverty, she begg'd in the Streets to support them. At last, some Friend of her Family told the Queen of the distressed way she was in; and in some Degree, how it came to pass, that neither her dead Husband nor her Relations might be blameable. The *Queen*, with much Goodness, told her Friend, That if she would leave that Woman, and go live with some Relation, she would take Care she should not want; and withal sent her Five Guineas, as an Earnest of a Monthly Pension; but notwithstanding, this infatuated Creature refus'd the *Queen's*

Favour, rather than part with this Family: And so, for their Support, begg'd in the Streets, the Remainder of her Days.

Sure, said the Lady, This poor Creature was under some Spell or Inchantment, or she could never have persisted, in so strange a manner, to oppose her Husband, and all her nearest Friends, and even her *Sovereign*. As they were descanting on this Subject, a Servant came and told them, that all was ready in the Arbour; and that the Gentlemen having finish'd their Bowl of *Punch*, were attending their coming, to share with them in a Dish of *Tea*, and *Welsh Flummery*.

[. . .]

On not facing the enemy's cannon

from *Millenium Hall* (1762)
by SARAH SCOTT (1723–1795)

In this extract from Millenium Hall, *Sarah Scott's utopian novel of a female community, the ladies of Millenium Hall explain to their male visitor why they do not themselves marry, although they are prepared to provide dowries for their female servants and other local young women to do so. Sarah Scott, before her marriage, was a Miss Robinson, younger sister of the woman who, as Mrs Montague, became one of the century's most celebrated 'Blues' (bluestockings, or learned ladies). Scott's own experience of marriage had been wretched. She was rescued – though from what is not quite clear – by her father and brothers who removed her from the marital home little more than twelve months after the wedding. After a brief convalescence at her sister's house she went to live with her inseparable friend, Lady Barbara Montagu (no relation to Scott's brother-in-law), and remained with her until Lady Bab's death nine years later in 1765. The two women lived either in Bath or the nearby village of Batheaston at a time when Charlotte Charke was working as a prompter at the Bath theatre. Sarah Scott and Lady Bab were theatre-goers. We must hope they did not hear Charlotte Charke's voice too often!*

My cousin told me that Miss Mancel gave the young bride a fortune, and that she might have her share of employment and contribute to the provision for her family had stocked her dairy and furnished her with poultry. This, Mrs Maynard added, was what they did for all the young women they brought up, if they proved deserving; shewing, likewise, the same favour to any other girls in the parish who, during their single state, behaved with remarkable industry and sobriety. By this mark of distinction they were incited to a proper behaviour, and appeared more anxious for this benevolence on account of the honour that arose from it than for the pecuniary advantage.

As the ladies' conduct in this particular was uncommon, I could not forbear telling them, that I was surprised to find so great encouragement given to matrimony by persons whose choice shewed them little inclined in its favour.

'Does it surprise you,' answered Mrs Morgan smiling, 'to see people promote that in others which they themselves do not choose to practise? We consider matrimony as absolutely necessary to the good of society; it is a general duty; but as, according to all ancient tenures, those obliged to perform knight's service, might, if they chose to enjoy their own firesides, be excused by sending deputies to supply their places; so we, using the same privilege substitute many others, and certainly much more promote wedlock than we could do by entering into it ourselves. This may wear the appearance of some devout persons of a certain religion who, equally indolent and timorous, when they do not choose to say so many prayers as they think their duty, pay others for supplying their deficiencies.'

'In this case,' said I, 'your example is somewhat contradictory, and should it be entirely followed, it would confine matrimony to the lower rank of people, among whom it seems going out of fashion, as well as with their superiors; nor indeed can we wonder at it, for dissipation and extravagance are now become such universal vices that it requires great courage in any to enter into an indissoluble society. Instead of being surprised at the common disinclination to marriage, I am rather disposed to wonder when I see a man venture to render himself liable to the expenses of a woman who lavishes both her time and money on every fashionable folly, and still more, when one of your sex subjects herself to be reduced to poverty by a husband's love for gaming, and to neglect by his inconstancy.'

'I am of your opinion,' said Miss Trentham, 'to face the enemy's cannon appears to me a less effort of courage than to put our happiness into the hands of a person who perhaps will not once reflect on the importance of the trust committed to his or her care. For the case is pretty equal as to both sexes, each can destroy the other's peace.

Marriage (1900)
MARY COLERIDGE (1861–1907)

Mary Coleridge was a descendant of the Romantic poet Samuel Taylor Coleridge, and although she initially established her reputation with prose fiction, is herself best known as a poet.

Coleridge's circle of women friends, to which she was constantly adding, was enormously important in her intellectual, spiritual and emotional development. Her intense inner life ran parallel with practical political activity. Unusually well-educated herself, with a knowledge of six languages including Greek and Hebrew, she taught at the Working Men's College, a forerunner of the Workers' Educational Association.

Poems by Mary E. Coleridge, edited by Henry Newbolt, was published in 1907 after her death. It, together with a later volume, Gathered Leaves from the Prose of Mary E. Coleridge, *with a Memoir by Edith Sichel, became touchstones for lesbian readers who recognised in the particular nature of Mary Coleridge's emotional and spiritual struggles something of their own lives. All who knew her are agreed that she had a genius for friendship; two friends bear testimony to it in the penultimate section of this book entitled 'Farewells'.*

> No more alone sleeping, no more alone waking,
>   Thy dreams divided, thy prayers in twain;
> Thy merry sisters to-night forsaking,
>   Never shall we see thee, maiden, again.

Never shall we see thee, thine eyes glancing,
   Flashing with laughter and wild in glee,
Under the mistletoe kissing and dancing,
    Wantonly free.

There shall come a matron walking sedately,
   Low-voiced, gentle, wise in reply.
Tell me, O tell me, can I love her greatly?
All for her sake must the maiden die!

The Farmer's Bride
CHARLOTTE MEW (1869–1928)

*This poem is probably Charlotte Mew's best-known piece of work. First
published in 1916, it was much anthologised for decades, and I first encountered it, as a schoolgirl of twelve, in the anthology we used in the late 1950s
in the first form of my Surrey Grammar School. Even then I realised that,
despite the heterosexual situation the poem describes, this woman poet had
a very particular understanding of what it means and how it feels to be an
object of horror or disgust to a woman one loves and desires.*

Three Summers since I chose a maid,
Too young maybe – but more's to do
At harvest-time than bide and woo.
   When us was wed she turned afraid
Of love and me and all things human;
Like the shut of a winter's day.
Her smile went out, and 'twasn't a woman –
   More like a little frightened fay.
      One night, in the Fall, she runned away.

'Out 'mong the sheep, her be,' they said,
'Should properly have been abed;

But sure enough she wasn't there
Lying awake with her wide brown stare.
So over seven-acre field and up-along across the down
    We chased her, flying like a hare
    Before our lanterns. To Church-Town
        All in a shiver and a scare
    We caught her, fetched her home at last
        And turned the key upon her, fast.

She does the work about the house
As well as most, but like a mouse:
        Happy enough to chat and play
        With birds and rabbits and such as they,
        So long as men-folk keep away.
'Not near, not near!' her eyes beseech
When one of us comes within reach.
        The women say that beasts in stall
        Look round like children at her call.
        I've hardly heard her speak at all.

Shy as a leveret, swift as he,
Straight and slight as a young larch tree,
Sweet as the first wild violets, she,
To her wild self. But what to me?

The short days shorten and the oaks are brown,
    The blue smoke rises to the low grey sky,
One leaf in the still air falls slowly down,
    A magpie's spotted feathers lie
On the black earth spread white with rime,
The berries redden up to Christmas-time.
    What's Christmas-time without there be
    Some other in the house than we!

She sleeps up in the attic there
Alone, poor maid. 'Tis but a stair

Betwixt us. Oh! my God! the down,
The soft young down of her, the brown,
The brown of her — her eyes, her hair, her hair!

'Unfathered the child clings to the wall of the heart'
MAUREEN DUFFY

Unfathered the child clings to the wall of the heart:
The seed I cannot embed in your flesh sprouts in the mind
To tendril, leaf and flower while the unborn riot
Joyful in the parks and gardens of never will be.
I would watch you through nine months
Sail of our love together my ship and sea,
Where I swim free or am wave breaking on your shore,
Run up through the soft molluscular caverns of your body
And leave my ocean life limpet to the embrace
Of your flesh, so proud you can conceive my queen
Cat-walking stiff legged
Against our bellying burgeon of light.

There are things that can't be said,
Doors shut that I daren't push
Yet you open them freely with an 'if'
And 'I would like'.
Unused to presents, to precious awards,
I do not answer, stumble over jutting words.
Our children whisper in my head
But most that mothering you I glimpse by proxy
That I would penetrate, stir with my shuddering blood,
Walks in my dreams. I tender my eunuch rage,
The wooden sword that snaps on steel reason,
Yet know I am in you and the unborn children
Riot in our sun.

Scan

ESTHER ISAAC

*The name 'Shet' comes from Genesis, 4:25, recounting what happened after Cain killed Abel: 'And Adam knew his wife again; and she bare a son, and called his name Seth: For God, said she, hath appointed me another seed instead of Abel, whom Cain slew.' Seth (*Shet *in Hebrew) is the child of a new beginning, the reassertion of life after death.*

Even now I'd like to give you something still more intimate
a hand entering your mouth
a finger on your tongue
a fist to close on softly
without a word or mark

turning you inside out
after a trace of blood
Susie duty ultrasonographer
scans this screen of fleeting images for signs
of defects or defection

she tells you straight

day 42
length from crown to rump
just half an inch
fingers just in bud
which by day 56
might touch the lips
and maybe go between
you'll see the eyes sit straight

look the heart beats strong

you shrink and hide your face
pregnant
and dying on the ridges of burning earth
that rock inside you

once you craved your mother's blood
and crumbling bone made flesh
dreaming
after her death
a monthly dream of change
of Aphrodite
walking a fall of foam
or Sappho singing

to her only daughter
lifting your head
out of your bloodless hands

alone in an empty room
stacked with the ghosts of children
their faces turned to smoke

you took just half an inch of sperm
newly ejaculated
warm inside a tube

saw yourself transfigured
mother of one living
(but still
how many dead)

19 weeks
Susie discloses the evident logic of embryogenesis
a scroll of images
an intertext of bone and blood
and his own sharp inimitable fingerprints

a perfect minute body
the anatomy of consolation
curls like an ammonite
away from here
prised out of time
way out of touch
somewhere becoming a homeless distant relative
whom you can't rehouse

only women can be truly intimate
you whisper afterwards
if he could have been yours
taking a cigarette

your hair light on my breasts
I touch a knot of limbs flexed under your skin
and stroke his head
until he feels asleep

and then my mouth finds you salt and warm and moaning

love surely when he's born
this child
surely
we'll call him Shet

Changes
SALLY CLINE

He no longer wears a plait.
He no longer keeps chickens.
The way the Radicals can.
No longer the same person
Or Man.

Now he wears short hair
Now he is the Department's Chairperson
Or Man.

His wife is no longer kept with the chickens.
She runs loose with no shoes.
The way Radical Wives can.
She does not quite look the same person.
Does not act quite according to plan.

He encourages her freedom.
Admires her aplomb.
(He calls her Mom)
He buys her new shoes.
He discovers
She has outgrown them.

He discovers
She has discovered another life.
He discovers
She has discovered
Another
Radical Wife.

He wishes they still kept chickens.

At Averham
U. A. FANTHORPE

Here my four-year-old father opened a gate,
And cows meandered through into the wrong field.

I forget who told me this. Not, I think,
My sometimes reticent father. Not much I know

About the childhood of that only child. Just
How to pronounce the name, sweetly deceitful

In its blunt spelling, and how Trent
Was his first river. Still here, but the church

Closed now, graveyard long-grassed,
No one to ask in the village. Somewhere here,

I suppose, I have a great-grandfather buried,
Of whom nothing is known but that, dying, he called

My father's mother from Kent to be forgiven.
She came, and was. And came again

To her sister, my great-aunt, for
Her dying pardon too. So my chatty mother,

But couldn't tell what needed so much forgiving,
Or such conclusive journeys to this place.

Your father, pampered only brother
Of many elder sisters, four miles away,

Grew up to scull on this river. My father,
Transplanted, grew up near poets and palaces,

Changed Trent for Thames. Water was in his blood;
In a dry part of Kent his telephone exchange

Was a river's name; he went down to die
Where Arun and Adur run out to the sea.

Your father, going north, abandoned skiffs for cars,
And lived and died on the wind-blasted North Sea shore.

They might have met, two cherished children,
Among nurses and buttercups, by the still silver Trent,

But didn't. That other implacable river, war,
Trawled them both in its heady race

Into quick-march regiments. I don't suppose they met
On any front. They found our mothers instead.

So here I stand, where ignorance begins,
In the abandoned churchyard by the river,

And think of my father, his mother, her father,
Your father, and you. Two fathers who never met,

Two daughters who did. One boy went north, one south,
Like the start of an old tale. Confusions

Of memory rise: rowing, and rumours of war,
And war, and peace; the secret in-fighting

That is called marriage. And children, children,
Born by other rivers, streaming in other directions.

You like the sound of my father. He would
Have loved you plainly, for loving me.

Reconciliation is for the quick, quickly. There isn't enough
Love yet in the world for any to run to waste.

Misfit
from *Feminist Fables* (1981)
SUNITI NAMJOSHI

Finally she died and went to heaven. Everyone was nice. The King of Heaven was kindly and patriarchal, even grandfatherly. He seemed to like her. Whenever she caught his eye, he always smiled. It was made very plain that there was a place for her there. If she wished to fit in, she could quite easily. She in her turn was pleasant enough, never rude; but she took to seeking out isolated corners, and going off by herself, and, in general, avoiding society. One day, when the King of Heaven was passing through a great hall, he found her there, staring out of a window. He put his arms around her shoulders. 'What's the matter,' he said, 'Don't you feel at home? Why are you unhappy?' She wanted to cry and be a little girl again and say she was sorry, but all she said was, 'It's very like home. That's what bothers me.'

Just Friends?

It's a curious phrase, 'just friends'. It seems to suggest that there's something 'rarther mere', as Daisy Ashford would say, about friendship. But friendship may be a passion, as many of the women you will meet in this section knew full well. It is perfectly capable of outlasting, ousting or replacing conventional marriage.

There used to be a nice neat view of life, much promulgated in certain academic circles, which said that there weren't really any such things as lesbians until about 1850: up until then there were just women who sometimes 'did' things with other women, but that did not, as we would say now, 'affect their sense of their own identity'. And, anyway, most women didn't 'do' anything; they just had feelings, instead. Friends, apparently, are never lovers. I never did believe it, and fortunately a great deal of recent research suggests I don't have to.

The emotional range encompassed in the next few pages is wide: light flirtation, desperate yearning, incoherent adulation, relief and gratitude. From Wollstonecraft, near tragedy; from Edgeworth, broad farce; and, from Amy Levy, a gallant effort to make light of a heavy heart.

Question and answer?

Both the poems which follow implicitly set up an opposition between hetero-sexuality and female friendship and could be seen as two halves of a dialogue. Although we have no evidence that Katherine Philips knew the poem by Edmund Waller or was directly responding to it, her poem not only appears to answer some of his charges but even emphasises many of the same words, and, in the final verse, replicates one of Waller's key rhymes, 'control/soul'. Waller's poem ricochets between idealisation of female friendship as celestial (associated with Venus's doves and Cupid's wings) and fierce resentment at the ladies' 'cunning change of hearts' which enables them to elude Cupid's 'darts'; Waller likens this to an act of fiscal fraud, the 'design' whereby debtors evade the law by making over their property to someone else. Katherine Philips, 'Orinda', insists on the innocence of her and Lucasia's 'design'; her version of love between women is highly spiritualised, yet her exultation over the 'bridegroom' and the 'crown-conqueror', both of whom can possess only 'pieces of earth', suggests more corporeal and material concerns.

On the Friendship Betwixt
Two Ladies
EDMUND WALLER (1606–1687)

Tell me, lovely, loving pair!
Why so kind, and so severe?
Why so careless of our care,
Only to yourselves so dear?

By this cunning change of hearts,
You the power of love control;
While the boy's eluded darts
Can arrive at neither soul.

For in vain to either breast
Still beguiled love does come,
Where he finds a foreign guest,
Neither of your hearts at home.

Debtors thus with like design,
When they never mean to pay,
That they may the law decline,
To some friend make all away.

Not the silver doves that fly,
Yoked in Cytherea's car;
Not the wings that lift so high,
And convey her son so far;

Are so lovely, sweet, and fair,
Or do more ennoble love;
Are so choicely matched a pair,
Or with more consent do move.

To My Excellent Lucasia,
On Our Friendship
KATHERINE PHILIPS (1632–1664)

I did not live until this time
Crown'd my felicity,
When I could say without a crime,
I am not thine, but thee.

This carcass breath'd, and walkt, and slept,
So that the world believ'd
There was a soul the motions kept;
But they were all deceiv'd.

For as a watch by art is wound
To motion, such was mine:
But never had Orinda found
A soul till she found thine;

Which now inspires, cures and supplies,
And guides my darkened breast:
For thou art all that I can prize,
My joy, my life, my rest.

No bridegroom's nor crown-conqueror's mirth
To mine compar'd can be:
They have but pieces of the earth,
I've all the world in thee.

Then let our flames still light and shine,
And no false fear controul,
As innocent as our design,
Immortal as our soul.

A trio of flirts

There is a certain sort of love poetry, written to women by women, in which it is not clear whether the writer herself desires the woman addressed, or whether she shares with her addressee the delicious knowledge that each of them is, or may be, desired by men. In the space created by this ambiguity, there is room for safe flirtation of a clearly erotic sort. Three such poems appear below.

Lady Mary Wortley Montagu (1689–1762) was not immune to the lure of female beauty, nor ignorant of sexual diversity: later in life she and her friend Lord Hervey both fell in love with a bisexual Italian man who resisted her (he went on to become a favourite of Frederick the Great). Elizabeth Rowe (1674–1737) was married to a man thirteen years her junior and lamented him in verse when he died after five years of marriage. Lady Sophia Burrell (?1750–1802) was married twice. Sometimes one is tempted to say, with Queen Charlotte, George III's consort, 'Cela n'empêche pas'.

Impromptu to a Young Lady Singing
(c. 1720s)
LADY MARY WORTLEY MONTAGU

Sing, Gentle Maid, reform my breast,
And soften all my Care;
Thus I can be some moments blest,
And easy in Despair.
The power of Orpheus lives in you;
The raging Passions of my Soul subdue,
And tame the Lions and the Tygers there.

To Celinda
ELIZABETH ROWE

I

I can't, Celinda, say, I love,
　　But rather I adore,
When with transported eyes I view
　　Your *shining* merits o'er.

II

A frame so spotless and serene,
　　A virtue so refined;
And thoughts as great, as e'er was yet
　　Grasped by a *female mind*.

III

There love and honour dressed in all
　　Their *genuine charms* appear,
And with a pleasing force at once
　　They conquer and endear.

IV

Celestial flames are scarce more bright,
　　Than those your worth inspires,
So Angels love and so they burn
　　In just such holy fires.

V

Then let's my dear *Celinda* thus
　　Blest in our selves contemn
The treacherous and deluding arts,
　　Of those *base things called men*.

To Emma
LADY SOPHIA BURRELL

Why, pretty rogue! do you protest
The trick of stealing you detest?
'Tis what you are doing ev'ry day,
Either in earnest or in play;
Cupid and you, 'tis said, are cousins,
(*Au fait* in stealing hearts by dozens,)
Who make no more of shooting 'sparks',
Than school-boys do of wounding larks;
Nay, what is worse, 'tis my belief,
Tho' known to be an arrant thief,
Such powers of witchcraft are your own,
That justice slumbers on her throne;
And shou'd you be arraign'd in court
For practising this cruel sport,
In spite of all the plaintiff's fury,
Your SMILE wou'd bribe both JUDGE and JURY.

from *Letters* by Anna Seward (1742–1809)

Anna Seward, often called 'The Swan of Lichfield' by her contemporaries, was one of the best-known poets of her day. Her emotions were largely directed towards other women, chief of whom was Honora Sneyd, who later became one of Maria Edgeworth's stepmothers. Here are two extracts from letters written about the young Honora in the 1760s.

You know the Lichfield young women do not play at cards. Six or seven of us were loitering at the windows and round the card-tables – expectation too busy with us for us to be busy with our needles. The beau was presented by his sister to every one in turn, and judiciously made no particular address to my sister. He said, gallantly enough, that he had pleasure in seeing his native country the richest in beauty of any nation through whose cities he had passed.

Our glowing Nannette was there, with her large and languishing hazle eyes, warm cheek, and the tender fascination of her smile. Eliza W—, in all her acquiline beauty and with that air of grandeur, though hardly yet sixteen, whose form so often reminds me of a passage in Ossian: 'Lovely, with her raven hair, is the white-bosomed daughter of Sorglan.' She also, whose charms are in their summer-ripeness, whose name seems to have been prophetic of her seldom-equalled beauty, the celebrated Helen White; yet has her cast of countenance more of Raphael's Madonna, than of that less-chastened loveliness with which imagination invests the faithless wife of Menelaus.

Miss A— also was in the group; of shape correct, and of air sprightly, with my sister, the fair bride-elect, whose form is so light and elegant, whose countenance has so much modest intelligence, and by her side Honora, 'fresh and beautiful as the young day-star when he bathes his fair beams in the dews of spring'. Often, when Mr. Porter's attention was otherwise engaged, she looked up in my sister's face with eyes moistened by solicitous tenderness.

This dear child will not live; I am perpetually fearing it, notwithstanding the clear health which crimsons her cheek and glitters in her eyes. Such an early expansion of intelligence and sensibility partakes too much of the angelic, too little of the mortal nature, to tarry long in these low abodes of frailty and of pain, where the harshness of authority, and the impenetrability of selfishness, with the worse mischiefs of pride and envy, so frequently agitate by their storms, and chill by their damps, the more ingenious and purer spirits, scattered, not profusely, over the earth.

This child seems angel before she is woman; how consummate shall she be if she should be woman before she is actually angel! What delight must then result to me from the consciousness that my sister and myself have been instrumental in the cultivation of talents and of virtues, in which the imagination, the sensibility, and warm disdain of every grovelling propensity, which are, I flatter myself, characteristic of one monitress, shall be united with the sweetness, the unerring discretion, and self-command of the other! She will, by all those who know how to appreciate excellence, be acknowledged, like Miranda, 'to have been formed of every creature's best'.

*   *   *

I begin to count the hours till Monday morning; yet this pleasure of expectation, perhaps more sweet and vivid than any reality which can crown it, is not without alloy, not without a mixture of regret. My amiable cousin will feel her retirement more lonely and deprived, for having had it enlivened during a whole month, by society so dear to her. That consciousness is painful. How I wish she might be permitted to return with us! but my aunt and uncle will not hear of it.

It is evening. Half an hour ago my fair cousin and myself were walking on the grass-plat, upon which our chamber window looks. The sun was setting splendidly; but, looking up, I saw an object more bright, more lovely – the face of my beauteous Honora at the open casement, packing up a little box which we were to take home with us. She leaned forward, bending upon me her fine eyes, luminous with joy, then lifted them up with a smile of delight, and clasped her dear hands together. I need not observe that it was the thoughts of our approaching return which produced this silent eloquence of pleasure. She would have restrained it, I well know, from respect to poor Miss Martin's very opposite sensations, had not that dear girl's eyes, heavy with regret, been fixed upon the ground, and therefore incapable of seeing an emanation whose lustre must have pained her.

Extracts from 'Llangollen Vale' (1796)
ANNA SEWARD

In April 1778, Miss Sarah Ponsonby leapt out of a window and made her way to her beloved cousin, Lady Eleanor Butler, with whom she eloped. Pursued by their horrified families, and dragged home, these two Anglo-Irish aristocrats nevertheless eventually made good their escape once more and crossed the Irish Sea. After many trials and vexations they set up house in the little Welsh town of Llangollen where they lived together for more than fifty years in a union broken only by the death, in 1829, of Lady Eleanor, at the age of ninety. Sarah Ponsonby, her junior by sixteen years, died just two years later. The Ladies and their heavily Gothicised rustic retreat at Plas Newydd drew admiration from many of their most celebrated contemporaries, including Wordsworth, Wellington, Lady Caroline Lamb and Sir Walter Scott. Yet some tongues wagged unkindly, and in 1790 the Ladies asked another friend, Edmund Burke, whether they should sue the author of a newspaper article about them, entitled 'Extraordinary Female Affection', in which the 'masculine' Lady Eleanor and 'effeminate' Miss Ponsonby were equivocally described. Very sensibly he advised them to do nothing (although he himself had successfully sued those who wondered, in the 1780s, why Mr Burke was 'soft' on sodomites, when he opposed the use of the pillory, with its often fatal results, as a punishment for sodomy).

Like much of Western Europe, Anna Seward was entranced by the Ladies. In 1796 she wrote an extremely over-excited poem celebrating them and the Vale of Llangollen to which they had brought international renown. This poem is sometimes so ecstatic and enthusiastic in its elevated passion that Seward's actual meaning becomes elusive! Lady Eleanor Butler and Miss Sarah Ponsonby appear here in poetic guise as Eleonora and Zara. The Ladies have been assimilated completely into a version of Gothic, and Miss Seward is anxious to assert not only the purity of the friendship between these positively vestal ladies, but also of the landscape itself. The footnotes are her own.

Now with a Vestal lustre glows the VALE,
   Thine, sacred FRIENDSHIP, permanent as pure
In vain the stern Authorities assail.
   In vain Persuasion spreads her silken lure,
High-born, and high-endow'd, the peerless TWAIN,[1]
Pant for coy Nature's charms 'mid silent dale, and plain.

---

[1] *Peerless twain.* RIGHT HONORABLE LADY ELEANOR BUTLER, and MISS PONSONBY, now seventeen years resident in Llangollen Vale and whose Guest the Author had the honor to be during several delightful days of the late Summer.

This Eleonora, and her ZARA's mind,
   Early tho' genius, taste and fancy flow'd,
Tho' all the graceful ARTS their powers combined,
   And her last polish brilliant Life bestow'd,
The lavish Promises, in Youth's soft morn,
Pride, Pomp, and Love, her friends, the sweet Enthusiasts scorn.

Then rose the Fairy Palace of the Vale,
   Then bloom'd around it the Arcadian Bowers;
Screen'd from the storms of Winter, cold and pale,
   Screen'd from the fervors of the sultry hours,
Circling the lawny crescent, soon they rose,
To letter'd ease devote, and friendship's blest repose.

Smiling they rose beneath the plastic hand
   Of Energy and Taste; – nor only they,
Obedient Science hears the mild command,
   Brings every gift that speeds the tardy day,
Whate'er the pencil sheds in vivid hues,
Th'historic tome reveals, or sings the raptur'd Muse.

How sweet to enter, at the twilight grey,
   The dear, minute Lyceum[1] of the Dome,
When, thro' the colour'd crystal, glares the ray,
   Sanguine and solemn 'mid the gathering gloom,
While glow-worm lamps diffuse a pale, green light,
Such as in mossy lanes illume the starless night.

[1] *Lyceum*, – the *Library*, fitted up in the Gothic taste, the painted windows of that form. In the elliptic arch of the door, there is a prismatic lantern of variously tinted glass, containing two large lamps with their reflectors. The light they shed resembles that of a Volcano, gloomily glaring. Opposite, on the chimney-piece, a couple of small lamps, in marble reservoirs, assist the prismatic lantern to supply the place of candles, by a light more consonant to the style of the partment, the pictures it contains of absent friends, and its aërial music.

Then the coy Scene, by deep'ning veils o'erdrawn,
   In shadowy elegance seems lovelier still;
Tall shrubs, that skirt the semi-lunar lawn,
   Dark woods, that curtain the opposing hill;
While o-er their brows the bare cliff faintly gleams,
And, from its paly edge, the evening-diamond[1] streams.

What strains Æolian thrill the dusk expanse,
   As rising Gales with gentle murmurs play,
Wake the loud chords, or every sense intrance,
   While in subsiding winds they sink away!
Like distant choir, 'When pealing organs blow',
And melting voices blend, majestically slow.

'But, ah! what hand can touch the strings so fine,
Who up the lofty diapason roll
Such sweet, such sad, such solemn airs divine,
Thus let them down again into the soul!'[2]
The prouder sex as soon, with virtue calm,
Might win from those bright Pair pure Friendship's spotless palm.

What boasts Tradition, what th'historic Theme,
   Stands it in all their chronicles confest
Where the soul's glory shines with clearer beam,
   Than in our sea-zon'd bulwark of the West
When, in this Cambrian Valley, Virtue shows
Where, in her own soft sex, its steadiest lustre glows?

[1] Evening-Star.
[2] These lines, with inverted commas, are from [James] Thomson's *Castle of Indolence*.

Lady Eleanor Butler wearing the
Croix St. Louis. Why the award was made
has never been totally clear...

by Kate Charlesworth

Friendship versus marriage

from *Mary, A Fiction*
MARY WOLLSTONECRAFT (1759–1797)

For Mary Wollstonecraft, as for so many women of her period, intimate and ardent friendships with other women so often seemed to promise more than heterosexual courtship and marriage. But the more it matters, the more it hurts. . . . In Mary, A Fiction *(1788), the heroine's passionate attachment to her friend Ann echoes Mary Wollstonecraft's own equally passionate attachment to Fanny Blood, whom Mary had loved since the age of sixteen and whose death in childbirth she had witnessed.* Mary, A Fiction *becomes, in part, an elegy for that lost relationship.*

Chapter VIII

I mentioned before, that Mary had never had any particular attachment, to give rise to the disgust that daily gained ground. Her friendship for Ann occupied her heart, and resembled a passion. She had had, indeed, several transient likings; but they did not amount to love. The society of men of genius delighted her, and improved her faculties. With beings of this class she did not often meet; it is a rare genus; her first favourites were men past the meridian of life, and of a philosophic turn.

Determined on going to the South of France, or Lisbon; she wrote to the man she had promised to obey. The physicians had said change of air was necessary for her as well as her friend. She mentioned this, and added, 'Her comfort, almost her existence, depended on the recovery of the invalid she wished to attend; and that should she neglect to follow the medical advice she had received, she should never forgive herself, or those who endeavoured to prevent her.' Full of her design, she wrote with more than usual freedom; and this letter was like most of her others, a transcript of her heart.

'This dear friend,' she exclaimed, 'I love for her agreeable qualities, and substantial virtues. Continual attention to her health, and the tender office of a nurse, have created an affection very like a maternal one –

I am her only support, she leans on me – could I forsake the forsaken, and break the bruised reed – No – I would die first! I must – I will go.'

She would have added, 'you would very much oblige me by consenting;' but her heart revolted – and irresolutely she wrote something about wishing him happy. – 'Do I not wish all the world well?' she cried, as she subscribed her name – It was blotted, the letter sealed in a hurry, and sent out of her sight; and she began to prepare for her journey.

By the return of the post she received an answer; it contained some common-place remarks on her romantic friendship, as he termed it; 'But as the physicians advised change of air, he had no objection.'

Chapter IX

There was nothing now to retard their journey; and Mary chose Lisbon rather than France, on account of its being further removed from the only person she wished not to see.

They set off accordingly for Falmouth, in their way to that city. The journey was of use to Ann, and Mary's spirits were raised by her recovered looks – She had been in despair – now she gave way to hope, and was intoxicated with it. On ship-board Ann always remained in the cabin; the sight of the water terrified her: on the contrary, Mary, after she was gone to bed, or when she fell asleep in the day, went on deck, conversed with the sailors, and surveyed the boundless expanse before her with delight. One instant she would regard the ocean, the next the beings who braved its fury. Their insensibility and want of fear, she could not name courage; their thoughtless mirth was quite of an animal kind, and their feelings as impetuous and uncertain as the element they plowed.

They had only been a week at sea when they hailed the rock of Lisbon, and the next morning anchored at the castle. After the customary visits, they were permitted to go on shore, about three miles from the city; and while one of the crew, who understood the language, went to procure them one of the ugly carriages peculiar to the country, they waited in the Irish convent, which is situated close to the Tagus.

Some of the people offered to conduct them into the church, where there was a fine organ playing; Mary followed them, but Ann preferred staying with a nun she had entered into conversation with.

One of the nuns, who had a sweet voice, was singing; Mary was struck with awe; her heart joined in the devotion; and tears of gratitude and tenderness flowed from her eyes. My Father, I thank thee! burst from her – words were inadequate to express her feelings. Silently, she surveyed the lofty dome; heard unaccustomed sounds; and saw faces, strange ones, that she could not yet greet with fraternal love.

*　　*　　*

One afternoon, which they had engaged to spend together, Ann was so ill, that Mary was obliged to send an apology for not attending the tea-table. The apology brought them on the carpet; and the mother, with a look of solemn importance, turned to the sick man, whose name was Henry, and said: 'Though people of the first fashion are frequently at places of this kind, intimate with they know not who; yet I do not choose that my daughter, whose family is so respectable, should be intimate with any one she would blush to know elsewhere. It is only on that account, for I never suffer her to be with any one but in my company,' added she, sitting more erect; and a smile of self-complacency dressed her countenance.

'I have enquired concerning these strangers, and find that the one who has the most dignity in her manners, is really a woman of fortune.' 'Lord, mamma, how ill she dresses:' mamma went on; 'She is a romantic creature, you must not copy her, miss; yet she is an heiress of the large fortune in ——shire, of which you may remember to have heard the Countess speak the night you had on the dancing-dress that was so much admired; but she is married.'

She then told them the whole story as she heard it from her maid, who picked it out of Mary's servant. 'She is a foolish creature, and this friend that she pays as much attention to as if she was a lady of quality, is a beggar.' 'Well, how strange!' cried the girls.

'She is, however, a charming creature,' said her nephew. Henry sighed, and strode across the room once or twice; then took up his violin, and played the air which first struck Mary; he had often heard her praise it.

The music was uncommonly melodious, 'And came stealing on the senses like the sweet south.' The well-known sounds reached Mary as she sat by her friend – she listened without knowing that she did – and shed tears almost without being conscious of it. Ann soon fell asleep, as she had taken an opiate. Mary, then brooding over her fears, began to imagine she had deceived herself – Ann was still very ill; hope had beguiled many heavy hours; yet she was displeased with herself for admitting this welcome guest. – And she worked up her mind to such a degree of anxiety, that she determined, once more, to seek medical aid.

No sooner did she determine, than she ran down with a discomposed look, to enquire of the ladies who she should send for. When she entered the room she could not articulate her fears – it appeared like pronouncing Ann's sentence of death; her faultering tongue dropped some broken words, and she remained silent. The ladies wondered that a person of her sense should be so little mistress of herself; and began to administer some common-place comfort, as, that it was our duty to submit to the will of Heaven, and the like trite consolations, which Mary did not answer; but waving her hand, with an air of impatience, she exclaimed, 'I cannot live without her! – I have no other friend; if I lose her, what a desart will the world be to me.' 'No other friend,' re-echoed they, 'have you not a husband?'

Mary shrunk back, and was alternately pale and red. A delicate sense of propriety prevented her replying; and recalled her bewildered reason. – Assuming, in consequence of her recollection, a more composed manner, she made the intended enquiry, and left the room. Henry's eyes followed her while the females very freely animadverted on her strange behaviour.

The scales fall

from *Angelina, or, l'amie inconnue* (1801)
by MARIA EDGEWORTH (1768–1849)

Anne Warwick, alias Angelina, has run away from her guardian, the fashion-able Lady Di Chillingworth, to live with her 'unknown friend', the novelist 'Araminta', author of The Woman of Genius. *Neither the note Angelina leaves behind nor the gushing letter from 'Araminta' (whose over-heated prose more than matches Anna Seward's over-heated verse), sheds much light on the situation. Angelina's departure creates consternation in one household, her arrival creates panic in another.*

'With whom did she go off?'

'With nobody,' cried Lady Diana – 'there's the wonder.'

'With nobody! – Incredible! – She had certainly some admirer, some lover, and she was afraid, I suppose, to mention the business to you.'

'No such thing, my dear: there is no love at all in the case: indeed, for my part, I cannot in the least comprehend Miss Warwick, nor ever could. She used, every now and then, to begin and talk to me some nonsense about her hatred of the forms of the world, and her love of liberty, and I know not what; and then she had some female correspon-dent, to whom she used to write folio sheets, twice a week, I believe; but I could never see any of these letters.

[...]

'I protest I know nothing of the matter, but that, one morning, Miss Warwick was nowhere to be found, and my maid brought me a letter, of one word of which I could not make sense: the letter was found on the young lady's dressing-table, according to the usual custom of eloping heroines. Miss Burrage, do show Lady Frances the letters – you have them somewhere; and tell my sister all you know of the matter, for I declare, I'm quite tired of it; besides, I shall be wanted at the card-table.'

Lady Diana Chillingworth went to calm her sensibility at the card-table; and Lady Frances turned to Miss Burrage, for farther information.

'All I know,' said Miss Burrage, 'is, that one night I saw Miss Warwick putting a lock of frightful hair into a locket, and I asked her whose it was. – "My amiable Araminta's," said Miss Warwick. "Is she pretty?" said I. "I have never seen her," said Miss Warwick; "but I will show you a lovely picture of her mind!" – and she put this long letter into my hand. I'll leave it with your ladyship, if you please; it is a good, or rather a bad hour's work to read it.'

'*Araminta!*' exclaimed Lady Frances, looking at the signature of the letter – 'this is only a nom de guerre, I suppose.'

'Heaven knows!' answered Miss Burrage; 'but Miss Warwick always signed her epistles Angelina, and her *unknown friend's* were always signed Araminta. I do suspect that Araminta, whoever she is, was the instigator of this elopement.'

Araminta's letter:

'Yes, my Angelina! our hearts are formed for that higher species of friendship, of which common souls are inadequate to form an idea, however their fashionable puerile lips may, in the intellectual inanity of their conversation, profane the term. Yes, my Angelina, you are right – every fibre of my frame, every energy of my intellect, tells me so. I read your letter by moon-light! The air balmy and pure as my Angelina's thoughts! The river silently meandering! – The rocks! – The woods! – Nature in all her majesty. Sublime confidante! sympathizing with my supreme felicity.

[...]

The garnish-tinselled wand of fashion has waved in vain in the illuminated halls of folly-painted pleasure; my Angelina's eyes have withstood, yes, without a blink! the dazzling enchantment. – And will she – no, I cannot – I will not think so for an instant – will she now submit her understanding, spell-bound, to the soporific charm of nonsensical words, uttered in an awful tone by that potent enchantress, *Prejudice?* – The declamation, the remonstrances of self-elected judges of right and wrong, should be treated with deserved contempt by superior minds, who claim the privilege of thinking and acting for themselves. The words *ward* and *guardian* appal my Angelina! but what are legal technical formalities, what are human institutions, to the view of shackle-scorning Reason? – Oppressed, degraded, enslaved, – must our unfortunate sex for ever submit to sacrifice their rights, their pleasures, their *will*, at the altar of public opinion; whilst the shouts of interested priests, and idle spectators, raise the senseless enthusiasm of the self-devoted victim, or drown her cries in the truth-extorting moment of agonizing nature! – You will not perfectly understand, perhaps, to what these last exclamations of your Araminta allude: – But, chosen friend of my heart! – when we meet – and O let that be quickly! – my cottage longs for the arrival of my unsophisticated Angelina! – when we meet you shall know all – your Araminta, too, has had her sorrows – Enough of this! – But her Orlando has a heart, pure as the infantine god of love could, in his most perfect mood, delight at once to wound, and own – joined to an understanding – shall I say it? – worthy to judge of your Araminta's – And will not my sober-minded Angelina prefer, to all that palaces can afford, such society in a cottage? – I shall reserve for my next the description of a cottage, which I have in my eye, within view of –; but I will not anticipate. – Adieu, my amiable Angelina. – I enclose, as you desire, a lock of my hair. – Ever, unalterably, your affectionate, though almost heart-broken, Araminta.

  April, 1800. *Angelina Bower!*
  So let me christen my cottage!'

What effect this letter may have on *sober-minded* readers in general can easily be guessed; but Miss Warwick, who was little deserving of this epithet, was so charmed with the sound of it, that it made her totally forget to judge of her amiable Araminta's mode of reasoning. 'Garnish-tinselled wands' – 'shackle-scorning Reason' – 'isolation of the heart' – 'soul-rending eloquence' – with 'rocks and woods, and a meandering river – balmy air – moon-light – Orlando – energy of intellect – a cottage – and a heart-broken friend,' made, when all mixed together, strange confusion in Angelina's imagination. She neglected to observe, that her Araminta was in the course of two pages – 'almost heart-broken' – and in the possession of – 'supreme felicity.' Yet Miss Warwick, though she judged so like a simpleton, was a young woman of considerable abilities: her want of what the world calls common sense arose from certain mistakes in her education. She had passed her childhood with a father and mother, who cultivated her literary taste, but who neglected to cultivate her judgment: her reading was confined to works of imagination; and the conversation which she heard was not calculated to give her any knowledge of realities. Her parents died when she was about fourteen, and she then went to reside with Lady Diana Chillingworth, a lady who placed her whole happiness in living in a certain circle of high company in London. Miss Warwick saw the follies of the society with which she now mixed; she felt insupportable ennui from the want of books and conversation suited to her taste; she heard with impatience Lady Diana's dogmatical advice; observed, with disgust, the meanness of her companion, Miss Burrage, and felt with triumph the superiority of her own abilities. It was in this situation of her mind that Miss Warwick happened, at a circulating library, to meet with a new novel, called 'The Woman of Genius.' – The character of Araminta, the heroine, charmed her beyond measure; and having been informed, by the preface, that the story was founded on facts in the life of the authoress herself, she longed to become acquainted with her; and addressed a letter to 'The Woman of Genius,' at her publisher's. The letter was answered in a highly flattering, and consequently, very agreeable style, and the correspondence continued for nearly two years; till, at length, Miss W. formed a strong desire to see her *unknown friend*.

[. . .]

Miss Warwick determined to accept of her *unknown friend's* invitation to Angelina Bower – a charming romantic cottage in South Wales, where, according to Araminta's description, she might pass her halcyon days in tranquil, elegant retirement.

[. . .]

Meeting 'Araminta'

Before we introduce Angelina to her 'unknown friend,' we must relate the conversation, which was actually passing between the amiable Araminta and her Orlando, whilst Miss Warwick was waiting in the fruit shop. Our readers will be so good as to picture to themselves a woman, with a face and figure which seemed to have been intended for a man, with a voice and a gesture capable of setting even man, 'imperial man,' at defiance. – Such was Araminta – She was, at this time, sitting cross-legged in an armchair at a tea-table, on which, beside the tea equipage, was a medley of things, of which no prudent tongue or pen would undertake to give a correct list. – At the feet of this fair lady, kneeling on one knee, was a thin, subdued, simple-looking quaker, of the name of Nathaniel Gazabo.

'But now, Natty,' said Miss Hodges, in a voice more masculine than her looks, 'You understand the conditions – If I give you my hand, and make you my husband, it is upon condition, that you never contradict any of my opinions; do you promise me that?'

'Yea, verily,' – replied Nat.

'And you promise to leave me entirely at liberty to act, as well as to think, in all things as my own independent understanding shall suggest?'

'Yea, verily,' – was the man's response.

'And you will be guided by me in all things?'

'Yea, verily.'

'And you will love and admire me all your life, as much as you do now?'

'Yea, verily.'

'Swear,' said the unconscionable woman.

'Nay, verily,' replied the meekest of men, 'I cannot swear, my Rachel, because a quaker; but I will affirm.'

'Swear, swear,' cried the lady in an impetuous tone, 'or I will never be your Araminta.'

'I swear,' said Nat Gazabo, in a timid voice.

'Then, Natty, I consent to be Mrs Hodges Gazabo. Only remember always to call me your dear Araminta.'

'My dear Araminta! thus,' said he, embracing her, 'thus let me thank thee, my dear Araminta.'

It was in the midst of these thanks that the maid interrupted the well-matched pair, with the news that a young lady was below, who was in a great hurry to see Miss Hodges.

'Let her come,' said Miss Hodges; 'I suppose 'tis only one of the Miss Carvers – Don't stir, Nat; it will vex her so to see you kneeling to me – Don't stir, I say.'

'Where is she? Where is my Araminta?' cried Miss Warwick, as the maid was trying to open the outer passage door for her, which had a bad lock.

'Get up, get up, Natty; and get some fresh water in the tea-kettle –
Quick!' cried Miss Hodges, and she began to clear away some of the
varieties of literature, &. which lay scattered about the room. Nat, in
obedience to her commands, was making his exit with all possible speed,
when Angelina entered exclaiming,

'My amiable Araminta! – My unknown friend.'

'My Angelina! My charming Angelina!' cried Miss Hodges.

Miss Hodges was not the sort of person our heroine expected to see!
– and to conceal the panic, with which the first sight of her unknown
friend struck her disappointed imagination, she turned back to listen to
the apologies, which Nat Gazabo was pouring forth about his awkwardness and the tea-kettle.

'Turn, Angelina, ever dear!' cried Miss Hodges, with the tone and
action of a bad actress, who is rehearsing an embrace. – 'Turn, Angelina,
ever dear. Thus, thus let us meet to part no more.'

'But her voice is so loud,' said Angelina to herself, 'and her looks so
vulgar, and there is such a smell of brandy! How unlike the elegant
delicacy I had expected in my unknown friend!' – Miss Warwick involun-
tarily shrunk from the stifling embrace.

'You are overpowered, my Angelina, lean on me;' said her Araminta.

Nat Gazabo re-entered with the tea-kettle.

'Here's *boiling* water, and we'll have fresh tea in a trice – the young
lady's over-tired seemingly – here's a chair, Miss, here's a chair;' cried
Nat. Miss Warwick *sunk* upon the chair: Miss Hodges seated herself
beside her, continuing to address her in a theatrical tone.

'This moment is bliss unutterable! my kind, my noble-minded
Angelina, thus to leave all your friends for your Araminta!' suddenly
changing her voice, 'set the tea-kettle, Nat!'

'Who is this Nat, I wonder?' thought Miss Warwick.

'Well, and tell me,' said Miss Hodges, whose attention was awkwardly
divided between the ceremonies of making tea and making speeches –
'and tell me, my Angelina – That's water enough, Nat – and tell me
my Angelina, how did you find me out?'

'With some difficulty, indeed, *my Araminta*.' Miss Warwick could
hardly pronounce the words.

'So kind, so noble-minded,' continued Miss Hodges, 'and did you

receive my last letter – three sheets? – And how did you contrive –
Stoop the kettle *do* Nat.'

'O this odious Nat! how I wish she would send him away;' thought
Miss Warwick.

'And tell me, my Araminta, my Angelina I mean, how did you
contrive your elopement – and how did you escape from the eye of
your aristocratic Argus – how did you escape from all your unfeeling
persecutors – tell me, tell me, all your adventures, my Angelina! – Snuff
the candle, Nat:' and Miss Hodges, who was cutting bread and butter,
which she did not do with the celebrated grace of Charlotte in the
Sorrows of Werter.

'I'll tell you all, my Araminta,' whispered Miss Warwick, 'when we
are by ourselves.'

'O, never mind Nat,' whispered Miss Hodges.

'Could'nt you tell him,' rejoined Miss Warwick, 'that he need not
wait any longer?'

'*Wait*, my dear! why, what do you take him for?'

'Why, is he not your footman?' whispered Angelina.

'My footman! – Nat!' – exclaimed Miss Hodges, bursting out a laughing, 'my Angelina took you for a footman.'

'Good Heavens! what is he?' said Angelina, in a low voice.

'Verily,' said Nat Gazabo, with a sort of bashful simple laugh, 'Verily,
I am the humblest of her servants.'

'And does not my Angelina – spare my delicacy,' said Miss Hodges:
'Does my Angelina not remember, in any of my long letters, the name
of – Orlando – There he stands.'

'Orlando! – Is this gentleman your Orlando, of whom I have heard
so much?'

'He! he! he!' simpered Nat – 'I am Orlando, of whom you have heard
so much – and she – (pointing to Miss Hodges) she is to-morrow
morning, God willing, to be Mistress Hodges Gazabo.'

'Mrs Hodges Gazabo my Araminta!' said Angelina with astonishment
which she could not suppress.

'Yes, my Angelina: so end "The Sorrows of Araminta" – Another
cup? – do I make the tea too sweet?' said Miss Hodges, whilst Nat
handed the bread and butter to the ladies officiously.

Anne Lister visits the Ladies of Llangollen

from the Diaries of Anne Lister
(1791–1840)

In 1822 Anne Lister made a visit which took on something of the character of a pilgrimage to Llangollen Vale (as hymned earlier by Anna Seward). Her purpose was to visit the Ladies, although in the event she saw only the younger – Miss Sarah Ponsonby – since the eighty-four-year-old Lady Eleanor Butler was ill in bed. The touching passages which follow make it clear how important the Ladies were to other women such as Anne Lister: they were the living proof that two women could form a life-long attachment in a shared home and could do so while winning respect and international reputation. Note how anxiously Anne asks for details (hints and tips?) about the two Ladies' shared life – do they quarrel, for example (No, never, and if they should have the merest difference of opinion they take good care that no one else should discern it). This is a rare opportunity for Anne to obtain first-hand information about how a loving, all-female household may work – managing both the economies of the home and the heart.

Note, too, the importance of literature to the Ladies, allied with the anxiety not to be thought ferocious 'Blues': Miss Ponsonby, for example, is relieved to be able to say that she has no first-hand knowledge of Latin or Greek, although that may also be connected with an anxiety about being thought to read heterodox, unGodly or anti-Christian pagan authors. This is very different from the way in which Anne Lister is familiar with and uses references to 'bad' authors, such as the obscene satirist Juvenal, and the sexually open Ovid, when sounding out other women's sexual attitudes (as we saw earlier in 'Betwixt and Between'). After her return from Llangollen, Anne used her women friends' responses to the Ladies and their love as a touchstone to determine character and, sometimes, sexuality.

Anne's own dips and depressions during and after the visit are interesting. Is it because there is an uncertainty about whether the Ladies are lovers in the fullest sexual sense, and therefore whether it is safe or fitting for the very sexual Anne to see them as hopeful portents of possibilities for her own future

life? Obviously, the seriousness of Lady Eleanor's illness at her fairly
advanced age also brings mortality menacingly close.

The rose which Miss Ponsonby cut for Anne is clearly going to be an
important keepsake and talisman. In the account of her visit which she wrote
to Sibbella MacLean (also given below), Lister says that she originally urged
Miss Ponsonby not to spoil the plant by taking the flower from it and Miss
Ponsonby replied: 'No! No! It may spoil its beauty for the present, but 'tis
only to do it good afterwards.' An undoubted horticultural truth, her response
seems also to resonate with additional meanings − transmission, generation
and continuity: a token that Miss Ponsonby recognises Anne Lister as a
younger kindred spirit, and wishes her well.

The year is 1822.

Tuesday 23 July [Llangollen]

A drop or 2 of rain just after setting off & a shower for about the 3rd
mile from Llangollen. Heavy rain just after we got in. Mrs Davis received
us at the door & came into our rooms to answer our inquiries after
Lady Eleanor Butler. Mrs Davis was called up at one last night, & they
thought her ladyship would have died. She was, however, rather better
this morning. The physician does not seem to apprehend danger but
Mrs Davis is alarmed & spoke of it in tears. Miss Ponsonby, too, is
alarmed & ill herself, on this account. Pain in her side. 'She is a lady,'
said Mrs Davis, 'of very strong ideas; but this would grieve her, too.'
Mrs Davis had only known them 13 or 14 years, during which time she
had lived at this house but she had always seen them 'so attached, so
amiable together', no two people ever lived more happily. They like all
the people about them, are beloved by all & do a great deal of good.
Lady Eleanor has the remains of beauty. Miss Ponsonby was a very fine
woman. Lady Eleanor Butler about 80. Miss Ponsonby 10 or 12 years
younger. The damp this bad account cast upon my spirits I cannot
describe. I am interested about these 2 ladies very much. There is a
something in their story & in all I have heard about them here that,
added to other circumstances, makes a deep impression.
[. . .]
Mrs Davis being going to inquire after Lady Eleanor Butler, my aunt
& I walked with her to wait for her giving an answer to our inquiries.

The physician there. Strolled about for 10 minutes &, he not being gone & it threatening to rain, returned & only just got in before a tremendously heavy shower. Then sat down & wrote the above of today. I feel better for this writing. In fact, come what may, writing my journals – thus, as it were, throwing my mind on paper – always does me good. Mrs Davis just returned. Brought a good account of her ladyship & a message of thanks for our inquiries from Miss Ponsonby, who will be glad to see me this evening to thank me in person. Shall [go] about 6½ or 7, just after dinner. This is more than I expected. I wonder how I work my way & what she will think of me. Mrs Davis wishes me to give all the comfort, all I can, & not to mention that I know of her having been called up last night. Dinner at 6. Before dinner, about two hours upstairs washing & cutting my toenails, putting clean things on.

At 7, went to Plasnewydd & got back at 8. Just an hour away & surely the walking there & back did not take more than 20 minutes. Shewn into the room next the library, the breakfast room, waited a minute or 2, & then came Miss Ponsonby. A large woman so as to waddle in walking but, tho', not taller than myself. In a blue, shortish-waisted cloth habit, the jacket unbuttoned shewing a plain plaited frilled habit shirt – a thick white cravat, rather loosely put on – hair powdered, parted, I think, down the middle in front, cut a moderate length all round & hanging straight, tolerably thick. The remains of a very fine face. Coarsish white cotton stockings. Ladies slipper shoes cut low down, the foot hanging a little over. Altogether a very odd figure. Yet she had no sooner entered into conversation than I forgot all this & my attention was wholly taken by her manners & conversation. The former, perfectly easy, peculiarly attentive & well, & bespeaking a person accustomed to a great deal of good society. Mild & gentle, certainly not masculine, & yet there was a *je-ne-sais-quoi* striking. Her conversation shewing a personal acquaintance with most of the literary characters of the day & their works. She seemed sanguine about Lady Eleanor's recovery. Poor soul! My heart ached to think how small the chance. She told me her ladyship had undergone an operation 3 times – the sight of one eye restored – couching by absorption. I said I believed it was neither a painful nor dangerous operation. She seemed to think it both the one & the other. Mentioned the beauty of the place – the books I had noticed

in the rustic library. She said Lady Eleanor read French, Spanish &
Italian – had great knowledge of ancient manners & customs, understood
the obsolete manners & phrases of Tasso remarkably well. Had written
elucidatory notes on the 1st 2 (or 4, I think) books of Tasso, but had
given away the only copy she ever had. Contrived to ask if they were
classical. 'No,' said she. 'Thank God from Latin & Greek I am free.'
[. . .]
As people got older, she said, they were more particular. She was almost
afraid of reading *Cain*, tho' Lord Byron had been very good in sending
them several of his works. I asked if she had read *Don Juan*. She was
ashamed to say she had read the 1st canto.

She asked if I would walk out. Shewed me the kitchen garden. Walked
round the shrubbery with me. She said she owned to their having been
42 years there. They landed first in South Wales, but it did not answer
the accounts they had heard of it. They then travelled in North Wales
&, taken with the beauty of this place, took the cottage for 31 years –
but it was a false lease & they had had a great deal of trouble & expense.
It was only 4 years since they had bought the place. Dared say I had a
much nicer place at home. Mentioned its situation, great age, long time
in the family, etc. She wished to know where to find an account of it.
Said it had been their humble endeavour to make the place as old as
they could. Spoke like a woman of the world about my liking the place
where I was born, etc. Said I was not born there. My father was a
younger brother but that I had the expectation of succeeding my uncle.
'Ah, yes,' said she, 'you will soon be the master & there will be an end
of romance.' 'Never! Never!' said I. I envied their place & the happiness
they had had there. Asked if, dared say, they had never quarrelled. 'No!'
They had never had a quarrel. Little differences of opinion sometimes.
Life could not go on without it, but only about the planting of a tree,
and, when they differed in opinion, they took care to let no one see it.

At parting, shook hands with her and she gave me a rose. I said I
should keep it for the sake of the place where it grew. She had before
said she should be happy to introduce me some time to Lady Eleanor.
I had given my aunt's compliments & inquiries. Said she would have
called with me but feared to intrude & was not quite well this evening.
She, Miss Ponsonby, gave me a sprig of geranium for my aunt with her

compliments & thanks for her inquiries. Lady Eleanor was asleep while I was there.

[. . .]

I came away much pleased with Miss Ponsonby & sincerely hoping Lady Eleanor will recover to enjoy a few more years in this world. I know not how it is, I felt low after coming away. A thousand moody reflections occurred, but again, writing has done me good . . . I mean to dry & keep the rose Miss Ponsonby gave me. 'Tis now 10¼. Sat talking to my aunt. Came upstairs at 11.10.

Monday 29 July [Halifax]

Crossed the 1st page of the 1st sheet written to M— yesterday. Determined to send it this morning, that she may have an account of our arrival at home . . . the ends of my paper contain the following . . . 'Charmed as I am with the landscape & loveliness of the country [of Wales], I do not envy it for home. I should not like to live in Wales – but, if it must be so, and I could choose the spot, it should be Plasnewydd at Llangollen, which is already endeared even to me by the association of ideas. Well, therefore, may it be on this account invaluable to its present possessors. My paper is exhausted; it has worn out my subject perhaps sufficiently. I am again seated quietly in my own room at Shibden where the happiest hours of my life have been spent with you & whence I shall always feel a peculiar satisfaction in assuring you that I am now & for ever, Mary, faithfully & affectionately yours.'

[*Anne described her meeting with Miss Ponsonby to a friend in York, Miss Sibbella MacLean, with whom she frequently corresponded.*]

Saturday 3 August [Halifax]

. . . If any of your friends are going to Llangollen, pray recommend them to the King's Head or New Hotel, kept by Mrs Davis. A very comfortable house. Everything good & Welsh mutton in greater perfection than we had it anywhere else. Never ate anything so excellent. Lady Eleanor Butler was seriously ill. An inflammatory complaint. She had been couched. 3 operations by absorption. The sight of one eye nearly restored. Caught cold by going out too soon & staying out too long, and late, in the evening. On our return she was rather better. Miss Ponsonby, by especial favour, admitted me & I spent an hour with her most agreeably. She had been alarmed, but was returning to good spirits, about the recovery of her friend. There was a freshness of intellect – a verdure of amusing talent which, with heart & thorough good breeding, made her conversation more time beguiling than I could have imagined. She told me they had been 42 years there. 'Tis the prettiest little spot I ever saw – a silken cord on which the pearls of taste are strung. I could be happy here, I said to myself, where hope fulfilled might still 'with bright ray in smiling contrast gild the vital day.' You know, Miss Ponsonby is very large & her appearance singular. I had soon forgotten all this. Do not, said I, give me that rose, 'twill spoil the beauty of the plant. 'No! No! It may spoil its beauty for the present, but 'tis only to do it good afterwards.' There was a something in the manner of this little simple circumstance that struck me exceedingly . . . Foolscap sheet from M— . . . She seems much interested about Lady Eleanor Butler & Miss Ponsonby and I am agreeably surprised (never dreaming of such a thing) at her observation, 'The account of your visit is the prettiest narrative I have read. You have at once excited & gratified my curiosity. Tell me if you think their regard has always been platonic & if you ever believed pure friendship could be so exalted. If you do, I shall think there are brighter amongst mortals than I ever believed there were.' . . . I cannot help thinking that surely it was not platonic. Heaven forgive me, but I look within myself & doubt. I feel the infirmity of our nature & hesitate to pronounce such attachments uncemented by something more tender still than friendship. But much, or all, depends upon the story of their former lives, the period passed before they lived together, that feverish dream called youth.

Saturday 10 August [Halifax]

Mrs Saltmarshe drove, in their gig, her sister, Mrs Waterhouse, to call here. They came at 1 & staid rather more than ½ hour. Mentioned my having seen Miss Ponsonby . . . Not a little to my surprise, Emma launched forth most fluently in dispraise of the place. A little baby house & baby grounds. Bits of painted glass stuck in all the windows. Beautifully morocco-bound books laid about in all the arbours, etc., evidently for shew, perhaps stiff if you touched them & never opened. Tasso, etc., etc. Everything evidently done for effect. She thought they must be 2 romantic girls &, as I walked with her to see her off, she said she had thought it was a pity they were not married; it would do them a great deal of good. Mrs Saltmarshe was less pleased [displeased?] with the place than she was – but when she came to get back to the inn, she agreed it was not worth going to see. Little bits of antiques set up here & there. They themselves were genuine antiques – 80 or 90! She hoped I should not despise her taste. I merely replied most civilly, 'No!' I was delighted to hear her account by way of contrast to what I had thought myself . . . Note from Mary Priestley – a very proper one – very attentive in her to write to me so soon. She will be glad to see me any time & hopes I will spend a long day with her . . . I have several times said to my aunt that, of all the people here, I liked Mary Priestley & Emma Saltmarshe the best, but doubted between the 2. Emma's remarks this morning & Mary's note this afternoon have made up my mind on this point in favour of the latter, as, I think *pour toujours*.

To Lallie
(Outside the British Museum)
AMY LEVY (1861–1889)

Sometimes poets seek to conceal their more painful emotions behind the metrical forms more usually associated with light verse. I think this is what Amy Levy has chosen to do in the poem that follows. In these most artful verses, some of love lyric's most enduring clichés struggle against rhymes and rhythms which constantly threaten to undercut them. And does the comic spirit win here? The poem's last line seems to leave the question open.

'Lallie' is thought to be a pet name for the art historian, essayist and short-story writer, Violet Paget (1856–1935), better known by her male pseudonym, 'Vernon Lee'. Another of Levy's poems, 'To Vernon Lee', appears later in the book (see 'Of Women's Gardens'). Levy, the first Jewish woman to be an undergraduate of Newnham College, Cambridge, won considerable acclaim as a poet during her short life. The young Oscar

Wilde much admired her work, reviewed it favourably and published some of it in Woman's World, *the magazine he then edited. She eventually committed suicide, by taking poison, in her parents' house.*

Up those Museum steps you came,
And straightway all my blood was flame.
   O Lallie, Lallie!

The world (I had been feeling low)
In one short moment's space did grow
   A happy valley.

There was a friend, my friend, with you;
A meagre dame, in peacock blue
   Apparelled quaintly:

This poet-heart went pit-a-pat;
I bowed and smiled and raised my hat;
   You nodded – faintly.

My heart was full as full could be;
You had not got a word for me,
   Not one short greeting;

That nonchalant small nod you gave
(The tyrant's motion to the slave)
   Sole mark'd our meeting.

Is it so long? Do you forget
That first and last time that we met?
   The time was summer;

The trees were green; the sky was blue;
Our host presented me to you –
   A tardy comer.

You look'd demure, but when you spoke
You made a little, funny joke,
        Yet half pathetic.

Your gown was grey, I recollect,
I think you patronized the sect
        They call 'æsthetic.'

I brought you strawberries and cream,
I plied you long about a stream
        With duckweed laden;

We solemnly discussed the – heat.
I found you shy and very sweet,
        A rosebud maiden.

Ah me, to-day! You passed inside
To where the marble gods abide:
        Hermes, Apollo,

Sweet Aphrodite, Pan; and where,
For aye reclined, a headless fair
        Beats all fairs hollow.

And I, I went upon my way,
Well – rather sadder, let us say;
        The world looked flatter.

I had been sad enough before,
A little less, a little more,
        What *does* it matter?

'Closely I watched it, hour by hour'
MARY COLERIDGE (1861–1907)

Closely I watched it, hour by hour,
  I almost thought I saw it grow,
When first the bud became a flower,
  I do not know.

Closely I watched thee, O my dove,
  I almost thought I knew thee well.
When liking blossomed into love,
  I cannot tell.

To an Old Friend
MARY COLERIDGE

Now when the sweet sunny weather
Quickens all that once was dead
    I remember how we two,
    You and I, I and you,
Wandered about the streets together,
Reading the books that had to be read,
Saying the things that cannot be said.

The world was young, and we were younger
In those bright forgotten days,
    I remember how we two,
    You and I, I and you,
Read and read for the spirit's hunger,
Walked in the old familiar ways,
Talked and talked for each other's praise.

The world is young, but we are older,
Many a book we shall read no more —
    I remember how we two,
      You and I, I and you,
Vowed that love should not grow colder,
That we would love as we loved before,
And the years should make us love the more.

Romantic Agonies

Erotic passion, thwarted, spurned, denied (sometimes even by the woman who feels it), swirls through this section. Self-denial and renunciation of the beloved may bring its own masochistic gratification, particularly when it is inflected by religion. Masochism and sadism may be intimately intertwined, as they are in Dickens's 'History of a Self-Tormentor' and Swinburne's 'Anactoria'. The idea of the lesbian as 'beautiful evil' is sometimes written off as a product of male hostility, but 'Marie-Madeleine' is not the only lesbian poet to find it irresistibly compelling. For some, the falling out of faithful friends, even when it does not lead to the renewing of love, provides abundant opportunities for an orgy of recrimination, self-pity and passionate despair. But not all despair is performance and not all pain is pleasurable: Charlotte Mew is not the only woman in this book who will eventually take her own life.

Which expounds the most exalted
nature of love
Poem No. 179
SOR JUANA INÉS DE LA CRUZ (?1648–1695)

Perhaps of all romantic agonies the most agonising is to desire the thing one knows one must not have. The Mexican poet, Juana de Asbaje y Ramírez de Santillana (more commonly known as Sor Juana Inés de la Cruz) was one of the most learned women of her generation. She writes that at seven years of age, she desperately desired to disguise herself as a man in order to go to university.

The poem that appears below glorifies love as renunciation. It may be true that we needs must love the highest when we see it, but we also have to learn to keep our hands off it. Like much of Sor Juana's work, this poem, one of a sequence to Lysis, is intricate and highly wrought, full of word-play of a kind dauntingly difficult to translate. I am extremely grateful to my friend, Gillian Spraggs, for translating it nevertheless.

I love Lysis, but I make no pretence
that Lysis to my courtship should respond,
since if I judge her beauty's to be gained
I slight her honour and my own good sense.
Not to attempt's the one thing I'm attempting:
since I know that to merit such nobility
no virtue is enough, and it's stupidity
to persevere despite this understanding.
Her loveliness I conceive a thing so holy
that my devoted fervour does not mean
to give to hope even a slender entry:
therefore my happiness I for hers resign
so as not to win her and see her treated wrongly
and even think how sad I'd feel to see her mine.

Translated by Gillian Spraggs

Mary Shelley is reproachful

from a letter

Mary Shelley (1797–1851) married her poet husband at nineteen and was widowed within five years. Before and during her marriage and throughout her long years of widowhood she was often much exercised by her passionate feelings for other women, just as her mother, Mary Wollstonecraft, had been before her (see extract from Mary *in 'Marriage Lines and Family Matters'). Friendships ardently embraced invariably turned sour and ended acrimoniously. As she herself said, 'It is hazardous for a woman to marry a woman'. Nevertheless, she gallantly came to the aid of a friend, Mary Diana Dods, who was fully determined to take this perilous course. Mary Shelley helped her to acquire a passport in a man's name. She continued to give very practical assistance to Dods and her 'spouse' when they set up house together in 1827 and lived successfully for many years as man and wife.*

The extract below comes from a letter in 1828 to Jane Williams, whose husband Edward Williams had drowned along with Percy Bysshe Shelley in 1822. Jane and Mary clung to each other for comfort, and perhaps more than that: in a letter to Leigh Hunt written after their return from Italy to England, Mary had described herself as 'wedded' to Jane, whom she saw as her only source of happiness. The two women fell out, however, when Mary discovered that Jane had been regaling their friends with stories about the unhappiness of the Shelley ménage and Percy Bysshe Shelley's infidelities (including his passes at her); relations were not helped by Jane's marriage to Thomas Jefferson Hogg, whom Mary found difficult. The letter follows on from a meeting a few days before, at which Mary had confronted Jane with what she knew.

[?51 George Street] Thursday
Morning [?14 February 1828]

Since Monday, I have been ceaselessly occupied by the scene, begun & interrupted, which filled me with a pain, that now thrills me as I revert to it. I then strove to speak, but your tears overcame me, while the struggle must have given me an appearance of coldness – Often – how often have I wept at instances of want of affection from you, and that you should complain of me, seemed the reproach of a benefactress to an ingrate.

If I revert to my devotion to you it is to prove that no worldly motives could estrange me from the partner of my miseries – the sweet girl whose beauty grace & gentleness were to me so long the sole charms of my life – Often leaving you at Kentish Town I have wept from the overflow of affection – Often thanked God who had given you to me – Could any but yourself have destroyed such engrossing & passionate love? – And what are the consequences of the change? – When I first heard that you did not love me, <I felt> every hope of my life deserted me – the depression I sunk under, and to which <in consequence> I am now a prey, undermines my health – How many many hours this dreary winter, I have paced my solitary room, driven nearly to madness as I could not expel from my mind the <circumstances> Memories of harrowing import that one after another intruded themselves. It was not long ago that eagerly desiring death – tho' death should only be oblivion, I thought that how to purchase oblivion of what was revealed to me last July, a torturous death would be a bed of Roses. At least, most lovely One, my love for you was not unworthy of its object – I have committed many faults – the remorse of love haunts me often & brings bitter tears to my eyes – but for four years I committed not one fault towards you – In larger, in minute things your pleasure and satisfaction were my objects, & I gave up every thing that is all the very little I could give up to them – I make no boast, heaven knows had you loved me you were worth all – more than all the idolatry with which my heart so fondly regarded you.

from *Little Dorrit*
CHARLES DICKENS (1812–1870)

Dickens's central female characters can often be depressingly faithful to one particular stereotype of mid-Victorian womanhood: sweet maids who (in Charles Kingsley's notorious formulation) are good rather than clever. Yet his fiction also reveals a consistent fascination with women on the margins, and with women who do not conform or fit neatly into the place which is supposedly theirs. Independently quirky characters, such as Betsy Trotwood, intrigue him, and female courage, whether of body (like Mrs Bagnet's in Bleak House*) or spirit (such as Nancy's in* Oliver Twist*), is an attribute he values highly.*

In his work we occasionally see portraits, created in a spirit of admiration and respect, of women very similar to those who will appear some years later in the works of the European sexologists, as they seek to identify and categorise the 'contra-sexuals', the 'inverts', the members of the 'third' and 'intermediate' sex. (I think of the splendid Miss Abbey Potterson, the landlady who effortlessly rules her river-side pub, The Six Jolly Fellowship-Porters, and watches with tender solicitude over her little maid of all work.)

In this extract from Little Dorrit *(1855–1857), we are given an insight into an altogether more troubling – and troubled – creature: Miss Wade, a character who delights in tormenting others, even as she torments herself.*

The History of a Self-Tormentor

I have the misfortune of not being a fool. From a very early age I have detected what those about me thought they hid from me. If I could have been habitually imposed upon, instead of habitually discerning the truth, I might have lived as smoothly as most fools do.

My childhood was passed with a grandmother; that is to say, with a lady who represented that relative to me, and who took that title on herself. She had no claim to it, but I – being to that extent a little fool – had no suspicion of her. She had some children of her own family in her house, and some children of other people. All girls; ten in number, including me. We all lived together and were educated together.

I must have been about twelve years old when I began to see how determinedly those girls patronised me. I was told I was an orphan. There was no other orphan among us; and I perceived (here was the first disadvantage of not being a fool) that they conciliated me in an insolent pity, and in a sense of superiority. I did not set this down as a discovery, rashly. I tried them often. I could hardly make them quarrel with me. When I succeeded with any of them, they were sure to come after an hour or two, and begin a reconciliation. I tried them over and over again, and I never knew them wait for me to begin. They were always forgiving me, in their vanity and condescension. Little images of grown people!

One of them was my chosen friend. I loved that stupid mite in a passionate way that she could no more deserve than I can remember without feeling ashamed of, though I was but a child. She had what they called an amiable temper, an affectionate temper. She could distribute, and did distribute pretty looks and smiles in every one among them. I believe there was not a soul in the place, except myself, who knew that she did it purposely to wound and gall me!

Nevertheless, I so loved that unworthy girl that my life was made stormy by my fondness for her. I was constantly lectured and disgraced for what was called 'trying her;' in other words charging her with her little perfidy and throwing her into tears by showing her that I read her heart. However, I loved her faithfully; and one time I went home with her for the holidays.

She was worse at home than she had been at school. She had a crowd of cousins and acquaintances, and we had dances at her house, and went out to dances at other houses, and, both at home and out, she tormented my love beyond endurance. Her plan was to make them all fond of her – and so drive me wild with jealousy. To be familiar and endearing with them all – and so make me mad with envying them. When we were left alone in our bedroom at night, I would reproach her with my perfect knowledge of her baseness; and then she would cry and cry and say I was cruel, and then I would hold her in my arms till morning: loving her as much as ever, and often feeling as if, rather than suffer so, I could so hold her in my arms and plunge to the bottom of a river – where I would still hold her after we were both dead.

It came to an end, and I was relieved. In the family there was an aunt who was not fond of me. I doubt if any of the family liked me much; but I never wanted them to like me, being altogether bound up in the one girl. The aunt was a young woman, and she had a serious way with her eyes of watching me. She was an audacious woman, and openly looked compassionately at me. After one of the nights that I have spoken of, I came down into a greenhouse before breakfast. Charlotte (the name of my false young friend) had gone down before me, and I heard this aunt speaking to her about me as I entered. I stopped where I was, among the leaves, and listened.

The aunt said, 'Charlotte, Miss Wade is wearing you to death, and this must not continue.' I repeat the very words I heard.

Now, what did she answer? Did she say, 'It is I who am wearing her to death, I who am keeping her on a rack and am the executioner, yet she tells me every night that she loves me devotedly, though she knows what I make her undergo?' No; my first memorable experience was true to what I knew her to be, and to all my experience. She began sobbing and weeping (to secure the aunt's sympathy to herself), and said, 'Dear aunt, she has an unhappy temper; other girls at school, besides I, try hard to make it better; we all try hard.'

Upon that the aunt fondled her, as if she had said something noble instead of despicable and false, and kept up the infamous pretence by replying, 'But there are reasonable limits, my dear love, to everything, and I see that this poor miserable girl causes you more constant and useless distress than even so good an effort justifies.'

The poor miserable girl came out of her concealment, as you may be prepared to hear, and said, 'Send me home.' I never said another word to either of them, or to any of them, but 'Send me home, or I will walk home along, night and day!' When I got home, I told my supposed grandmother that, unless I was sent away to finish my education somewhere else before that girl came back, or before any one of them came back, I would burn my sight away by throwing myself into the fire, rather than I would endure to look at their plotting faces.

Anactoria
A. C. SWINBURNE (1837–1909)

The poetry of Swinburne intoxicated readers during the middle years of Victoria's reign; undergraduates are said to have swept, arm-in-arm, through the streets of Oxford, chanting his irresistibly rhythmical lines and revelling in the daring sensuality and anguished eroticism of his subjects. Love, desire and pain were inextricably mixed for Swinburne, in life as in art, and his poetry returns again and again to women who both inflict and suffer pain. 'Anactoria' is a poem spoken in Sappho's voice, and addressed to one of the beloved women whose absence the original Sappho mourned. It provided for subsequent decades one of the most influential models for lesbian poetry and the lesbian poet, and for subsequent treatments of Sappho herself. Swinburne's influence is clear in many poems in this book, including some of those by 'Michael Field' and 'Marie Madeleine'.

τίνος ἀυ τὺ πειθοῖ
μάψ σαγηνευσας φιλότατα:
SAPPHO

My life is bitter with thy love; thine eyes
Blind me, thy tresses burn me, thy sharp sighs
Divide my flesh and spirit with soft sound,
And my blood strengthens, and my veins abound.
I pray thee sigh not, speak not, draw not breath;
Let life burn down, and dream it is not death.
I would the sea had hidden us, the fire
(Wilt thou fear that, and fear not my desire?)
Severed the bones that bleach, the flesh that cleaves
And let our sifted ashes drop like leaves.
I feel thy blood against my blood: my pain
Pains thee, and lips bruise lips, and vein stings vein.
Let fruit be crushed on fruit, let flower on flower,
Breast kindle breast, and either burn one hour.

Why wilt thou follow lesser loves? are thine
Too weak to bear these hands and lips of mine?
I charge thee for my life's sake, O too sweet
To crush love with thy cruel faultless feet,
I charge thee keep thy lips from hers or his,
Sweetest, till theirs be sweeter than my kiss:
Lest I too lure, a swallow for a dove,
Erotion or Erinna to my love.
I would my love could kill thee; I am satiated
With seeing thee live, and fain would have thee dead.
I would earth had thy body as fruit to eat,
And no mouth but some serpent's found thee sweet.
I would find grievous ways to have thee slain,
Intense device, and superflux of pain;
Vex thee with amorous agonies, and shake
Life at thy lips, and leave it there to ache;
Strain out thy soul with pangs too soft to kill,
Intolerable interludes, and infinite ill;
Relapse and reluctation of the breath,
Dumb tunes and shuddering semitones of death.
I am weary of all thy words and soft strange ways,
Of all love's fiery nights and all his days,
And all the broken kisses salt as brine
That shuddering lips make moist with waterish wine,
And eyes the bluer for all those hidden hours
That pleasure fills with tears and feeds from flowers,
Fierce at the heart with fire that half comes through,
But all the flowerlike white stained round with blue;
The fervent underlid, and that above
Lifted with laughter or abashed with love;
Thine amorous girdle, full of thee and fair,
And leavings of the lilies in thine hair.
Yea, all sweet words of thine and all thy ways,
And all the fruit of nights and flower of days,
And stinging lips wherein the hot sweet brine
That Love was born of burns and foams like wine,

And eyes insatiable of amorous hours,
Fervent as fire and delicate as flowers,
Coloured like night at heart, but cloven through
Like night with flame, dyed round like night with blue
Clothed with deep eyelids under and above —
Yea, all thy beauty sickens me with love;
Thy girdle empty of thee and now not fair,
And ruinous lilies in thy languid hair.
Ah, take no thought for Love's sake; shall this be,
And she who loves thy lover not love thee?
Sweet soul, sweet mouth of all that laughs and lives,
Mine is she, very mine; and she forgives.
For I beheld in sleep the light that is
In her high place in Paphos, heard the kiss
Of body and soul that mix with eager tears
And laughter stinging through the eyes and ears;
Saw Love, as burning flame from crown to feet,
Imperishable, upon her storied seat;
Clear eyelids lifted toward the north and south,
A mind of many colours, and a mouth
Of many tunes and kisses; and she bowed,
With all her subtle face laughing aloud,
Bowed down upon me, saying, 'Who doth thee wrong,
Sappho?' but thou — thy body is the song,
Thy mouth the music; thou art more than I,
Though my voice die not till the whole world die;
Though men that hear it madden; though love weep,
Though nature change, though shame be charmed to sleep.
Ah, wilt thou slay me lest I kiss thee dead?
Yet the queen laughed from her sweet heart and said:
'Even she that flies shall follow for thy sake,
And she shall give thee gifts that would not take,
Shall kiss that would not kiss thee' (yea, kiss me)
'When thou wouldst not' — when I would not kiss thee!
Ah, more to me than all men as thou art,
Shall not my songs assuage her at the heart?

Ah, sweet to me as life seems sweet to death,
Why should her wrath fill thee with fearful breath?
Nay, sweet, for is she God alone? hath she
Made earth and all the centuries of the sea,
Taught the sun ways to travel, woven most fine
The moonbeams, shed the starbeams forth as wine,
Bound with her myrtles, beaten with her rods,
The young men and the maidens and the gods?
Have we not lips to love with, eyes for tears,
And summer and flower of women and of years?
Stars for the foot of morning, and for noon
Sunlight, and exaltation of the moon;
Waters that answer waters, fields that wear
Lillies, and langour of the Lesbian air?
Beyond those flying feet of fluttered doves,
Are there not other gods for other loves?
Yea, though she scourge thee, sweetest, for my sake,
Blossom not thorns and flowers not blood should break.
Ah that my lips were tuneless lips, but pressed
To the bruised blossom of thy scourged white breast!

Three Poems by 'Marie Madeleine'
(the Baronin von Puttkamer) (1881–1944)

In 1898 'Marie Madeleine' (later the Baronin von Puttkamer) created pleasurable shock waves in Germany with her first volume of poems, published under what her English translator, somewhat ingenuously, called 'the curious title, Auf Kypros'. In fact the title, with its clear reference to 'the Cyprian' (Aphrodite, the goddess of love, born from the foam of the seas around Cyprus), made it very clear that these would be poems of sexual love. They included some addressed to women.

Ferdinand Kappey wrote in his Introductory Note to his 1907 translation, Hydromel and Rue*:*

Perhaps the most remarkable feature in connection with the poems was the age at which they were written, for the author had only just reached her seventeenth year at the date of their publication. The volume here presented should thus afford another example of that strange precocity which, with its amazing intuitions, may be said to forecast an experience and display a knowledge of those psychic influences and sexual emotions either entirely withheld from or but dimly perceived through the channels of normal youth.

He also added later that the original volume had shared, with Marie Bashkirt-seff's work, 'the same disregard of the restrictions which convention imposes on the treatment of the sexual theme.'

These *1907 translations from* Hydromel and Rue *draw heavily on the idiom created several decades earlier by Swinburne, whose 'Anactoria', which appears above, became the source and model of a particular sort of lesbian love-poem — love as doom and suffering. It was a model which some lesbians found as attractive as any dubiously fascinated heterosexual male. ('Marie Madeleine' would probably have known its Baudelairean versions.) I have retained Kappey's Edwardian translation because it typifies so finely the particular 'tone of voice' used by much of the period's poetry when it speaks of the 'Beautiful Evil' of 'Sapphic Loves'. Here are all the stock clichés of the period: love as poison; kisses as wounds; the challenge purity offers to vice; the desire to despoil the beloved; the whiteness of bodies that 'gleam'; the shiveringly excited use of blasphemous imagery and analogies for lesbian loves, the fist shaken at heaven and the terror of hell. As with so much lesbian(ish) poetry of the period, it is often difficult to distinguish between the temporary attitudinising of adolescence and what will prove to be more permanent and deeply rooted conflicts.*

Crucifixion

Nailed to a cross, your beauty still aglow,
   A fierce incarnate agony you seem;
Like purple wounds upon a field of snow
   My scarring kisses on your body gleam.

How thin your fair young face, your limbs how spare,
　　How frail upon your breast the blossom lies!
But oh! the torch of lust is flaming there
　　Through darkness and in triumph from your eyes.

When you, a virgin sword unstained, yet fierce
　　To brook affront, came trusting unto me,
Your innocence was like a sword to pierce,
　　And I desired to stain your purity.

I gave you of the poison that was mine,
　　My sorrow and my passion — all I gave;
And now behold the depth of my design:
　　A tortured soul too late for tears to save.

That I might now re-fashion from the dust
　　My shattered altars, and redeem the loss!
Madonna, with the kindled eyes of lust,
　　'Twas I who nailed you naked to the cross.

The Last Desire

Like ghostly fingers all night long the rain
　　Taps at the window-pane;
Among the shivering leaves the wind makes moan,
And all my heart goes out to you again —
　　You, who were once my own.

Framed in a mist of unaccustomed light,
　　Your face, grown sad and white,
Looks down — your parted lips so strangely red!
I would that you had passed beyond the night,
　　I would that you were dead!

That o'er your shameful body, joyless child,
　　The healing earth were piled;
That you again might burst the bonds of death,
And rise to scent — a lily undefiled —
　　The Dawn's inviolate breath.

Foiled Sleep

Ah me! I cannot sleep at night;
　　And when I shut my eyes, forsooth,
I cannot banish from my sight
　　The vision of her slender youth.

She stands before me lover-wise,
　　Her naked beauty fair and slim,
She smiles upon me, and her eyes
　　With over-fierce desire grow dim.

Slowly she leans to me. I meet
　　The passion of her gaze anew,
And then her laughter, clear and sweet,
　　Thrills all the hollow silence through.

O, siren, with the mocking tongue!
　　O beauty, lily-sweet and white!
I see her, slim and fair and young,
　　And ah! I cannot sleep at night.

Three Poems by Mary Coleridge
(1861–1907)

Why?

Why is she set so far, so far above me,
 And yet not altogether raised above?
I would give all the world that she should love me,
 My soul that she should never learn to love.

A Moment

The clouds had made a crimson crown
 Above the mountains high.
The stormy sun was going down
 In a stormy sky.

Why did you let your eyes so rest on me,
 And hold your breath between?
In all the ages this can never be
 As if it had not been.

Mistaken

I never thought that you could mourn
 As other women do.
A blossom from your garland torn,
A jewel dropped that you had worn,
 What could that be to you?

You never heard the human sound
   Of wailing and despair.
Nor faithful proved nor faithless found,
You lived and moved in beauty crowned,
   Content with being fair.

If I had known those eyes could weep
   That used to sparkle so,
You had been mine to love, to keep,
But all too late I probed the deep
   And all too late I know.

Ne me tangito
CHARLOTTE MEW (1869–1928)

This poem was written in 1916, and probably shortly after an unfortunate encounter with the novelist May Sinclair. Sinclair claimed to have been subjected to an unwanted seduction attempt by Mew, and promptly regaled literary London with highly coloured versions of the episode, much to Mew's intense distress.

'This man . . . would have known who and what manner of woman
this is: for she is a sinner.'   S. Luke vii. 39.

Odd, *You* should fear the touch,
   The first that I was ever ready to let go,
   I, that have not cared much
For any toy I could not break and throw
To the four winds when I had done with it. You need not fear the
   touch,
Blindest of all the things that I have cared for very much
In the whole gay, unbearable, amazing show.

True — for a moment — no, dull heart, you were too small,
Thinking to hide the ugly doubt behind that hurried puzzled little
  smile:
Only the shade, was it, you saw? but still the shade of something
  vile:
                    Oddest of all!
So I will tell you this. Last night, in sleep,
Walking through April fields I heard the far-off bleat of sheep
And from the trees about the farm, not very high,
A flight of pigeons fluttered up into an early evening mackerel sky;
              Someone stood by and it was you:
              About us both a great wind blew.
              My breast was bared
              But sheltered by my hair
              I found you, suddenly, lying there,
Tugging with tiny fingers at my heart, no more afraid:
              The weakest thing, the most divine
              That ever yet was mine,
              Something that I had strangely made,
              So then it seemed —
The child for which I had not looked or ever cared,
          Of whom, before, I had never dreamed.

Self or Other?

'Opposites attract, likes repel', so say the laws of science, and the adage has long been a stick with which to beat those who take their lovers from members of their own sex. Desiring likeness, lesbians, like their male homosexual brothers, have often been accused of narcissism. But the choice of likeness is not an easy option and opens up a host of painful questionings, as we struggle to recognise our own divided selves and the boundaries which do or should distinguish us from the women we love. The other woman may be one's younger self, a reflection in a mirror or in the troubled waters of a river; conversely, what seems to be a part of one's own body may be a part of someone else's. Sometimes, indeed, it is not quite clear just how many women there are in these poems.

Sappho to Philaenis
JOHN DONNE (?1573–1631)

Donne's Sappho explains at some length how she is at a loss for words to describe her beloved Philaenis, or to find appropriate comparisons for her. The mutuality which there should be in love is absent from heterosexual embraces, she argues; in love between women, the difference between self and other is so slight as to be insignificant, and their 'dalliance' is so natural as to leave no trace.

Where is that holy fire, which Verse is said
    To have? is that enchanting force decay'd?
Verse that draws Nature's works, from Nature's law,
    Thee, her best work, to her work cannot draw.
Have my tears quench'd my old Poetic fire;
    Why quench'd they not as well, that of desire?
Thoughts, my mind's creatures, often are with thee,
    But I, their maker, want their liberty.
Only thine image, in my heart, doth sit,
    But that is wax, and fires environ it.
My fires have driven, thine have drawn it hence;
    And I am robb'd of Picture, Heart, and Sense.
Dwells with me still mine irksome Memory,
    Which, both to keep, and lose, grieves equally.
That tells me how fair thou art: Thou art so fair,
    As gods, when gods to thee I do compare,
Are graced thereby; and to make blind men see,
    What things gods are, I say they're like to thee.
For, if we justly call each silly man
    A little world, What shall we call thee then?

Thou art not soft, and clear, and straight, and fair,
 As Down, as Stars, Cedars, and Lilies are,
But thy right hand, and cheek, and eye, only
 Are like thy other hand, and cheek, and eye.
Such was my Phao awhile, but shall be never,
 As thou wast, art, and oh, may'st thou be ever.
Here lovers swear in their idolatry,
 That I am such; but Grief discolours me.
And yet I grieve the less, lest Grief remove
 My beauty, and make me unworthy of thy love.
Plays some soft boy with thee, oh there wants yet
 A mutual feeling which should sweeten it.
His chin, a thorny hairy unevenness
 Doth threaten, and some daily change possess.
Thy body is a natural Paradise,
 In whose self, unmanur'd, all pleasure lies,
Nor needs perfection; why shouldst thou then
 Admit the tillage of a harsh rough man?
Men leave behind them that which their sin shows,
 And are as thieves traced, which rob when it snows.
But of our dalliance no more signs there are,
 Than fishes leave in streams, or Birds in air.
And between us all sweetness may be had;
 All, all that Nature yields, or Art can add.
My two lips, eyes, thighs, differ from thy two,
 But so, as thine from one another do;
And, oh, no more; the likeness being such,
 Why should they not alike in all parts touch?
Hand to strange hand, lip to lip none denies;
 Why should they breast to breast, or thighs to thighs?
Likeness begets such strange self-flattery,
 That touching myself, all seems done to thee.
Myself I embrace, and mine own hands I kiss;
 And amorously thank myself for this.
Me, in my glass, I call thee; but alas,
 When I would kiss, tears dim mine eyes, and glass.

O cure this loving madness, and restore
   Me to me; thee, my half, my all, my more.
So may thy cheeks' red outwear scarlet dye,
   And their white, whiteness of the Galaxy,
So may thy mighty, amazing beauty move
   Envy in all women, and in all men, love,
And so be change, and sickness, far from thee,
   As thou by coming near, keep'st them from me.

Moods and Thoughts
AMY LEVY (1861–1889)

The Old House

In through the porch and up the silent stair;
   Little is changed, I know so well the ways; –
Here, the dead came to meet me; it was there
   The dream was dreamed in unforgotten days.

But who is this that hurries on before,
   A flitting shade the brooding shades among? –
She turned, – I saw her face, – O God, it wore
   The face I used to wear when I was young!

I thought my spirit and my heart were tamed
   To deadness; dead the pangs that agonise.
The old grief springs to choke me. – I am shamed
   Before that little ghost with eager eyes.

O turn away, let her not see, not know!
   How should she bear it, how should understand?
O hasten down the stairway, haste and go,
   And leave her dreaming in the silent land.

Two Poems by Mary Coleridge
(1861–1907)

The Other Side of a Mirror

I sat before my glass one day,
    And conjured up a vision bare,
Unlike the aspects glad and gay,
    That erst were found reflected there –
The vision of a woman, wild
    With more than womanly despair.

Her hair stood back on either side
    A face bereft of loveliness.
It had no envy now to hide
    What once no man on earth could guess.
It formed the thorny aureole
    Of hard unsanctified distress.

Her lips were open – not a sound
    Came through the parted lines of red.
Whate'er it was, the hideous wound
    In silence and in secret bled.
No sigh relieved her speechless woe,
    She had no voice to speak her dread.

And in her lurid eyes there shone
    The dying flame of life's desire,
Made mad because its hope was gone,
    And kindled at the leaping fire
Of jealousy, and fierce revenge,
    And strength that could not change nor tire.

Shade of a shadow in the glass,
  O set the crystal surface free!
Pass — as the fairer visions pass —
  Nor ever more return, to be
The ghost of a distracted hour,
  That heard me whisper, 'I am she!'

'True to myself am I'

'To thine own self be true;
And it must follow, as the night the day,
Thou canst not then be false to any man.'

True to myself am I, and false to all.
  Fear, sorrow, love, constrain us till we die.
  But when the lips betray the spirit's cry,
The will, that should be sovereign, is a thrall.
Therefore let terror slay me, ere I call
  For aid of men. Let grief begrudge a sigh.
  'Are you afraid?' — 'unhappy?' 'No!'
      The lie
About the shrinking truth stands like a wall.
'And have you loved?' 'No, never!' All the
      while,
  The heart within my flesh is turned to stone.
Yea, none the less that I account it vile,
  The heart within my heart makes speechless
      moan,
  And when they see one face, one face alone,
The stern eyes of the soul are moved to smile.

Poem XX
from *Twenty-One Love Poems* (1974–1976)
ADRIENNE RICH

That conversation we were always on the edge
of having, runs on in my head,
at night the Hudson trembles in New Jersey light
polluted water yet reflecting even
sometimes the moon
and I discern a woman
I loved, drowning in secrets, fear wound round her throat
and choking her like hair. And this is she
with whom I tried to speak, whose hurt, expressive head
turning aside from pain, is dragged down deeper
where it cannot hear me,
and soon I shall know I was talking to my own soul.

'When we lie together'
C. M. DONALD

When we lie together, our legs
enmesh and entangle,
become somewhat autonomous,
like a friendly octopus.
I am astonished at that leg
that won't move when I tell it to
(being, presumably, one of yours).

Small Female Skull
CAROL ANN DUFFY

With some surprise, I balance my small female skull in my
   hands.
What is it like? An ocarina? Blow in its eye.
It cannot cry, holds my breath only as long as I exhale,
mildly alarmed now, into the hole where the nose was,
press my ear to its grin. A vanishing sigh.

For some time, I sit on the lavatory seat with my head
in my hands, appalled. It feels much lighter than I'd thought;
the weight of a deck of cards, a slim volume of verse,
but with something else, as though it could levitate.
   Disturbing.
So why do I kiss it on the brow, my warm lips to its papery
   bone,

and take it to the mirror to ask for a gottle of geer?
I rinse it under the tap, watch dust run way, like sand
from a swimming-cap, then dry it – firstborn – gently
with a towel. I see the scar where I fell for sheer love
down treacherous stairs, and read that shattering day like
   braille.

Love, I murmur to my skull, then louder, other grand
   words,
shouting the hollow nouns in a white-tiled room.
Downstairs they will think I have lost my mind. No. I only
   weep
into these two holes here, or I'm grinning back at the joke,
   this is
a friend of mine. See, I hold her face in trembling, passionate
   hands.

Tattooed (1999)
ESTHER ISAAC

*In this poem, where multiple layers of meaning and identity constantly merge
and blur, Esther Isaac explores some of the ways in which Jewish and lesbian
identity come together now, as they did in the past.*

                    . . . nothing hurts like grief.   Mark Doty

the image was barely in question
and when you left for home I found I had no choice

the tattooist
young brash new to the job
had trouble with the shape
all our stars she said *have five points*
and you're
asking for six . . . there may be a higher cost
it's a double triangle I said
one up against one . . . for which I know I'll have to pay
(your mouth your breasts your thighs leaving me every day)

and there's a warning here she said
picking out the pigment
you can't get rid of yellow
even with a laser
yellow leaves its mark
lasting as long as you
is that what you really want
a yellow star
barely an inch across

make it luminous
I said
I want to see it in the dark
each stark dyed point

let me tell you how it's done
she said
we need to keep the skin from going red
to prick you so as not to fetch up blood
then ease stain in the cuts

so when you're ready   say   she said
wiping my upper arm
(as if for inoculation)

up till 1942 I said
until they used this fine art of tattoo inside the camps
the 'helpers' used black pencil on the skin
so they could recognise and name the naked dead

and is this why you want this yellow star
she said
so even after you are dead
we'll still see who you are

Sisters

The feelings which sisters entertain for each other may be at least as passionate as those of more conventional lovers, and may well be tinged with their eroticism too; witness the poems by Christina Rossetti and E. J. Scovell.

By metaphorical extension, women united in suffering or struggle are also often 'sisters'. What more persuasive demonstration of sisterhood could we hope to find, for instance, than that enacted by the spirited coffee-house ladies of Covent Garden, who flocked to liberate the beleaguered Charlotte Charke (temporarily passing as 'Mr Brown') from her sojourn in the cells? And, for women writers, predecessors whose work and experience inspire and hearten may also be sisters, as Amy Lowell's poem makes clear.

Sadly, where there is sisterhood, there are often angry and resentful men; Andrew Marvell's complex poem 'Upon Appleton House' has many intricate political, religious and historical agendas to fulfil; but, helping to shape and colour them, as the extract here reveals, is a deep-rooted fear and suspicion of female communities.

from 'Goblin Market'
CHRISTINA ROSSETTI (1830–1894)

'Goblin Market' is a powerful tale of forbidden fruit and what happens to women who develop a taste for it. Rossetti plays on the eroticism of likeness between the sisters, Lizzie and Laura.

> Golden head by golden head,
> Like two pigeons in one nest,
> Folded in each other's wings,
> They lay down in their curtained bed:
> Like two blossoms on one stem,
> Like two flakes of new-fall'n snow,
> Like two wands of ivory
> Tipped with gold for awful kings.
> Moon and stars gazed in at them,
> Wind sang to them lullaby,
> Lumbering owls forbore to fly,
> Not a bat flapped to and fro
> Round their rest:
> Cheek to cheek and breast to breast
> Locked together in one nest.

But the impression of peace and harmony here is illusory: Laura, having succumbed to the lure of the goblins' enchanted wares, soon begins wasting away, deprived of what she craves for. Another young woman, Jeanie, has already pined to death after her encounter with the goblins and their fruits; no grass or flowers will grow on her grave. Lizzie, Laura's sister, must find a way to rescue Laura without tasting the fruit herself. Sisterhood, in Rossetti's poem, exemplifies the best kind of friendship – but it also partakes of violence and sensuous gratification.

'Good folk,' said Lizzie,
Mindful of Jeanie:
'Give me much and many:' –
Held out her apron,
Tossed them her penny.
'Nay, take a seat with us,
Honour and eat with us,'
They answered grinning:
'Our feast is but beginning.
Night yet is early,
Warm and dew-pearly,
Wakeful and starry:
Such fruits as these
No man can carry;
Half their bloom would fly,
Half their dew would dry,
Half their flavour would pass by.
Sit down and feast with us,
Be welcome guest with us,
Cheer you and rest with us.' –
'Thank you,' said Lizzie: 'But one waits
At home alone for me:
So without further parleying,
If you will not sell me any
Of your fruits tho' much and many,
Give me back my silver penny
I tossed you for a fee.' –
They began to scratch their pates,
No longer wagging, purring,
But visibly demurring,
Grunting and snarling.
One called her proud,
Cross-grained, uncivil;
Their tones waxed loud,
Their looks were evil.
Lashing their tails

They trod and hustled her,
Elbowed and jostled her,
Clawed with their nails,
Barking, mewing, hissing, mocking,
Tore her gown and soiled her stocking,
Twitched her hair out by the roots,
Stamped upon her tender feet,
Held her hands and squeezed their fruits
Against her mouth to make her eat.
White and golden Lizzie stood,
Like a lily in a flood, —
Like a rock of blue-veined stone
Lashed by tides obstreperously, —
Like a beacon left alone
In a hoary roaring sea,
Sending up a golden fire, —
Like a fruit-crowned orange-tree
White with blossoms honey-sweet
Sore beset by wasp and bee, —
Like a royal virgin town
Topped with gilded dome and spire
Close beleaguered by a fleet
Mad to tug her standard down.

One may lead a horse to water,
Twenty cannot make him drink.
Tho' the goblins cuffed and caught her,
Coaxed and fought her,
Bullied and besought her,
Scratched her, pinched her black as ink,
Kicked and knocked her,
Mauled and mocked her,
Lizzie uttered not a word;
Would not open lip from lip
Lest they should cram a mouthful in:
But laughed in heart to feel the drip

Of juice that syrupped all her face,
And lodged in dimples of her chin,
And streaked her neck which quaked like curd.
At last the evil people
Worn out by her resistance
Flung back her penny, kicked their fruit
Along whichever road they took,
Not leaving root or stone or shoot;
Some writhed into the ground,
Some dived into the brook
With ring and ripple,
Some scudded on the gale without a sound,
Some vanished in the distance.

In a smart, ache, tingle,
Lizzie went her way;
Knew not was it night or day;
Sprang up the bank, tore thro' the furze,
Threaded copse and dingle,
And heard her penny jingle
Bouncing in her purse,
Its bounce was music to her ear.
She ran and ran
As if she feared some goblin man
Dogged her with gibe or curse
Or something worse:
But not one goblin skurried after,
Nor was she pricked by fear;
The kind heart made her windy-paced
That urged her home quite out of breath with haste
And inward laughter.

She cried 'Laura,' up the garden,
'Did you miss me?
Come and kiss me.
Never mind my bruises,

Hug me, kiss me, suck my juices
Squeezed from goblin fruits for you,
Goblin pulp and goblin dew.
Eat me, drink me, love me;
Laura, make much of me:
For your sake I have braved the glen
And had to do with goblin merchant men.'

Laura started from her chair,
Flung her arms up in the air,
Clutched her hair:
'Lizzie, Lizzie, have you tasted
For my sake the fruit forbidden?
Must your light like mine be hidden,
Your young life like mine be wasted,
Undone in mine undoing
And ruined in my ruin,
Thirsty, cankered, goblin-ridden?' –
She clung about her sister,
Kissed and kissed and kissed her:
Tears once again
Refreshed her shrunken eyes,
Dropping like rain
After long sultry drouth;
Shaking with aguish fear, and pain,
She kissed and kissed her with a hungry mouth.

Her lips began to scorch,
That juice was wormwood to her tongue,
She loathed the feast:
Writhing as one possessed she leaped and sung,
Rent all her robe, and wrung
Her hands in lamentable haste,
And beat her breast.
Her locks streamed like the torch
Borne by a racer at full speed,

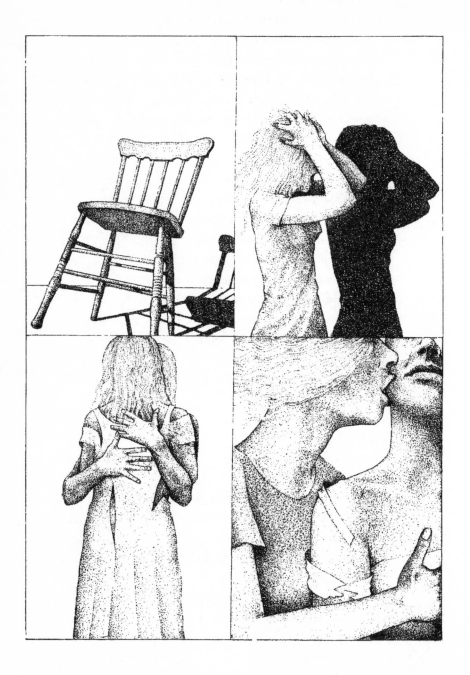

'Laura started from her chair': by Martin Ware

Or like the mane of horses in their flight,
Or like an eagle when she stems the light
Straight toward the sun,
Or liked a caged thing freed,
Or like a flying flag when armies run.

Swift fire spread thro' her veins, knocked at her heart,
Met the fire smouldering there
And overbore its lesser flame;
She gorged on bitterness without a name:
Ah! fool, to choose such part
Of soul-consuming care!
Sense failed in the mortal strife:
Like the watch-tower of a town
Which an earthquake shatters down,
Like a lightning-stricken mast,
Like a wind-uprooted tree
Spun about,
Like a foam-topped waterspout
Cast down headlong in the sea,
She fell at last;
Pleasure past and anguish past,
Is it death or is it life?

Life out of death.
That night long Lizzie watched by her,
Counted her pulse's flagging stir,
Felt for her breath,
Held water to her lips, and cooled her face
With tears and fanning leaves:
But when the first birds chirped about their eaves,
And early reapers plodded to the place
Of golden sheaves,
And dew-wet grass
Bowed in the morning winds so brisk to pass,
And new buds with new day

Opened of cup-like lilies on the stream,
Laura woke as from a dream,
Laughed in the innocent old way,
Hugged Lizzie but not twice or thrice;
Her gleaming locks showed not one thread of grey,
Her breath was sweet as May
And light danced in her eyes.

Days, weeks, months, years
Afterwards, when both were wives
With children of their own;
Their mother-hearts beset with fears,
Their lives bound up in tender lives;
Laura would call the little ones
And tell them of her early prime,
Those pleasant days long gone
Of not-returning time:
Would talk about the haunted glen,
The wicked, quaint fruit-merchant men,
Their fruits like honey to the throat
But poison in the blood;
(Men sell not such in any town:)
Would tell them how her sister stood
In deadly peril to do her good,
And win the fiery antidote:
Then joining hands to little hands
Would bid them cling together,
'For there is no friend like a sister
In calm or stormy weather;
To cheer one on the tedious way,
To fetch one if one goes astray,
To lift one if one totters down,
To strengthen whilst one stands.'

A Girl to Her Sister
E. J. SCOVELL (1907–1999)

A girl said to her sister, late, when their friends had gone:
'I wish there were no men on earth, but we alone.

'The beauty of your body, the beauty of your face –
Which now are greedy flames, and clasp more than themselves in
   light,
Pierce awake the drowsing air and boast before the night –
Then should be of less account than a dark reed's grace,
All summer growing in river mists, unknown –
The beauty of your body, the beauty of my own.

'When we two talk together, the words between us pass
Across long fields, across drenched, upland fields of grass,
Like words of men who signal with flags in clear weather.
When we two are together, I know before you speak
Your answers by your head's turn and shadows on your cheek –
Running of wind on grass, to bring our thoughts together.

'We should live as though all day were the day's first hour,
All light were the first daylight, that whistles from so far,
That stills the blood with distance. We should live as though
All seasons were the earliest spring when only birds are mating,
When the low, crouched bramble remembers still the snow
And woods are but half unchained from the winter's waiting.
We should be gay together, with pleasures primrose-cool,
Scattered and quick as spring's are, by thicket and chill pool.

'Oh, to-night,' the girl said, 'I wish that I could sit
All my life here with you, for ever unlit.
To-morrow I shall love again the summer's valour,
Heavy heat of noon, and the night's mysteries,
And love like the sun's touch, that closes up my eyes –
To-morrow; but to-night,' she said, as night ran on,
'I wish there were no love on earth but ours alone.'

Subtle nuns

from 'Upon Appleton House, to my Lord Fairfax'
ANDREW MARVELL (1621–1678)

*Enclosed communities of women frequently attract hostility and pleasurably
shocked allegations of rampant 'unnatural vice'. Convents and nuns, in particular, have fuelled much over-excited censure down the centuries. For sturdy
English Protestants in the years following the Reformation, Sapphic nuns
become a vivid metaphor for the devious subtlety and pernicious seductions
of that most Whorish of all religions, the Scarlet woman, Rome herself.*

XII

Near to this gloomy Cloysters Gates
There dwelt the blooming Virgin *Thwates*;
Fair beyond Measure, and an Heir
Which might Deformity make fair.
And oft She spent the Summer Suns
Discoursing with the *Suttle Nunns*.
Whence in these Words one to her weav'd,
(As 'twere by Chance) Thoughts long conceiv'd.

XIII

'Within this holy leisure we
Live innocently as you see.
These Walls restrain the World without,
But hedge our Liberty about.
These Bars inclose that wider Den
Of those wild Creatures, called Men.
The Cloyster outward shuts its Gates,
And, from us, locks on them the Grates.

XIV

'Here we, in shining Armour white,
Like *Virgin Amazons* do fight.
And our chast *Lamps* we hourly trim,
Lest the great *Bridegroom* find them dim.
Our *Orient* Breaths perfumed are
And Holy-water of our Tears
Most strangly our Complexion clears.

XV

'Not Tears of Grief; but such as those
With which calm Pleasure overflows;
Or Pity, when we look on you
That live without this happy Vow.
How should we grieve that must be seen
Each one a *Spouse*, and each a *Queen*;
And can in *Heaven* hence behold
Our brighter Robes and Crowns of Gold?

XVI

'When we have prayed all our Beads,
Some One the holy *Legend* reads;
While all the rest with Needles paint
The Face and Graces of the *Saint*.
But what the Linnen can't receive
They in their Lives do interweave.
This Work the *Saints* best represents;
That serves for *Altar's Ornaments*.

XVII

'But much it to our work would add
If here your hand, your Face we had:
By it we would *our Lady* touch;
Yet thus She you resembles much.
Some of your Features, as we sow'd,
Through ev'ry *Shrine* should be bestow'd.
And in one Beauty we would take
Enough a thousand *Saints* to make.

XVIII

'And (for I dare not quench the Fire
That me does for your good inspire)
'Twere Sacriledge a Man t'admit
To holy things, for *Heaven* fit.
I see the *Angels* in a Crown
On you the Lillies show'ring down:
And round about you Glory breaks,
That something more then humane speaks.

XIX

'All Beauty, when at such a height,
Is so already consecrate.
Fairfax I know; and long ere this
Have mark'd the Youth, and what he is.
But can he such a *Rival* seem
For whom you *Heav'n* should disesteem?
Ah, no! and 'twould more Honour prove
He your *Devoto* were, then Love.

XX

'Here live beloved, and obey'd:
Each one your Sister, each your Maid.
And, if our Rule seem strictly pend,
The Rule it self to you shall bend.
Our *Abbess* too, now far in Age,
Doth your succession near presage.
How soft the yoke on us would lye,
Might such fair Hands as yours it tye!

xxi

'Your voice, the sweetest of the Quire,
Shall drawn *Heav'n* nearer, raise us higher.
And your Example, if our Head,
Will soon us to perfection lead.
Those Virtues to us all so dear,
Will straight grow Sanctity when here:
And that, once sprung, increase so fast
'Till Miracles it work at last.

XXII

'Nor is our *Order* yet so nice,
Delight to banish as a Vice.
Here Pleasure Piety doth meet;
One perfecting the other Sweet.
So through the mortal fruit we boyl
The Sugars uncorrupting Oyl:
And that which perisht while we pull,
Is thus preserved clear and full.

XXIII

'For such indeed are all our Arts;
Still handling Natures finest Parts.
Flow'rs dress the Altars; for the Clothes,
The Sea-born Amber we compose;
Balms for the griev'd we draw; and Past[e]s
We mold, as Baits for curious tast[e]s.
What need is here of Man? unless
These as sweet Sins we should confess.

XXIV

'Each Night among us to your side
Appoint a fresh and Virgin Bride;
Whom if *our Lord* at midnight find,
Yet Neither should be left behind.
Where you may lye as chast in Bed,
As Pearls together billeted.
All Night embracing Arm in Arm,
Like Chrystal pure with Cotton warm.

XXV

'But what is this to all the store
Of Joys you see, and may make more!
Try but a while, if you be wise:
The Tryal neither Costs, nor Tyes.[']
Now *Fairfax* seek her promis'd faith:
Religion that dispensed hath;
Which She hence forward does begin;
The *Nuns* smooth Tongue has suckt her in.

XXVI

Oft, though he knew it was in vain,
Yet would be valiantly complain.
'Is that this *Sanctity* so great,
An Art by which you finly'r cheat?
Hypocrite Witches, hence *avant*,
Who though in prison yet inchant!
Death only can such Theeves make fast,
As rob though in the Dungeon cast.

XXVII

'Were there but, when this House was made,
One Stone that a just Hand had laid,
It must have fall'n upon her Head
Who first Thee from thy Faith misled.
And yet, how well soever ment,
With them 'twould soon grow fraudulent:
For like themselves they alter all,
And vice infects the very Wall.

XXVIII

'But sure those Buildings last not long,
Founded by Folly, kept by Wrong.
I know what Fruit their Gardens yield,
When they it think by Night conceal'd.
Fly from their Vices. 'Tis thy state,
Not Thee, that they would consecrate.
Fly from their Ruine. How I fear
Though guiltless lest thou perish there.[']

Ladies to the rescue

from *A Narrative of the Life of Mrs Charlotte Charke* (1755)

Arrested for debt during one of her many prolonged spells in men's clothes ('being then for some very substantial reasons, en cavalier*'), Charlotte Charke is rescued by the somewhat disreputable sisterhood of the Covent Garden coffee-house keepers. These women may call Charke 'poor Sir Charles', but it is fairly clear that they know what as well as whom they are rescuing.*

What to do in this terrible Exigence I could not tell, as I had but a Day and a Half longer to be at Large, if I could not produce a second Bail. I tried all Means, but in vain; and, on the *Friday* following, was obliged to surrender, and lay that Night in *Jackson's-Alley*, at the Officer's House.

I had not been there Half an Hour, before I was surrounded with all the Ladies who kept Coffee-Houses in and about the *Garden*, each offering Money for my Ransom: But nothing then could be done, without the Debt and Costs; which, though there was, I believe, about a dozen or fourteen Ladies present, they were not able to raise. As far as their Finances extended, they made an Offer of 'em; and would have given Notes jointly or separately, for the Relief of poor *Sir Charles*, as they were pleased to stile me. 'Tis true, the Officer would willingly have come into their kind Propositions, as he was truly sensible of my Indigence; but, being closely watched by the Creditor, who would, on no Terms be brought to any Composition, all their Efforts were ineffectual.

After two or three Hours wasted in fruitless Entreaties, it growing late, they left me to bewail the terrible Scene of Horror that presented to my tortured View; and, with a Heart overcharged with Anguish, and hopeless of Redress, I retired to my Dormitory, and passed the Night in bitterest Reflections on my melancholly Situation.

My poor Child, who was then but eight Years of Age, and whose sole Support was on her HAPLESS, FRIENDLESS MOTHER, knew not what was become of me, or where to seek me; and, with watchful Care, wore away the tedious Night, in painful Apprehensions of what really had befallen me.

About Seven next Morning, I dispatched a Messenger to my poor little suffering Infant; who soon came to me, with her Eyes over-flowed with Tears, and a Heart full of undissembled Anguish. She immediately threw her Head upon my Bosom, and remained in speechless Grief, with which I equally encountered her. For some Time the Child was so entirely sensible of our Misfortunes, and of the Want of Means of being extricated from them, 'twas with Difficulty I soothed her into a Calm. Alas! what has the POOR and FRIENDLESS TO HOPE FOR! surrounded with Sorrows of such a Nature, that even People in tolerable Circumstances find some Perplexity, when so ASSAILED, to OVERCOME?

I sat down and wrote eight and thirty Letters before I stirred out of my Chair, some of which went where I thought NATURE might have put in HER CLAIM, but I could obtain no Answer; and, where I LEAST EXPECTED, I FOUND REDRESS!

My poor little Wench was the melancholly Messenger, and neither eat or drank 'till she had faithfully discharged the Trust I reposed in her. To be short, the very Ladies who had visited me the Night before, brought with them the late Mrs. *Elizabeth Hughes*; who, by Dint of her laying down a Couple of Guineas, and a Collection from the rest, with a Guinea from Mrs. *Douglass* in the *Piazza*, I was set at Liberty; and the Officer advised me to change Hats with him, that being the very Mark by which I was unfortunately distinguished, and made known to him.

My Hat was ornamented with a beautiful Silver Lace, little the worse for wear, and of the Size which is now the present Taste; the Officer's a large one, cocked up in the Coachman's Stile, and weightened with a horrible Quantity of Crape, to secure him from the Winter's Cold.

As to my Figure, 'tis so well known it needs no Description; but my Friend, the Bailiff, was a very short, thick, red-faced Man: Of such a Corpulency, he might have appeared in the Character of *Falstaff*, without the artful Assistance of Stuffing, and his Head proportionable to his Body, consequently we each of us made very droll Figures; he with his little laced Hat, which appeared on his Head of the Size of those made for the *Spanish* Ladies, and my unfortunate Face smothered under his, that I was almost as much incommoded as when I marched in the Ditch, under the insupportable Weight of my Father's.

The Sisters
AMY LOWELL (1874–1925)

The American poet Amy Lowell muses on the dialogues she wishes she could have had with three earlier sisters of the pen.

> Taking us by and large, we're a queer lot
> We women who write poetry. And when you think
> How few of us there've been, it's queerer still.
> I wonder what it is that makes us do it,
> Singles us out to scribble down, man-wise,
> The fragments of ourselves. Why are we
> Already mother-creatures, double-bearing,
> With matrices in body and in brain?
> I rather think that there is just the reason
> We are so sparse a kind of human being;
> The strength of forty thousand Atlases
> Is needed for our every-day concerns.
> There's Sapho, now I wonder what was Sapho.
> I know a single slender thing about her:
> That, loving, she was like a burning birch-tree

All tall and glittering fire, and that she wrote
Like the same fire caught up to Heaven and held there,
A frozen blaze before it broke and fell.
Ah, me! I wish I could have talked to Sapho,
Surprised her reticences by flinging mine
Into the wind. This tossing off of garments
Which cloud the soul is none too easy doing
With us to-day. But still I think with Sapho
One might accomplish it, were she in the mood
To bare her loveliness of words and tell
The reasons, as she possibly conceived them,
Of why they are so lovely. Just to know
How she came at them, just to watch
The crisp sea sunshine playing on her hair,
And listen, thinking all the while 'twas she
Who spoke and that we two were sisters
Of a strange, isolated little family.
And she is Sapho — Sapho — not Miss or Mrs.,
A leaping fire we call so for convenience;
But Mrs. Browning — who would ever think
Of such presumption as to call her 'Ba.'
Which draws the perfect line between sea-cliffs
And a close-shuttered room in Wimpole Street.
Sapho could fly her impulses like bright
Balloons tip-tilting to a morning air
And write about it. Mrs. Browning's heart
Was squeezed in stiff conventions. So she lay
Stretched out upon a sofa, reading Greek
And speculating, as I must suppose,
In just this way on Sapho; all the need,
The huge, imperious need of loving, crushed
Within the body she believed so sick.
And it was sick, poor lady, because words
Are merely simulacra after deeds
Have wrought a pattern; when they take the place
Of actions they breed a poisonous miasma

Which, though it leave the brain, eats up the body.
So Mrs. Browning, aloof and delicate,
Lay still upon her sofa, all her strength
Going to uphold her over-topping brain.
It seems miraculous, but she escaped
To freedom and another motherhood
Than that of poems. She was a very woman
And needed both.

                If I had gone to call,
Would Wimpole Street have been the kindlier place,
Or Casa Guidi, in which to have met her?
I am a little doubtful of that meeting.
For Queen Victoria was very young and strong
And all-pervading in her apogee
At just that time. If we had stuck to poetry,
Sternly refusing to be drawn off by mesmerism
Or Roman revolutions, it might have done.
For, after all, she is another sister,
But always, I rather think, an older sister
And not herself so curious a technician
As to admit newfangled modes of writing —
'Except, of course, in Robert, and that is neither
Here nor there for Robert is a genius.'
I do not like the turn this dream is taking,
Since I am very fond of Mrs. Browning
And very much indeed should like to hear her
Graciously asking me to call her 'Ba.'
But then the Devil of Verisimilitude
Creeps in and forces me to know she wouldn't.
Convention again, and how it chafes my nerves,
For we are such a little family
Of singing sisters, and as if I didn't know
What those years felt like tied down to the sofa.
Confounded Victoria, and the slimy inhibitions
She loosed on all us Anglo-Saxon creatures!
Suppose there hadn't been a Robert Browning.

No 'Sonnets from the Portuguese' would have been written
They are the first of all her poems to be,
One might say, fertilized. For, after all,
A poet is flesh and blood as well as brain
And Mrs. Browning, as I said before,
Was very, very woman. Well, there are two
Of us, and vastly unlike that's for certain.
Unlike at least until we tear the veils
Away which commonly gird souls. I scarcely think
Mrs. Browning would have approved the process
In spite of what had surely been relief;
For speaking souls must always want to speak
Even when bat-eyed, narrow-minded Queens
Set prudishness to keep the keys of impulse.
Then do the frowning Gods invent new banes
And make the need of sofas. But Sapho was dead
And I, and others, not yet peeped above
The edge of possibility. So that's an end
To speculating over tea-time talks
Beyond the movement of pentameters
With Mrs. Browning.
               But I go dreaming on,
In love with these my spiritual relations.
I rather think I see myself walk up
A flight of wooden steps and ring a bell
And send a card in to Miss Dickinson.
Yet that's a very silly way to do.
I should have taken the dream twist-ends about
And climbed over the fence and found her deep
Engrossed in the doing of a humming-bird
Among nasturtiums. Not having expected strangers,
She might forget to think me one, and holding up
A finger say quite casually: 'Take care.
Don't frighten him, he's only just begun.'
'Now this,' I well believe I should have thought,
'Is even better than Sapho. With Emily

You're really here, or never anywhere at all
In range of mind.' Wherefore, having begun
In the strict centre, we could slowly progress
To various circumferences, as we pleased.
We could, but should we? That would quite depend
On Emily. I think she'd be exacting,
Without intention possibly, and ask
A thousand tight-rope tricks of understanding.
But, bless you, I would somersault all day
If by so doing I might stay with her.
I hardly think that we should mention souls
Although they might just round the corner from us
In some half-quizzical, half-wistful metaphor.
I'm very sure that I should never seek
To turn her parables to stated fact.
Sapho would speak, I think, quite openly,
And Mrs. Browning guard a careful silence,
But Emily would set doors ajar and slam them
And love you for your speed of observation.

Strange trio of my sisters, most diverse,
And how extraordinarily unlike
Each is to me, and which way shall I go?
Sapho spent and gained; and Mrs. Browning,
After a miser girlhood, cut the strings
Which tied her money-bags and let them run;
But Emily hoarded — hoarded — only giving
Herself to cold, white paper. Starved and tortured,
She cheated her despair with games of patience
And fooled herself by winning. Frail little elf,
The lonely brain-child of a gaunt maturity,
She hung her womanhood upon a bough
And played ball with the stars — too long — too long —
The garment of herself hung on a tree
Until at last she lost even the desire
To take it down. Whose fault? Why let us say,

To be consistent, Queen Victoria's.
But really, not to over-rate the queen,
I feel obliged to mention Martin Luther,
And behind him the long line of Church Fathers
Who draped their prurience like a dirty cloth
About the naked majesty of God.
Good-bye, my sisters, all of you are great,
And all of you are marvellously strange,
And none of you has any word for me.
I cannot write like you, I cannot think
In terms of Pagan or of Christian now.
I only hope that possibly some day
Some other woman with an itch for writing
May turn to me as I have turned to you
And chat with me a brief few minutes. How
We lie, we poets! It is three good hours
I have been dreaming. Has it seemed so long
To you? And yet I thank you for the time
Although you leave me sad and self-distrustful,
For older sisters are very sobering things.
Put on your cloaks, my dears, the motor's waiting.
No, you have not seemed strange to me, but near,
Frightfully near, and rather terrifying.
I understand you all, for in myself —
Is that presumption? Yet indeed it's true —
We are one family. And still my answer
Will not be any one of yours, I see.
Well, never mind that now. Good night! Good night!

Lessons for Life

Schoolgirl crushes on female teachers, and on each other, are traditionally regarded with a mixture of condescending sympathy and ribald mirth, yet their importance has often proved incalculable.

It would have been possible to fill a whole book with accounts of such attachments, drawn from fact and fiction, life and literature. In them we would encounter a passionate swirl of emotions – ardour, embarrassment, rage, confusion, fear and gratitude. Such a book might include Sappho's relations with her girl pupils more than two thousand years ago; or Dorothy Bussy's Olivia, with its hauntingly elegiac reworking of her own Wimbledon schooldays, transposed to a flawed Eden on the outskirts of Paris; or Maureen Duffy's fine tribute to Evelyn, her English teacher, in That's How It Was. On a very different note, Nancy Spain's gleeful dissection of the emotions rampantly at work in her select, south-coast boarding school, Radclyffe Hall, would have its place; nor should such a book omit the lyrics of Meg Christian's splendidly tongue-in-cheek, sing-along song, 'Ode to a Gym Teacher', dedicated to a 'big strong woman, the first to come along who showed me being female meant you still could be strong!'. And how could one exclude all those schoolgirl yarns crammed with loves and tiffs, fallings out and makings up? Who would be without them?

Well, quite a lot of people, actually. From the 1880s, when the expansion of girls' secondary education took off, through to the inter-war years, various self-appointed authorities inveighed against the dangers of 'unhealthy' school attachments' and 'unduly influential' teachers. Efforts were even made in the late 1920s to bar spinsters from teaching in girls' schools.

It is a not altogether surprising irony that some of the fiercest opponents of passionate attachments between schoolgirls and their mistresses have written about them so well. 'Clemence Dane', for instance, whose 1917 novel Regiment of Women contains a charismatic teacher who is as irresistible as she is lethal. This brief section has just a tiny handful of texts, where fine teachers and terrible ones do battle over their girls, and where the girls themselves watch, wonder and judge.

from *Regiment of Women* (1917)
'CLEMENCE DANE' (1888–1965)

Two extracts from Regiment of Women, *the best-selling first novel of 'Clemence Dane' (Winifred Ashton). Clare Hartill, a brilliant but dangerously charismatic teacher, all but succeeds in detaching a younger colleague, Alwynne Durand, from her Aunt Elsbeth, and from heterosexuality. Dane's fiercely hostile book is nevertheless surprisingly sympathetic and perceptive in its treatment of Clare's psychology. The first extract shows Clare's impact upon her pupils; in the second, Aunt Elsbeth, who has come to beg Clare to give up Alwynne, speaks her mind to Clare at last.*

One of Alwynne's duties was the conduct of a small 'extra' class, consisting of girls, who, for reasons of stupidity, ill-health or defective grounding, fell too far below the average of knowledge in their respective classes. She devoted certain afternoons in the week to coaching them, and was considered to be unusually successful in her methods. She could be extremely patient, and had quaint and unorthodox ways of insinuating facts into her pupils' minds. As she told Elsbeth, she invented their memories for them. She was sufficiently imaginative to realize their difficulties, yet sufficiently young to dream of developing, in due course, all her lame ducks into swans. She was intensely interested in hearing how her coaching had succeeded; her pleasure at an amended place in class was so genuine, her disappointment at a collapse so comically real, yet so devoid of contempt, so tinged with conviction that it was anybody's fault but the culprit's, that either attitude was an incentive to real effort. Like Clare, she did not suffer fools gladly, but unlike Clare, she had not the moral courage to be ruthless. Stupidity seemed as terrible to her as physical deformity; she treated it with the same touch of motherliness, the same instinctive desire to spare it realization of its own unsightliness.

Her rather lovable cowardice brought a mixed reward; she stifled in sick-rooms, yet invalids liked her well; she was frankly envious of Clare's circle of brilliant girls and as inevitably surrounded by inarticulate adorers, who bored her mightily, but whose clumsy affection she was too kind-hearted to suppress.

It had been well for Alwynne, however, that her following was of the duller portion of the school. This Clare could endure, could countenance; such boy-bishopry could not affect her own sovereignty, and her subject's consequence increased her own. But to see Alwynne swaying, however unconsciously, minds of a finer type, would not have been easy for Clare. She had grown very fond of Alwynne; but the sentiment was proprietary; she could derive no pleasure from her that was not personal, and, in its most literal sense, selfish. She was unmaternal to the core. She could not see her human property admired by others with any sensation but that of a double jealousy; she was subtly angered that Alwynne could attract, yet was caught herself in the net of those attractions, and unable to endure to watch them spread for any but herself.

Alwynne, quite unconscious of the trait, had at first done herself harm by her unfeigned interest in Clare's circle. It took the elder woman some suspicious weeks to realize that Alwynne lacked completely her own *dompteuse* instinct, her craving for power; that she was as innocent of knowledge of her own charm as unwedded Eve; that her impulse to Clare was an impulse of the freshest, sweetest, hero-worship; but the realization came at last, and Clare opened her hungry heart to her, and, warmed by Alwynne's affection, wondered that she had hesitated so long.

Alwynne never guessed that she had been doubted. Clare was proud of her genuine skill as a character reader – had been a little pleased to give Alwynne proof of her penetration when occasion arose; and Alwynne, less trained, less critical, thought her omniscient, and never dreamed that the motives of her obscurest actions, the sources of her most veiled references were not plain to Clare. Secure of comprehension, she went her way: any one in whom Clare was interested must needs attract her: so she took pains to become intimate with Clare's adorers, from a very real sympathy with their appreciation of Clare, whom she no more grudged to them than a priestess would grudge the unveiling of her goddess to the initiate. She received their confidences, learned their secrets, fanned the flame of their enthusiasms. Too lately a schoolgirl herself, too innocent and ignorant to dream of danger, she did her loyal utmost in furtherance of the cult, measuring the artificial and unbalanced emotions she encountered by the rule of her own saner affection, and, in her desire to see her friend appreciated, in all good faith utilized her degree of authority to encourage what an older woman would have recognized and combated as incipient hysteria.

Gradually she became, through her frank sympathy, combined with her slightly indeterminate official position, the intermediary, the interpreter of Clare to the feverish school. Clare herself, her initial distrust over, found this useful. She could afford to be moody, erratic, whimsical; to be extravagant in her praises and reproofs; to deteriorate, at times, into a caricature of her own bizarre personality, with the comfortable assurance that there was ever a magician in her wake to steady her tottering shrines, mix oil with her vitriol, and prove her pinchbeck gold.

Fatal, this relaxation of effort, to a woman of Clare's type. Love of some sort was vital to her. Of this her surface personality was dimly, ashamedly aware, and would, if challenged, have frigidly denied; but the whole of her larger self knew its need, and saw to it that that need was satisfied. Clare, unconscious, had taught Clare, conscious, that there must be effort – constant, straining effort at cultivation of all her alluring qualities, at concealment of all in her that could repulse – effort that all appearances of complete success must never allow her to relax. She knew well the evanescent character of a schoolgirl's affection; so well that when her pupils left the school she seldom tried to retain her hold upon them. Their letters would come thick as autumn leaves at first; she rarely answered, or after long intervals; and the letters dwindled and ceased. She knew that, in the nature of things, it must be so, and had no wish to prolong the farewells.

Also, her interest in her correspondents usually died first; to sustain it required their physical nearness. But every new year filled the gaps left by the old, stimulated Clare to fresh exertion.

So the lean years went by. Then came vehement Alwynne – no schoolgirl – yet more youthful and ingenuous than any mistress had right to be, loving with all the discrimination of a fine mind, and all the ardour of an affectionate child. Here was no question of a fleeting devotion that must end as the schooldays ended. Here was love for Clare at last, a widow's cruse to last her for all time. Clare thanked the gods of her unbelief, and, relaxing all effort, settled herself to enjoy to the full the cushioning sense of security; the mock despot of their pleasant, earlier intercourse becoming, as she bound Alwynne ever more closely to her, albeit unconsciously, a very real tyrant indeed.

Yet she had no intention of weakening her hold on any lesser member of her coterie. Alwynne was too ingenuous, too obviously subject through her own free impulse, to entirely satisfy: Clare's love of power had its morbid moments, when a struggling victim, head averted, pleased her. There was never, among the new-comers, a child, self-absorbed, nonchalant or rebellious, who passed a term unmolested by Miss Hartill. Egoism aroused her curiosity, her suspicion of hidden lands, virgin, ripe for exploration; indifference piqued her; a flung gauntlet she welcomed with frank amusement. She had been a rebel in her own time, and had ever a thrill of sympathy for the mutinies she relentlessly crushed. War, personal war, delighted her; she was a mistress of tactics, and the certainty of eventual victory gave zest to her campaigns. She did not realize that the strain upon her childish opponents was very great. The finer, the more sensitive the character, the more complete the eventual defeat, the more permanent its effects. Clare was pitiless after victory: not till then did she examine into the nature thus enslaved, seldom did she find it worth the trouble of the skirmish. In most cases she gave semi-liberty; enough of smiles to keep the children feverishly at work to please her (the average of achievement in her classes was astounding), and enough of indifference to prevent them from becoming a nuisance. To the few that pleased her fastidious taste, she gave of her best, lavishly, as she had given to Alwynne. There are women to-day, old girls of the school, who owe Clare Hartill the best things of their lives, their wide knowledge, their original ideals, their hopeful futures and happy memories: to whom she was inspiration incarnate. The Clare they remember is not the Clare that Elsbeth knew, that Alwynne learned to know, that Clare herself, one bitter night, faced and blanched at. But which of them had knowledge of the true Clare, who shall say?

*　　*　　*

Clare was elaborately bored.

'Really, Miss Loveday, the subject does not interest me.'

'It must, for Alwynne's sake. Don't you realize your enormous responsibility? Don't you realize that when you keep Alwynne entangled in your apron strings, blind to other interests, when you cram her with poetry and emotional literature, when you allow her to attach herself passionately to you, you are feeding, and at the same time deflecting from its natural channel, the strongest impulse of her life – of any girl's life? Alwynne needs a good concrete husband to love, not a fantastic ideal that she calls friendship and clothes in your face and figure. You are doing her a deep injury, Miss Hartill – unconsciously, I know, or I should not be here – but doing it, none the less. If you will consider her happiness —'

Clare broke in angrily –

'I do consider her happiness. Alwynne tells you that I am essential to her happiness.'

'She may believe so. But she's not happy. She has not been happy for a long time. But she believes herself to be so, I grant you that. But consider the future. Shall she never break away? Shall she oscillate indefinitely between you and me, spend her whole youth in sustaining two old maids? Oh, Miss Hartill, she must have her chance. We must give her what we've missed ourselves.'

Clare appeared to be occupied in stifling a yawn. Her eyes were danger signals, but Elsbeth was not Alwynne to remark them.

'In one thing, at least, I do thoroughly agree with you. I don't think there is the faintest likelihood of Alwynne's wishing to marry at all at present, but I do feel, with you, that it is unfair to expect her to oscillate, as you rhetorically put it, between two old maids. I agree, too, that I have responsibilities in connection with her. In fact, I think she would be happier if she were with me altogether, and I intend to ask her to come and live here. I shall ask her to-night. Don't you think she will be pleased?'

Clare's aim was good. Elsbeth clutched at the arms of her chair.

'You wouldn't do such a thing?'

Clare laughed shrilly.

'I shall do exactly what your Mr. Lumsden wants to do. I'm not poor.

I can give her a home as well as he, if you are so anxious to get her off your hands. She seems to be going begging.'

Elsbeth rose.

'I'm wasting time. I'll say good-bye, Miss Hartill. I shouldn't have come. But it was for Alwynne's sake. I hoped to touch you, to persuade you to forego, for her future's sake, for the sake of her ultimate happiness, the hold you have on her. I sympathized with you. I knew it would be a sacrifice. I knew, because I made the same sacrifice two years ago, when you first began to attract her. I thought you would develop her. I am not a clever woman, Miss Hartill, and you are; so I made no stand against you; but it was hard for me. Alwynne did not make it easier. She was not always kind. But hearing you to-day, I understand. You made Alwynne suffer more than I guessed. I don't blame her if sometimes it recoiled on me. You were always cruel. I remember you. The others were always snails for you to throw salt upon. I might have known you'd never change. Do you think I don't know your effect on the children at the school? Oh, you are a good teacher! You force them successfully; but all the while you eat up their souls. Sneer if you like! Have you forgotten Louise? I tell you, it's vampirism. And now you are to take Alwynne. And when she is squeezed dry and flung aside, who will the next victim be? And the next, and the next? You grow greedier as you grow older, I suppose. One day you'll be old. What will you do when your glamour's gone? I tell you, Clare Hartill, you'll die of hunger in the end.'

from *The Child Manuela*
CHRISTA WINSLOE (1888–1944)

Although Christa Winsloe's novel, The Child Manuela, *was not published until 1934, it was in fact the basis of* Mädchen in Uniform *(*Schoolgirls in Uniform*), directed by Leontine Sagan in 1931 and one of the most famous of all anti-fascist films. The novel is set in a physically austere and emotionally brutal school for the daughters of high-ranking German officers. This is a 'total' institution, where subordination to the rules of caste and country is* *paramount; the girls are here to learn to be the wives and mothers of yet more officers. The school is credible both as itself and as a brilliantly extended metaphor for the totalitarian military state. To this school comes the motherless Manuela, a thirteen-year-old girl desperate to give and receive love. But Fräulein von Bernburg, the initially sympathetic young teacher who wins Manuela's selfless adoration, is herself too repressed and frightened to be able to accept it. In the passage below, we see how clearly Manuela recognises that her love for her (dead) mother is not the same as her love for Fräulein von Bernburg: here there is to be no safe and comforting pretence that lesbian and maternal loves, though they may sometimes overlap, are the same thing.*

Fräulein von Bernburg got up and went over to her wardrobe. After some searching she found what she was looking for. With a chemise in her hand, she came back to Lela and proffered it.

'The shoulder-straps will have to be taken in a bit; it'll be a little large for you, but you're still growing. . . .'

With both hands Manuela clutched what was given her, holding it to her bosom. Tears of joy welled up in her eyes.

'For me? No, it can't be . . .' she stammered. 'A thousand, thousand thanks! But it's a shame to give it to me. . . .'

Fräulein von Bernburg laughed to see Manuela's delight. She did not make any objection, either, when Manuela seized her hand and kissed it. But when Manuela tried to say something else her voice failed in her throat. Losing all self-control she burst out sobbing, and Fräulein von Bernburg had to support the reeling child in her arms. This kindly action brought down Manuela's last barrier, and Fräulein von Bernburg had to lead her to a chair and set her down on it. Wordlessly she waited until the child should somewhat recover herself.

Lela struggled for composure. Still sobbing and gasping she tried to apologize.

'I really don't know why I'm crying. I'm not really unhappy. Not the least little bit.' And wiping her eyes, in which the tears welled up again and again, she looked timidly up at Fräulein von Bernburg.

'Let the tears flow, child. That won't do you any harm. But, tell me – does this often happen? Are you homesick?'

'Homesick?' repeated Lela in amazement. 'No. . . .'

'And yet you simply do this kind of thing without any reason, all of a sudden. . . .' Fräulein von Bernburg's voice was warm, grave and tender.

'Oh, I don't know why – and just to-day I've been so happy – but sometimes . . .'

Fräulein von Bernburg pulled out a chair beside Manuela's and sat down quite close to her.

'Sometimes?' she prompted gently.

But Manuela could not go on. What she had to say could not be said to *her*, to her above all people. Fräulein von Bernburg waited, and then, somewhat disappointed, remarked:

'Haven't you any confidence in me?'

'I – I do,' stammered Manuela. 'But it's – it's too difficult to say.'

'Will you not try? Not if I tell you that I very, very much want to hear it?'

Lela clung to her hand and gazed at her bosom.

'When I go to bed at night and you shut the door behind you, then I . . . have such a longing for you because you're gone, and I have to keep looking at the door, and then I think: no, I mustn't, and I hold myself down in my bed. . . .'

Fräulein von Bernburg jumped up and turned her back to Manuela, whose eyes followed her.

'You're always so far away, so distant, I can never be close to you and never hold your hand and never kiss you, never get near you. . . .'

'But, my dear – tell me —'

Lela would not let her go on. She had suppressed herself too long. With both arms round the hips of the woman beside her she poured it all out.

'I can't, I can't help it. I love you, darling Fräulein von Bernburg. I love you so much, as much as my mother and ever so much more. Whenever I see your hands I feel drawn to touch them. Your voice when you call my name makes my heart turn over and carries me away – I can't help it, I love you, I love you. . . .'

Now Fräulein von Bernburg energetically seized the child's hands and freed herself. She walked away from her as far as possible, to the very wall, while Lela, panic-stricken over what she had done, followed her with her eyes.

By that time Fräulein von Bernburg had got herself in hand.

'Listen to me, Manuela. I can't have you saying that kind of thing to me. I think you are exaggerating your feelings, without intending to; things can't be as bad as all that. You must pull yourself together. One should be able to control oneself. Do you understand me? Every single person must exercise self-control, Manuela. I do so too!'

Manuela's eyes opened widely. She was too much of a child even to guess how much an admission of that kind cost the woman confronting her. She heard only the reprimand and submitted to it. Trembling and with a final sob she gave her promise.

'Yes, Fräulein von Bernburg.'

'And now there's something I must say to you, and you must take it sensibly.'

Her voice sounded gentler, and she again approached the child.

'I am very fond of you, Manuela, but all the same I cannot pay more attention to you than to the others; you know that, of course. Still, if ever you are in trouble you can always come to me.'

Gently she took Lela's head in her hands and tilted the girl's chin so that they looked in each other's eyes.

'Are you content now?'

'Thank you, a thousand thanks!' and once more Lela shyly and reverently kissed the beloved hand, that beautiful hand whose fragrance reminded her of lavender and of her mother.

from *The Chinese Garden* (1962)
ROSEMARY MANNING (1911–1988)

Rosemary Manning was best known to most people as the author of the extremely successful 'Green dragon' books for children. But she also wrote a number of distinguished novels for adults, and, in 1971, under the pseudonym 'Sarah Davys' and the title A Time and a Time, *she published an autobiographical account of a lesbian relationship whose failure culminated in a freakishly unsuccessful suicide attempt.*

Later, in 1980, and to my great pleasure, she 'came out' as a lesbian on a programme in L W T*'s* Gay Life *series which I was then presenting. Coming out at seventy was no small step for the ex-headmistress of a successful Hampstead preparatory school.*

Her heavily autobiographical novel, The Chinese Garden, *was set in Bampfield, a girls' boarding school, during 1928, the year in which Radclyffe Hall's* The Well of Loneliness *was published, prosecuted and banned for its unequivocal championing of lesbianism. Hall's book and its prosecution cast their shadow over those of the staff and pupils who have most reason to lament its fate. In this extract, Rachel Curgenven looks back to her last year at the school and recalls the sexually ambiguous triumvirate of mistresses who ruled it.*

Dictator though Chief was, the other two members of the triumvirate which fenced us from the world were more than mere lackeys. Each of them possessed a character of iron, which, joined by the rigid band of a common and apparently uncriticized ideal, dictated the shape of our youth.

The School was called Bampfield Girls' College. I think Miss Faulkner would have liked to call it Bampfield Ladies' College, since Cheltenham was one of her working models, but she hesitated at the plagiarism, and later even the 'Girls' was dropped. The reason for this was, I believe, that she had come by this time to regard us all as boys and did not wish to be reminded of the biological facts.

To Miss Murrill and to the members of the triumvirate, Chief was known as Dick, a tribute, I presume, to her masculinity. The second member of this trio, Mrs Watson, despite the evidence of a daughter, might also have been taken for a man, except that her rotund figure precluded all possibility of her wearing trousers. She, like Chief, wore her hair cropped, but her masculinity had nothing of sex about it. She was a grand old woman and a ripe eccentric. Her humour was, for a girls' school, somewhat Rabelaisian, her temper execrable, and her language of doubtful propriety, but there was about her an inalienable air of good breeding. She came of an ancient and cultured family, and showed it, despite the cropped hair, the sagging tweed skirts and the grubby habits (her room smelt abominably). She was known to her intimates as Punch, and the name fitted her exactly.

Her loyalty to Chief was incorruptible. Her keen intelligence and sceptical, inquiring mind could have made her critical, and I knew, later

on, that she never hesitated to argue with Chief, or present to her plainly
her own views on a situation, but publicly she gave not the slightest
indication that even the most monstrous pronouncements, the most
impracticable suggestions, on Chief's part, were alien to her own way
of thinking, and she supported them not merely with good humour but
with a personal bias which seemed to proclaim them reasonable. I have
never discovered the springhead of this devotion. Punch was condemned
to discomfort, for she lived in one of the most disagreeable, though
picturesque, corners of the house; she drew no salary and had devoted
a substantial portion of her capital to the school; and her work was a
mere dismal round of teaching in a school where the standard of scholar-
ship was low, and book-learning played a subordinate part to character
forming. Scripture must be taught, and Geography must appear on the
time-table. Punch took both, doling out to us the needful portions of
each, much as though it were a matter of brimstone and treacle. She
was only diverted – and diverting – when drawn into the bypaths of
knowledge. It became a matter of tactics to trail red herrings across her
path, and she relished the game hugely, casting aside with relief the
annotated edition of Genesis, or the out-of-date atlas, and embarking
on a detailed explanation of the eugenics of the ring-straked and spotted
cattle, or the supposed location of the land of the anthropophagi whose
heads do grow beneath their shoulders.

Punch's rooms were at the top of the house in the Tudor wing of
the building, and approached either by the old turret staircase, or from
the passages which ran right round the top of the school. Off these
passages lay twenty or twenty-five rooms, mostly very small. Some of
them were allotted to the junior staff, two or three to the prefects for
studies, while the larger ones were used as dormitories. They were
bitterly cold in winter and insufferably hot in summer, but they had a
magnificent view, and outside them was a stone parapet which was the
delight of daring spirits. Punch was too indolent and too absorbed in
her books to pay much attention to the children in these dormitories,
technically under her care and in her 'house'. They were notoriously
ill-behaved, and the lives of the prefects whose studies were near by
were made a misery by their lawlessness.

Punch's rooms were themselves of unbelievable squalor. In front of the small rusty grate lay a black and red rag hearth-rug, thick with crumbs and hair and coal-dust. In my early days, a dog repellent with age, rheumy of eye and for the most part hairless, lived on this mat. Later he was replaced by a corpulent dachshund whom Punch took everywhere with her at the end of a lead at least ten feet long, fixed to her waistband. With this creature she could be seen from afar off in park and pleasure gardens, a vast rolling barrel of a woman, with a small, fourlegged bottle-shaped dog panting along at a distance of ten feet, the two joined by what appeared to be an umbilical cord.

On the far side of her rooms were the domestic quarters, which ran along one side of the house and were sealed off from the studies and upper dormitories by a locked door. Men and maid servants slept in these tiny attic rooms, an arrangement which the presence of Punch was supposed to regularize. Once, I saw the rooms, I have no idea why. Perhaps it was after the end of term when I had stayed on for a few days. I remember I walked the length of that corridor from the prefects' studies to Punch's quarters. Below me were the noble wrought-iron gates of Chief's private garden, the green turf, the flower-beds a blaze of colour, and the dark yew hedge bordering its brightness. I turned from these windows to look into the rooms, for the doors were open, and I was so sickened that I could hardly refrain from running down that corridor. In those little airless garrets was the most piggish squalor I had ever seen. Beds were unmade, chamber-pots unemptied, chests of drawers lurched sideways, lacking a leg, or hung half open to reveal a few discoloured clothes, and there emanated from those wretched cells, and from the unspeakable lavatory, a smell I shall never forget. Who knew of it? No one. Not even Punch, living within a few yards of that smell, thought it worth while to make those rooms more habitable.

The servants at Bampfield frightened me. They were brutish, but I did not at the time draw the necessary conclusions from what I saw that afternoon. I was only the more disgusted and fearful. One of the servants was an old woman called Bessie who was often to be found lurking in dark corners of the back stairs, and who was, I think, a natural. She spoke an unintelligible Somerset, in which the elisions 'ch'ill' and 'ch'ave' were common and almost the only distinguishable features of her barbaric speech. The servants were no one's responsibility. Their squalor was part of the corruption which festered underneath the smooth Palladian skin of Bampfield. It was one of the many contradictions of the place that Punch, who certainly must have known of that evil corridor, remained indifferent to it, and to the sordid discomforts of her own rooms, and yet displayed in her own person, despite the shabby evidence of her clothes, a fastidiousness, and in her bearing a quality which fitted with absolute harmony into the cultivated home she shared with her sister. I never knew her well enough to find the solution to this contradiction. I leave her in the picture as I saw her for six years, keen-eyed, weather-beaten, good-humoured yet irascible, with a face like one of Rembrandt's women, as wrinkled as a stored apple.

Miss Gerrard, the third member of the triumvirate, was a tall, severe, fine-looking woman, a 'handsome' woman, with blue eyes of the most piercing quality I have ever seen. Her hair was a golden-brown, rather stiff – almost *en brosse* – but at least it was not an Eton crop, and indeed she was not masculine. But neither was she truly feminine. She looked a woman, but somehow every ounce of femininity had been drained out of her and left her a splendid shell, animated by a fierce devotion to work and duty. I never knew her well. Some children were fond of her, but most of us feared her too much for affection. She left when I was about fourteen, and I never saw her again. I have often wondered why she went, and suspect (with no grounds whatever) that there was in her adamant nature a righteousness and high principle which could not in the end countenance the regime for which she was expected to work. We called her the Rock, and she was one of the very few women at Bampfield for whom I felt and still feel an honest respect.

When Miss Gerrard left, her place in the triumvirate was taken by Miss Murrill. She was mildly attractive, with curly hair and a small neat figure. She was lively, and, when in good humour, very charming. When I arrived at Bampfield she was not more than twenty-seven and engaged at the time in a fervent love affair with a local man, of which she later told me some most unsuitable details. Even after her affair came to nothing, she made some effort to retain her femininity. She never got as far as make-up, but she sometimes wore frocks. In keeping with the masculine principle of the place, Chief had christened her Georgie, her Christian name being Georgina.

Mrs Watson, Miss Gerrard and Miss Murrill were housemistresses. I knew only one of them, therefore, at all well, my contract with the other two being limited to the classroom. Though we all lived under one roof, different parts of the building were sacred to different houses; there were house colours and house mascots, and separate dining-rooms. The combined influence of the triumvirate was weaker, therefore, because it was diffused. It reached us in small draughts, in the history lesson, or the house match. Chief's influence, however, reached us wherever we were. Though she seldom met us in the classroom, dormitory or games field, she was present in those places where we were most vulnerable - the chapel and big hall – and she wandered the passages ceaselessly, so that we were always aware of her physical presence. She was not spying on us. It would be unfair to suggest this. She had a beautiful and melodious whistle and this she used as she walked the corridors, to warn us of her coming. She once told me that she had deliberately cultivated the art of whistling for this purpose. Because of this, I do not think I ever feared her as a remote, God-of-vengeance figure. I *did* fear her, but my fear was something far more subtle. I feared the idea of headship, the immanent power of which she was a manifestation. With her actual presence I was often on the best of terms. Yet I knew always that no matter how good-humouredly she fell in with my wildest schemes, no matter how flattering her warm interest in anything I wrote, I was subject to her pervasive will, by a process I was half-conscious of, yet incapable of rebelling against, for a part of my nature enjoyed and was gratified by it. If I am honest, I must admit that many children passed through Bampfield unscathed. If I was one of those who suffered, then it was, at least partly, my own fault, in that there was much that nourished the less creditable sides of my nature, and which I imbibed willingly.

The key figure to this aspect of my youth was Georgie Murrill. There was never a more untrue cliché than that which says we needs must love the highest when we see it. Not only did I like and enjoy the wrong things. I liked, and even loved, the wrong people. For Miss Burnett, to whom I owe so much of what has made life worth living, I felt no personal affection at all. I place on record now a belated tribute to her and to all she gave my adolescent mind. It does not matter to me that she was a failure personally. As far as I am concerned, she was a success, and in trying to discover the sources of my imaginative life, and the roots from which grew my mature self, I am inevitably led to Miss Burnett. Chief was less an influence than an atmosphere in which I breathed. It had certain virtues. It made me resistant to some things, but more prone to others, but I dare say this would have happened wherever I had been educated. My mind and heart were driven to find their nourishment in books and in my evocative and strange surroundings, by the rigid discipline of the school and the physical hardships imposed on us, and by the stifling atmosphere with which Chief surrounded us. I think I was fortunate that Bampfield gave me so much, even if in this negative manner. It furnished me, all unknowing, with a weapon which I was later able to turn against the worst elements it had encouraged in me. At another school I might have been 'made to pattern' and remained so, with no rebel vision to tear away the falsity. Other schools might have had no Chief, and no Miss Burnett. They would, I fear, have had plenty of Georgie Murrills. One was enough.

This young housemistress was addicted to mascots, hockey matches, nineteenth-century history and early Beethoven. It is difficult to resist the charm of such things when one is young, and many people, who have had too many Georgie Murrills in their lives, never grow out of such addictions. To all of them she succeeded in enlisting my devotion, with the exception of the hockey matches. I have nothing against the other three enthusiasms, but they can hardly be said to lead one on to maturity.

She also succeeded in enlisting my personal devotion, as no one else did at Bampfield, and this was an entirely limiting and wasteful experience. It is not possible for an adult to attempt to pull a child into her own adult world, and this is what Georgie Murrill attempted. She treated me as a confederate, elevated me to the position of a confidante and personal assistant in matters relating to the house of which I was later to be captain. She was incapable of seeing me as a child and a rather immature one. She played upon the arrogant side of my nature, allowing me to believe myself a far more grown-up and privileged person than I actually was. Put, as I thought, upon an equality with her, I took the same liberties, and made the same demands which I should have made of my contemporaries. It was unfortunate that I had no contemporaries for whom I cared anything. Bisto was soon to leave and Margaret was inaccessible. I learned to despise my fellow prefects when I became one – blown up by Georgie with self-esteem, and set apart from them in any case by my university work.

Chief, whatever her faults may have been, did not make the mistake of favouring me above my fellows. She encouraged and praised my writing, but she judged my character ruthlessly. She told me bluntly, when she had seen how I behaved as a prefect, that she would never make me head of the school, and she told me why. 'You have not learned to suffer fools gladly,' she said. 'Moreover, you are not reliable enough to be in such a position. Plainly, I do not trust you, completely.'

I was hurt, but she was right. Georgie Murrill, instead of supporting Chief in her verdict, undermined it, allowing me to recover with her the worthless and inflated self-esteem which Chief had refused me. I wish to be just to Chief, aware that I have ridiculed and criticized her. But I find it hard to be just to Georgie Murrill who took so much and gave so little, who sucked the life out of her favourites, but was herself too small and limited a personality to make such an operation in the least worth while to her victims. It is a truism that out of our most wretched and humiliating experiences there is usually something to be gained. I think Daniel might agree that the walk through the fiery furnace was worth the meeting with the three holy children. I am not going to shed tears because I spent my schooldays in a place where many of the staff were morally corrupt, the physical standards those of Dartmoor, the religion perverted and the games mistress a sadist. It looks a formidable list, but children will always be subjected to something. I was not beaten, as I had been at my previous school, by a gang of bullies. I was not underfed. I was not entirely ill-educated. But I find it necessary to place on record that Georgie Murrill, the least valuable in personality, the most trivial in mind, procured my affection and exploited it for her own ends. The full measure of her turpitude will be seen later, when her cowardly desire to appear on the side of the angels led her to jettison the child she should have protected. I think it is for the Georgie Murrills of this world that the millstones are reserved.

'At my new school'
C. M. DONALD

At my new school (I took
exams to get there, you know)
the headmistress is thin, dark,
and rather exciting.
                   She teaches
us geography, which she leaves
somewhat colourless, and she wields
power without sympathy.
                     They say

she is a lesbian. Her stockings
have seams up the back which
are always straight.
                   I was only
average at geography, but I knew
one day she would call me namelessly
into her study and tell me
something of overwhelming significance
that bonded us.
                   Unfortunately,
she omitted to do this.

Of Women's Gardens

Women and gardens (and the occasional serpent) have enjoyed a long association down the ages. Art and literature constantly place women in gardens and see them as gardens. Different periods produce intricate languages of flowers, whereby a posy chosen with sufficient care may speak whole volumes. Lesbian writing, too, has developed its own conventions concerning women, gardens, and what may be found in them. Many of the traditional associations – women as source and symbol of fruitfulness; goddesses as overseers of the seasons; gardens as symbolic landscapes of desire and loss – will be found here, always with a subtle tilt of perspective.

One of the critics of Ancient Greece said that 'Sappho's verses are few – and all roses'. On one level he meant simply that although the body of work was small, each poem in it was as perfect as a rose. On another level he was probably punning: the Greek word usually translated as rose can also signify the female genitals. Sappho's poems are roses twice over: perfect, and often expressive of sexual love between women.

You will find several roses in this section, appearing as talismans, gifts and symbols. In late nineteenth- and early twentieth-century writing by homosexual men and women, roses, especially wild ones, often take on a special, coded meaning: the wild rose represents homosexual love, the outlawed outsider, expelled or escaped from the ordered, tended 'garden' of conventional, heterosexual desire.

One Girl (1870)
(*a combination from Sappho*)
DANTE GABRIEL ROSSETTI (1828–1882)

Rossetti here has taken two of Sappho's scattered fragments and made one poem of them.

I

Like the sweet apple which reddens upon the topmost bough,
A-top on the top-most twig, – which the pluckers forgot,
   somehow, –
Forgot it not, nay, but got it not, for none could get it till now.

II

Like the wild hyacinth flower which on the hills is found,
Which the passing feet of the shepherds for ever tear and wound,
Until the purple blossom is trodden into the ground.

To Vernon Lee
AMY LEVY (1861–1889)

Amy Levy's poem (published in 1889) seems to play on a poetic code according to which the colour white stands for purity, celibacy or repression, and the colour red for impurity, desire and passion consummated. The exchange of flowers between the two women can nevertheless be read in strikingly different ways. Which woman is 'pure' and which 'impure'? What does it mean that the white flower is out of reach for one woman but not for the other? Is each woman to be 'read' according to the flower she gives, or the flower she receives? And what is the connection between the flowers (given and received) and the gifts of the gods, Hope and Despair?

For another poem by Amy Levy probably written to and about Vernon Lee, see 'To Lallie' in the earlier section of this book entitled 'Just Friends?'

On Bellosguardo, when the year was young,
We wandered, seeking for the daffodil
And dark anemone, whose purples fill
The peasant's plot, between the corn-shoots sprung.

Over the grey, low wall the olive flung
Her deeper greyness; far off, hill on hill
Sloped to the sky, which, pearly-pale and still,
Above the large and luminous landscape hung.

A snowy blackthorn flowered beyond my reach;
You broke a branch and gave it to me there;
I found for you a scarlet blossom rare.

Thereby ran on of Art and Life our speech;
And of the gifts the gods had given to each –
Hope unto you, and unto me Despair.

Rosa Rosarum
A. MARY F. ROBINSON (1857–1944)

This poem was probably written for Vernon Lee, like the one by Amy Levy which precedes it. Mary Robinson had already dedicated a volume of poems, A Handful of Honeysuckle (1878) to Lee, a collection which bears witness to the intense friendship between the two women. The title of this poem, 'Rosa Rosarum', ('rose of roses', a phrase sometimes associated with the Virgin Mary), may refer both to Lee herself and to the love the two women shared. Sappho's pagan roses are not far away, despite the presence of the 'convent-close'. Unlike the Levy poem, where the opposed meanings of red and white flowers are in conflict, we have here but the one red rose, an unambiguously sexual token. Unambiguous, but still problematic, since the

love it betokens is dangerous to reveal. Only when it — and the women? —
are dead can the poet be sure that 'never more the rose shall rise / To shame
us'.

Give me, O friend, the secret of thy heart
   Safe in my breast to hide,
So that the leagues which keep our lives apart
   May not ever our souls divide.

Give me the secrets of thy life to lay
   Asleep within my own,
Nor dream that it shall mock thee any day
   By any sign or tone.

Nay, as in walking through some convent-close,
   Passing beside a well,
Oft have we thrown a red and scented rose
   To watch it as it fell;

Knowing that never more the rose shall rise
   To shame us, being dead;
Watching it spin and dwindle till it lies
   At rest, a speck of red —

Thus, I beseech thee, down the silent deep
   And darkness of my heart,
Cast thou a rose; give me a rose to keep,
   My friend, before we part.

For, as thou passest down the garden-ways,
   Many a blossom there
Groweth for thee: lilies and laden bays,
   And rose and lavender.

But down the darkling well one only rose
  In all the year is shed;
And o'er that chill and secret wave it throws
  A sudden dawn of red.

On a Torso of Cupid (1895)
MATHILDE BLIND (1841–1896)

*In this poem, the statue of a classical god of love, though male, symbolises
and embodies the fallen fortunes of same-sex love (including love between
women) in late nineteenth-century England. The statue is mutilated, lost,
ignored, neglected, a mere fragment of a once-proud tradition. The garden
offers it a place of safe concealment until it and the love it represents reclaim
their power, as Blind urges them to do. This poem was written in the
heyday of English Decadence; appropriately, Arthur Symons, England's
arch-decadent poet, edited Blind's work posthumously.*

*Child of a Jewish father, stepdaughter of a German revolutionary leader
forced to flee with his family to England, Mathilde Blind worked for many
political movements, including campaigns for women's education and crofters'
land rights.*

Peach trees and Judas trees,
  Poppies and roses,
Purple anemones
  In garden closes!
Lost in the limpid sky,
Shrills a gay lark on high;
Lost in the covert's hush,
Gurgles a wooing thrush.

Look, where the ivy weaves,
    Closely embracing,
Tendrils of clinging leaves
    Round him enlacing,
With Nature's sacredness
Clothing the nakedness,
Clothing the marble of
This poor, dismembered love.

Gone are the hands whose skill
    Aimed the light arrow,
Strong once to cure or kill,
    Pierce to the marrow;
Gone are the lips whose kiss
Held hives of honeyed bliss;
Gone too the little feet,
Overfond, overfleet.

O helpless god of old,
    Maimed mid the tender
Blossoming white and gold
    Of April splendour!
Shall we not make thy grave
Where the long grasses wave;
Hide thee, O headless god,
Deep in the daisied sod?

Here thou mayst rest at last
    After life's fever;
After love's fret is past
    Rest thee for ever.
Nay, broken God of Love,
Still must thou bide above
While left for woe or weal
Thou hast a heart to feel.

I will now sing a short song
comparing my lover's
clitons to a pearl, and her
labia to a persimmon fruit
and her vagina to a vanilla
pod because quite frankly
that's the only way
I can cope with it all

by Jo Nesbitt

Pomegranates
'MICHAEL FIELD'

*In this poem (posthumously published in 1936), the myth of Proserpine
(Persephone) is used to represent the dying down and away of sexual desire
in one partner when serious illness, possibly fatal, strikes. (The Michael
Fields' conversion to Roman Catholicism, and the required relinquishing of
fleshly sins may also be at work here.) The pomegranates ('love apples')
represent desire and the rejection of it ('I do not want / The pomegranate').
Desire has its seasons: Spring, when desire, and the natural world, are young
and vital; Winter, when nature, and sometimes desire, seem dead. But, for
both the world and the beloved, new life and new longing are possible.*

Proserpine, Proserpine,
   Give us of lovely stems,
Give us your fruit –
We with pomegranates will crown our bowers,
   So feel the flowers,
   So fails desire –
So your fruit is ruddy as a fire.

Winter again, how quick,
   Comes! and my loved is sick:
   'Proserpine'.
Shuddering she pleads 'I do not want
   The pomegranate' –
   Desire in tears
Claims an eternity of love and years.

O Love, thy voice! . . . My breath
Warm on thee startles Death.
   Mythology
Shrivels as a ghost, beholding me

My lips, O Sweet,
 To thine the heat,
Stir of coals, immortal cherishing!

Nov. 8th, 1911

To the Winter Aphrodite
'MICHAEL FIELD'

*Here, as in 'Pomegranates', the death of love and desire is linked with the
passing of the seasons.*

O Winter Aphrodite! (O acute,
Ice-eating pains, thine arrows!) shivering
By thy cold altar-stones, to thee I bring
Thy myrtle with its Erebus-black fruit,
Locked up, provocative, profoundly mute,
Muter than snow or any melting thing,
Muter than fall'n winds, or bird's dead wing,
Secret as music of a fresh-struck lute
Laid by a little while and yet for aye –
By all that jealously thou dost enwomb,
By Sappho's words hid of thee in a tomb,
Pondered of thee where no man passeth by,
Use thou my heart awhile for Love's own room,
O Winter Aphrodite, ere I die!

But if our love be dying let it die
As the rose shedding secretly,
Or as a noble music's pause:
Let it move rhythmic as the laws
Of the sea's ebb, or the sun's ritual
When sovereignly he dies:
Then let a mourner rise and three times call
Upon our love, and the long echoes fall.

The Strawberry Plant
RUTH PITTER (1897–1992)

There seem to be links here between Sappho's perfect but unreachable 'apple'
and Ruth Pitter's strawberry.

Above the water, in her rocky niche,
She sat enthroned and perfect; for her crown
One bud like pearl, and then two fairy roses
Blanched and yet ardent in their glowing hearts:
One greenish berry spangling into yellow
Where the light touched the seed: one fruit achieved
And ripe, an odorous vermilion ball
Tight with completion, lovingly enclasped
By the close cup whose green chimed with the red,
And showered with drops of gold like Danaë:
Three lovely sister leaves as like as peas,
Young but full-fledged, dark, with a little down:
Two leaves that to a matron hue inclined;
And one the matriarch, that dressed in gold
And flushed with wine, thought her last days her best.
And here and there a diamond of dew
Beamed coolly from the white, smiled from the gold,
Silvered the down, struck lightning from the red.
The overhanging rock forbade the sun,
Yet was she all alight with water-gleams
Reflected, like the footlights at a play:
Perfection's self, and (rightly) out of reach.

from *The Chinese Garden* (1962)
ROSEMARY MANNING (1911–1988)

We have already encountered Bampfield, the repressive and corrupted girls'
school, earlier in this book, in the section entitled 'Lessons for Life'. Ugly
though much of Bampfield is, it holds an unexpected beauty at its heart. In
the park that surrounds it lies the all but hidden and forgotten Chinese Garden,
now derelict, still lovely. It is perfect but vulnerable, strange, beautiful, utterly
artificial. This garden is both a real place and a symbolic landscape through
which the young Rachel Curgenven begins at last to be able to articulate
hitherto dimly perceived truths about her own emotions and sexuality.

Chapter Ten

Meanwhile the mind, for pleasure less
Withdraws into its happiness;
The mind, that recess where each kind
Doth straight its own resemblance find.
Yet it creates, transcending these
Far other worlds and other seas.   Andrew Marvell

The fragile coat of rime stiffened over the long grass. Ice appeared in
the sluggish meanderings of the stream. The whole envelope of atmosphere in which Bampfield lay embalmed suddenly clarified, and contours
of the hills sharpened at the edges. It could now be seen that Moses was
several trees, not one. The smoke from the home farm chimneys drifted
up against the sallow green of the hill, and sounds became crystalline,
stones dropped into a well: the high-pitched creak of a cart, a dog
barking in distant cottages, and the birdlike notes of the church clock
were carried through the resonant, frosty air into the windows of the
school.

Rachel's perceptions became sharper, tauter, more distinct. The
elements of the life she was living separated into recognizable patterns,
like pictures of frost on glass. All that was distasteful to her at Bampfield
assumed palpable outlines. She could no longer accept their once-soft,

once-blurred contours. All that she loved and felt particular to herself, receded, diminished, behind a wall of glass, and she felt it beyond her reach. Bampfield, the real Bampfield, forced itself upon her senses – a place of dank, ill-smelling corridors, of fetid little corners where girls whispered, a place where cruelty dwelt under the guise of discipline, and corruption beneath a mask of beauty and moral tone. She felt herself trapped like a bird in its icy reality, involved inevitably in the decay, the corruption, the loathsomeness beneath the fine, glassy surface. It was no longer possible to extract from it the different essences, the pleasures, stupidities, horrors, humours, and turn upon each a separate personality. All were, with herself, embalmed in a frigid, transparent pattern.

No more parodies came from her pen. Life did not seem laughable any more and she was too immature for satire. She spent most of her time in the library, where the imposition of silence made it unnecessary to speak to others. Her creative urge was over, spent in the translation of Virgil. That inner world of pleasure was sealed off for her. Fortunately, work for University entrance gave Rachel a special time-table which often involved working at different hours from her fellows, and she was relieved to get away from the form-room, from the distraction of twenty other living minds, and to walk alone through the building, past closed doors, behind which tired and reddened faces pored over exercise books. She was even able on occasions to miss games for coaching and get out for solitary walks in the park or gardens when others were still in class.

It was on one of these occasions, during bright and frosty weather, that she decided to discover for herself what it was that Margaret had found and never communicated. She might have done this before but for an enlarged sense of honour, which prevented her from intruding upon another's secret world. And always she had hoped that Margaret herself would tell her but she had never done so. She purloined the pliers from one of the gardeners' sheds and walked down the lime avenue towards the deserted stables till she was out of sight of the house. Then she turned across the stream by its lowest bridge and back to the shrubbery on the far side. There was no one about. The frosty rushes creaked under her shoes. She found the place where Margaret entered, and, to salve her conscience, selected another part of the palings, several yards away. It took her some time to get the wire cut and the palings out. She was not so practical as Margaret. At last it was done and she climbed through into dense undergrowth. She was in a thicket of overgrown shrubs, azalea and rhododendron mostly, their tough twisted trunks meshed in bramble and nettle. Through this she pushed her way with some difficulty, drawn towards the centre of the plantation only by her sense of direction. Shiny boughs of laurel brushed a green wound over her sleeve. For a moment she hesitated, pulled up by the world of school, in which stained or torn clothes must be explained, absences justified. Then an obstinate desire to force her way into the heart of the place gave her impetus, and thrusting aside the brown stringy creepers, she pushed on through the undergrowth.

She emerged into a strange, secret world, a clear blue sky above, willows, a lake, a coloured pagoda, and a tiny bridge – the world of a willow-pattern plate.

The park stream ran right through the centre of the large plantation, and in the heart of it had been created two pools big enough to sail a boat on, and indeed the poor relic of a punt still lay rotting in the boathouse. The pools lay close together and the stream that joined them had been divided into two courses, making a tiny, almost circular island between the lakes. Here stood a summerhouse, built like a Chinese pagoda, and reached by two bridges, one over each stream, highly ornamented in the oriental style so that the whole scene, viewed from the point where she stood, possessed the formal beauty of a Chinese plate, its rim the fringe of trees around the still, shallow pools.

Rachel crossed a creaking, dilapidated bridge, and went into the tiny pagoda. Bells were still hanging under the painted eaves, their copper green with age, shrill and fragile when she touched them with her hand. It was inhabited only by spiders. The floorboards were rotten, and covered with bird droppings, and the once bright paint was blistered and faded. The quiet pools, greened over with weed, never-disturbed, the dense overgrown shrubbery which hedged it from the world without, the incongruous oriental appearance of the pagoda and its bridges, created an indescribable air of secrecy and strangeness. She entered an exotic world where she breathed pure poetry. It had the symmetry of Blake's tiger. It was the green thought in a green shade.

She wandered slowly about, mapping it out in her mind. Its dereliction did not distress her. She was used to decay and ruin. The Chinese garden still offered, in its broken bridges and peeling cupola, the symbols of a precise pattern, a perfection greater than itself. Its complex image held within it a world of images, unfolding to the heart unending sequences of dream. Rachel realized now why Margaret, after visiting the garden again, had no wish to bring anyone else into it. To do so would be to reduce it to the status of a playground. It was not that. Entering it, one shed one's reality and partook of its charmed atmosphere, like the hero of a fairy tale who, on reaching the enchanted palace, hears music from the air, and from cups presented by invisible hands, drinks a paradisal wine.

A few days later, term ended. Reluctantly I went home. Home with its passions, its poverty, its wall of misunderstanding between parents and children, brothers and sisters, made more impenetrable by the blood which cemented it — home was a place that I dreaded. The countryside around it furnished a certain measure of escape, but it was not an invariable comfort to me. It lacked the familiarity of Bampfield and its clearly defined limits. In the countryside around my home I was adrift. I wandered and came up against no familiar fencing. One might, I felt at times as I walked alone through the hazel copses, one might walk for ever and out of the world. There was too weak a centrifugal force to hold me to the hub of this universe. Thus my walks at home, lacking security, lacking a sense of possession, were always a faint source of fear. I was compelled to take them, yet I half hated them. They were the wrong sort of solitude, a solitude imposed rather than a solitude sought. I did not withdraw, as I did at Bampfield, into a secret world. I ran out into a desert to escape from home, and explored the unfamiliar with a kind of desperate hope that I would find in it something that would reassure me. When the end of the holidays came, I returned to Bampfield with a readiness that grieved my parents.

Travelling down in the train through the well-known landscape, now sodden with January rain, viewing the sheets of flood water over the Somersetshire meadows, I drew towards me the picture of Bampfield, its features, its touch, its smell, as if I were pulling towards me, by the hand, some loved and familiar figure. Resting serenely in my mind was the image of the Chinese garden. The disgust and tedium I had felt at the end of the previous term had been exorcised by absence. At the heart of Bampfield lay a world private to myself, and one which was so powerfully present to my thoughts that I did not need to visit it at once. It shed its enchanted light over those aspects of school for which I had recently felt so much detestation, and I found myself accepting again the life I had temporarily lost.

Spring Landscape from a Train (1985)
GILLIAN SPRAGGS

The train's percussion overrides my thoughts.
Steep banks abrade my eyes, then slip away;
the vista opens on a sunbright land.
A field of rough grass wakes to the wind's combing.
Behind a stand of trees a hidden pool
glints and is lost.
And now the hills close in
with curves that stir a pit behind the ribs.
My hand
tingles to explore a wooded cleft
and touch the landscape into ecstasy.
(Prickle of leafless twigs against my palm,
the earth opens smoothly for my fingers.)
And once
the trembling subsides,
and the hills resume their old familiar shapes,
I should like to lay my cheek
against a sun-warmed mound,
breathe its sharp scents,
and sleep.

Glimpses

Sometimes we have so little information about an author, a piece of writing, an historical episode, that we can only speculate. What is going on in the work; what was happening in the lives of authors or their characters? This section brings together a number of 'glimpses' into fragmented pasts. Sometimes the work is literally a fragment, as with the little alba or 'dawn song'. Sometimes the lives are ripped from their larger context and we know only the small piece that lies before us, as with the desolate set of family circumstances which Charles Ricketts records, or with the poignant episode recounted by a survivor of the concentration camp at Ravensbrück. More cheeringly, we see persistent traces of women happily loving women (as in Tom Wakefield's 'willdews' and Marie Maitland's litany of female lovers), even if they do so in hostile or uncomprehending times.

from a Maiden Chorus
'I sing the light of Agido'
ALCMAN (*fl.* 630 BC)

Gillian Spraggs, who has translated these verses, adds this note:

This fragment is part of a choral text written by a male poet for a choir of Spartan girls. Alcman flourished in the seventh century BC, in the generation before Sappho. The surviving fragments of his maiden choruses combine with other evidence (notably Plutarch's account of early Spartan culture in his *Life of Lycurgus*) to suggest a society in which female homoeroticism played a recognised and public part.

The interpretation of this fragment is fraught with difficulties; but the central situation is fairly clear. In the dawn of a festival day, a choir of girls sing a choral song as a musical offering to a goddess, the Lady of the Dawn. As part of their offering they present an object, possibly a plough, but more plausibly a robe. Meanwhile, their song includes several strophes in which the singers comment on the personal characteristics of their leaders: the sun-like Agido, and Hagesichora, who is not quite so beautiful, but who is exceptional in other ways. The name Hagesichora means chorus leader, and may be a title rather than a personal name. The girls (singing as though they were one person, which is a standard convention for choruses) say among other things that Hagesichora makes [them] weak, a phrase that can have sexual connotations.

The singers may have been members of a *thiasos*, or women's religious association, and were probably part of an initiation group. There are obvious parallels to the female-centred, homoerotic culture glimpsed in the fragments of Sappho. It has even been suggested that the occasion for which the chorus was written was the formal recognition within the *thiasos*, of a sexual bonding between two of its members, Agido and Hagesichora.

I sing the light of Agido:
I see her as the sun,
the sun that Agido invokes
to shine for us and testify.
But she who leads our choir
that famous one
she will not let me praise or fault
Agido in the least degree.
She seems herself to be
outstanding, as if someone put
among the herds a champion horse,
sturdy, with ringing hooves,
and bred from fleeting dreams.

Do you not see? The horse
is of a swift Italian strain.
The flowing mane of my cousin
blooms like the purest gold.
And the light that silvers her face
how can I tell you about it?
Such is Hagesichora.
She, who comes second in looks
only to Agido, will run
like a Scythian horse in a race,
pacing a horse from Lydia.
This night belongs to the gods;
as we carry the robe, the Pleiades
rise in the dawn to compete with us,
bright as the Dog Star.

No aid to us in the contest
is our wealth of crimson cloth,
nor a jewelled snake-bracelet,
a Lydian cap
(that treasure of soft-eyed girls);
not Nanno's hair, nor even Areta,
a goddess in looks;
not Sylacis and Cleïsisera.
Nor shall you go to Aenesimbrota's house,
and say, I wish Astaphis were mine;
that Philylla would look my way,
and Damareta, and lovely Vianthemis;
but Hagesichora makes me weak.

For she of the lovely ankles,
Hagesichora, is she not beside me,
and standing next to Agido
to praise with her our festival?
O gods, look kindly on our prayers.
For only the gods control
what will be in the end.
You who instruct the choir,
there is something I want to say,
but girl as I am, like an owl in the roof
I have only made pointless noise.
But she whom I long most to please
is the Lady of the Dawn,
for she has been our healer in our labours.
And Hagesichora is the means
by which the girls have come
to the peace that they've desired.
[. . .]

Dreaming of other women

from *The Interpretation of Dreams*
[*Oneirocritica*]
Artemidorus
(late second century AD)

If a woman dreams that she possesses another woman, she will share her secrets with the woman she has possessed. But if she is not familiar with the woman whom she possesses, she will attempt futile projects. But if a woman dreams that she is being possessed by another woman, she will be divorced from her husband or become a widow. She will learn, besides, the secrets of the woman with whom she has had sexual intercourse.

Translated by Gillian Spraggs

'All the birds are singing'
Anon., from an eleventh-century
manuscript

This is the first verse of a little mediaeval alba *(a dawn-poem, spoken by lovers when the night they have shared is over and they must part). It has long puzzled scholars and critics. Some argue that it makes best sense if it is read as spoken by a woman lover saying farewell to a female beloved. 'Amica cara' is the female form of 'dear friend' — if addressed to a man, it would have to read 'Amice care'.*

Cantant omnes volucres
iam lucescit dies.
Amica cara, surga sine me
per portas exire.

All the birds are singing,
already the day is growing light.
Dear friend, rise up without me
and go out through the gates.

'As phoebus in his spheris hicht'
[As Phoebus in his high spheres]
Anon., possibly by Marie Maitland

We do not know for certain who wrote this remarkable poem in which one woman declares her devotion and desire for another, and wishes that one or other of them — it seems not to matter which — could become a man so that the two of them might marry. Possibly it was written by or for Marie Maitland, a Scottish aristocrat, and the daughter of Richard Maitland, Lord Lethington (1496–1586), Keeper of the Great Seal of Scotland until 1567. Marie Maitland was born after 1528 and flourished before 1586. The poem survives in a manuscript and may be written in her hand.

This is a poem which treats love with a generous inclusiveness: although lover and beloved are both women, the poet evokes her love by constant comparison with some of the most famous unions and pairings to be found in mythology, history and the Bible. Planets, Heavenly siblings and married couples, male pairs and female ones, warrior lovers from Ancient Greece and Old Testament Israel, and, inevitably, Ruth and Naomi, are all invoked to do honour to this unknown woman poet's peerless Beloved.

As phoebus in his spheris hicht
precellis the kaip Crepusculein
and phoebe all the starris licht
your splendour so madame I wein
Dois onlie pas all feminine
In sapience superlative
Indewit with vertewis sa devine
as leirned pallas redivive.

And as be hid vertew unknawin
The admant drawis yron thairtill
your courtes nature so hes drawin
My hairt youris to continew still
Sa greit Joy dois my spreit fulfill
contempling your perfectioun
Ye weild me holie at your will
and raviss my affectioun.

Your perles Vertew dois provoike
and loving kyndness so dois move
My Mynd to freindschip reciproc
That treuth sall try sa far above
The auntient heroicis love
as salbe thocht prodigious
and plaine experience sall prove
Mair holie and religious.

In amitie perithous
to theseus wes not so traist
Nor Till Achilles patroclus
nor pilades to trew orest
Nor yit achates luif so lest
to gud Ænee nor sic freindschip
Dauid to Ionathan profest
nor Titus trew to kynd Iosip.

Nor yet Penelope I wiss
so luiffed ulisses in hir dayis
Nor Ruth the kynd moabitiss
Nohemie as the scriptire sayis
nor portia quhais worthie prayiss
inromaine historeis we reid
Qha did devoir the fyrie brayis
To follow brutus to the deid

Wald michtie Jove grant me the hap
With yow to have your brutus pairt
and metamorphosing our schap
my sex intill his vaill convert
No brutus then could caus ws smart
as we doe now unhappie wemen
Then sould we bayth with Joyfull hairt
honour and bliss the band of hymen

Yea certainlie we sould efface
Pollux and castories memorie
and gif that thay deservit place
amang the starris for loyaltie
Then our mair perfyte amitie
mair worthie recompence sould merit
In hevin eternall deitie
amang the goddis till Inherit.

And as we ar thocht till our wo
nature and fortoun doe coniure
and hymen also be our fo
Yit luif of vertew dois procuire
freindschip and amitie sa suire
with sa greit fervencie and force
Sa constantlie quhilk sall Induire
That not but deid sall ws divorce.

And thoucht adversitie ws vex
Yit be our freindschip salbe sein
Thair is mair constancie in our sex
Than ever amang men hes bein
no troubill / torment/ grief/ or tein
nor erthlie thing sall ws dissever
Sic constancie sall ws mantein
In perfyte amitie for ever.

A literal modernised version

As Phoebus (i.e., the sun) in the height of his sphere surpasses the cloak of twilight, and Phoebe (i.e., the moon) all the stars' light, so, madam, I believe that your splendour alone exceeds the whole female creation, endowed in superlative wisdom with virtues as divine as learned Pallas Athene come back to life.

And just as by hidden, unknown power the magnet draws iron to itself, so your gracious nature has drawn my heart to continue as yours still. Such great joy fills my spirit in contemplating your perfection that you control me wholly at your will and ravish my emotion.

Your peerless virtue provokes and your loving kindness so moves my mind to reciprocal friendship that loyalty will exert itself so far above the ancient heroes' love as shall be thought prodigious, and plain experience will prove more holy and religious.

Perithous was not so loyal in amity to Theseus, nor Patroclus to Achilles, nor Pylades to true Orestres, nor yet did Achates' love last so well towards good Æneas, nor did David profess such friendship to Jonathan, nor true Titus to kind Josippus.

Not even Penelope, I believe, so loved Ulysses in her days, nor Ruth, the kind Moabitess, so loved Naomi, as the Scripture says, nor Portia, whose worthy praise we read in Roman histories, who devoured the fiery coals in order to follow Brutus to the dead.

If only Mighty Jove would grant me the good fortune to have your Brutus' part with you and, metamorphosing our shapes, convert my sex into his form. No Brutus then could cause us the pain we suffer now, unhappy women. Then we should both, with joyful heart, honour and bless the band of Hymen.

Yes, certainly we should efface the memory of Pollux and Castor. And, if they deserved a place among the stars for loyalty, then our more perfect amity should merit a worthier recompense, to inherit eternal divinity among the gods in heaven.

And as we are, though Nature and Fortune, to our woe, conspire against us and Hymen also is our enemy, nevertheless Love through its power procures friendship and amity so certain, with such great fervency and force, which will endure so constantly, that nothing but death will divorce us.

And though adversity vex us, nevertheless it will be seen through our friendship that there is more constancy in our sex than there has ever been among men. No trouble, torment, grief or suffering, nor any earthly thing, will separate us. Such constancy will maintain us in perfect amity for ever.

A female husband

from *Journal de voyage*
MICHEL DE MONTAIGNE (1533–1592)

This extract from Montaigne's Journal de voyage *(his record of travels undertaken between June 1580 and November 1581) tells not of a single woman living and loving as a man but of a sizeable group. The ambivalent use of pronouns is Montaigne's own.*

Seven or eight girls from around Chaumont en Bassigny secretly planned together, a few years ago, to dress as men and go through the world living their lives in this way. One of them came to this place, Vitry, under the name of Marie, earning a living as a weaver, a well set up young man who became friends with everyone. At Vitry he became engaged to a woman who is still alive; but because of some disagreement between them, their bargain went no further. Afterwards he went on to Montirandet, still earning his living in the same trade; he fell in love with a woman, whom he married, and lived four or five months with her to her satisfaction, so people say; but having been recognized by someone from Chaumont, and the case brought to court, she was condemned to be hanged: *which she said she would rather undergo than return to her life as a girl.* And she was hanged for using forbidden devices to supplement the defect of her sex.

Extraordinary discovery at Poplar

from *The Gentleman's Magazine* (1766)

This story presents a striking contrast to Montaigne's unfortunate 'female husband'; two women living together, one 'passing' as a man, run an enormously profitable business (valued at £3,000) over more than three decades, and when the supposed man has to change back into a woman it seems as if nothing could be more straightforward. But there is another story behind this one, as Emma Donoghue points out in Passions Between Women: British Lesbian Culture, 1668–1801 *– a story of blackmail and unwilling exposure.*

A discovery of a very extraordinary nature was made at Poplar, where two women had lived together for six and thirty years, as man and wife, and kept a public house, without ever being suspected; but the wife happening to fall sick, and die, a few years before she expired, revealed the secret to her relations, made her will, and left legacies to the amount of half what she thought they were worth. On application to the pretended, she at first endeavoured to support her assumed character, but being closely pressed, she at length owned the fact, accommodated all matters amicably, put off the male, and put on the female character, in which she appeared to be a sensible well-bred woman, though in her male character she had always affected the plain plodding alehouse-keeper. It is said they had acquired in business money to the amount of 3000*l.* Both had been crossed in love when young, and had chosen this method to avoid further importunities.

Madame Vestris and her female admirers

from the Diaries of John Cam Hobhouse
(1786–1869)

An evening at the little theatre in the Haymarket provides unexpected sources of entertainment for Byron's friend, John Cam Hobhouse, as he reveals in his Diary for 25 July 1820. Madame Vestris, a celebrated actress who specialised in 'breeches parts', is playing Macheath in John Gay's The Beggar's Opera, *and attracting an alarmingly enthusiastic female following, who include some of the highest in the land. The inclusion among them of Lady Castlereagh, wife of the much-hated Foreign Secretary, gains an added piquancy in the light of contemporary rumours about her husband's (homo)-sexual tastes. It's nice to know Lord Castlereagh enjoyed his evening: two years later he would cut his throat for reasons that have always remained ambiguous.*

This extract includes an illusion to that famous poem by Sappho, whose opening line could be roughly translated as 'Happy the man who sits close

Madame Vestris as Macheath   Madame Vestris as herself in 1820

*to you'. Hobhouse quotes the line from a French translation by Boileau,
'Hereux qui, près de toi . . .', but significantly transforms Sappho's happy
man into a happy woman ('heureuse').*

I went to Kinnaird's dined there – then went with him & his brother
to little theatre & saw M[adam]e Vestris act Macheath – I was delighted
– Lord K[innaird] was told by M[adame]. V[estris]. that Lady C[aroline].
Lamb had sent for her to ask her to go to a masquerade and had
frightened her with certain testimonies of personal admiration – such as
squeezing &c. heureuse qui pres de toi . . . I saw Castlereagh in back
row of public box over the way smiling & clapping – some of the
company recognized me & cried Hobhouse for ever – I ran back &
kept out of sight – this was worth something for Castlereagh – I do
not know how it was but I rather liked to see the man unbending –
Morris the proprietor came into our box & told me that Lady Castlereagh
had been to see the opera three nights running.

A glimpse

from the Diary of Charles Ricketts

*This haunting paragraph comes from Charles Ricketts's Diary. Homosexual
himself, he and his lover, Charles Shannon, were for many years the next-door
neighbours of the aunt-and-niece poets 'Michael Field', whose work appears
throughout this volume. Ricketts was an eminent illustrator and book designer;
the books he created, including some by the Michaels, are among the most
beautiful of the English Decadence and early twentieth century.*

*This paragraph is just a poignant little glimpse into a virtually unknown
world of Victorian marriage in which lesbian wives tried to make something
work with sympathetic husbands. In this case, the husband is clearly homosexual, too – a mariage de convenance, perhaps, which, in the end, failed?*

Nov. 5 [1905]

Have been aghast at tragedy in paper. Two women in love, one of them consumptive and dying; both are readers of neurotic literature, telegraphing in cipher to each other with references to poems by Dowson and Arthur Symons. One of these telegrams is answered by relatives: 'Dora asleep.' The friend understands by that she is dead, and commits suicide. Whereupon the other dies. The woman who commits suicide is the wife of a blind parson arrested for sodomy, who gives evidence at the inquest. The blind parson, the hysterical wife, the friend, the neurotic literature, conjure up a picture which should have taken place in some corner of the world lit by a midnight sun. The wife bids farewell to the husband in a letter where she says, 'You are the only man I could love, the others disgust me!'

from *A Ravensbrück Memoir*
MICHELINE MAUREL

This extract comes from a memoir of life in Ravensbrück concentration camp, first published in France in 1958.

Kvieta

Late in the fall when it was already very cold, Michelle and I went to a 'party' in the Yugoslav quarters. There were songs and dances, and a young Czech girl did a classic number. It had been a long time since I had seen anything so beautiful. On my return to Block 3, I wrote a poem about it:

> *Danseuse au bras flexible et léger comme une aile,*
> *Danseuse, pourquoi danses-tu?*

> *Dancer, with arms so graceful, light as the wing of a bird,*
> *Oh, Dancer, why is it you dance?*

A whole page followed in which I speculated philosophically on the reasons a person felt impelled to dance. I did not suspect then that this poem was to save my life that winter.

One evening Sissy came to Block 3 to find me and to give me a little package wrapped in white paper. 'Kvieta sends you this. She read your verses and liked them very much.'

Sissy disappeared and left me standing there, utterly astounded, clutching half a loaf of bread. Only someone who has been as hungry as I can possibly understand my stupefaction. Half a loaf, when it wasn't even Christmas, when one least expected anything. . . . This was more than a miracle. I stood there, unable to believe my good fortune. Then joy – a wild joy – broke over me like a wave. I stuffed the bread under my dress, hurried to Michelle's bunk and called up to her.

From the sound of my voice, from my smile, she understood immediately that something had happened that had to do with food. Quickly she scrambled down from her third-tier bunk, and the two of us left the block and made for the washroom as fast as possible. Even though Michelle did not know the reason yet, she was smiling.

And there, behind the washroom, I showed her my treasure. I shared it with her. It was bread from the civilian world outside, bread that was just like cake.

'Hurrah for poetry,' said Michelle with tears in her eyes.

'Hurrah for the dance.'

We had already begun to eat it when the question occurred to us: What about Mitzy?

I forget now which of the two of us resolved the problem and in a spirit of unforgiveness dryly said, 'Mitzy has had some of Madame Montigny's chicken.' So we devoured it all ourselves. Forgive us, Mitzy.

I wrote Kvieta a note of thanks and gave it to Sissy, who worked in the same section of the factory. Not long after, Sissy brought me word that Kvieta would meet me in the washroom the next day, between the first and second roll call.

I went to the meeting, as excited as though I were keeping a lover's tryst. Kvieta, so slim and tall under her clean white kerchief, handed me a little package she had carried in her bowl and said, with a lovely smile, 'Tomorrow, same place.'

The roll call for work assignment followed immediately after the roll call of the blocks. I barely had time to find Michelle, to give her half the provisions and to join my squad, which was always one of the last to be counted.

My eyes sought out Kvieta's squad, just then getting under way by the gate. Feeling as though she could hear me, I whispered to myself, 'Thank you, Kvieta.' It would not be long before I would be eating the food, crumb by crumb, after we reached the workroom.

Thanks to Kvieta, I was able to survive that second winter. Over a period of several weeks of bitter cold, she gave me something almost every day: a bit of poppy-seed roll, a ham sandwich, some bacon, an apple, onions sometimes, or a little sugar. Whenever she appeared, so elegant under her white kerchief, I found myself comparing her to an angel.

Kvieta was the youngest of a family of ten, almost all of whom had been arrested. She had already seen her mother die at Auschwitz. Two of her sisters were with her at Neubrandenburg, and all three had big, black eyes, full of fire. They were all good-looking, refined and intelligent.

Kvieta made a point of seeing me as often as possible. It wasn't the easiest thing to do because the Czech block was at the other end of the camp from Block 3, and, besides, we had so little free time.

One Sunday she invited me to the Czech block. As I entered, an aroma of apples and smoked ham assailed me. Most of the women were seated around the tables, and there was no lack of anything on those tables: bread, rolls, biscuits, butter, sausages of all sizes, onions, apples, nuts and canned food. The bearing of these women was very different from that of the women in Block 3; even their expression was different. They weren't any less unhappy than the rest of us, but because they were less hungry, they may have felt the exile more keenly, the separation, the slavery and all those human sorrows that I had already put behind me.

The stove in their dormitory was lighted, and the humbler women huddled around it drying various articles of clothing. These were the 'slaves' of the ladies with food parcels.

When I told Kvieta that I didn't know how to thank her, she answered, 'Write; keep on writing. I am so happy when you are writing!'

And as for me, with a sandwich in my stomach and buoyed up by the prospect of another such gift the next day, I was writing more freely. The days were not so full of despair. I had something to look forward to.

On still another Sunday the Czech block gave a party. Kvieta danced without musical accompaniment, to a reading of a patriotic poem by her sister. It was very moving. After the performance, the other sister said to me, 'You know, of course, that she was dancing just for you.'

I had suspected something of the kind, and I was as upset about it as I could be at the time. A long while before, when I had been Kvieta's age, I had loved one of my teachers. Kvieta could give me her affection, if she wanted to; I would try not to let her down. I would give her as much affection as I could. This feeling was apparently as precious to her as bread. Once, as she was walking back to Block 3 with me in the evening, she suddenly caught me by the arm and kissed me. I returned the kiss. She seemed to glow with joy and then she turned and bounded away.

Not long after, an *officerine* surprised Kvieta reading one of my books of verses. The *officerine* beat her very hard and tore up the notebook. And still Kvieta defied her, saying she didn't care, she was glad. To punish her they sent her to the neighboring camp of Waldau.

We exchanged a few letters by means of some of the women who were transferred back to Neubrandenburg or sent to Waldau. But the sun had gone from the camp. Once again I began to fail very fast.

I saw Kvieta on the 'Open Road' on April 28, 1945. Our column, on its march westward, overtook a column from Waldau which had halted by the side of the road. Kvieta was sitting on the embankment, her legs hanging, arms limp. She saw me and recognized me. She looked at me, but she didn't have the strength to smile. No more could I. No smile, no pause, no turning back.

The Manhood of Margaret Allen

On the last Saturday of August 1948 the body of a woman, Mrs Nancy Chadwick, a sixty-eight-year-old widow, was discovered lying in the main road which linked the two Lancashire towns of Bacup and Rawtenstall. Although Mrs Chadwick was shabbily dressed, local people believed her to be, by local standards, modestly well off. She had been attacked only two years before, and her assailants stole £25. Presumably this was another robbery, but one which had gone badly wrong.

The following Wednesday, Margaret Allen, who lived in a house only yards from the spot where the body had been found, was charged with Mrs Chadwick's murder. She had already admitted killing Mrs Chadwick, not, she said, for money, but because she was in one of her 'funny moods'. She made a lucid statement in which she said that Mrs Chadwick had called at an inconvenient time, insisted on staying even though Margaret Allen made it clear she herself had been on the point of going out: 'I was in a nervy mood and she just seemed to get on my nerves although she had not said anything. I told her to go and she could see me some time else. But she seemed to insist on coming in. I happened to look round and saw a hammer in the kitchen. At this time we were talking just inside the kitchen with the front door shut. On the spur of the moment I hit her with the hammer. She gave a shout and that seemed to start me off more. I hit her a few times but I don't know how many. I pulled the body in my coal house.'

A jury of three women and nine men took some five hours to find Margaret Allen guilty of murder. They made no recommendation to mercy, although her Defending Counsel had entered a plea of insanity, arguing that this was an essentially unstable woman, now menopausal, and one who said she had had an operation that had 'made her into a man'. But her general lucidity, calm behaviour and powers of rational argument militated against her being found insane by the M'Naghten Rules by which madness is judicially defined, and she was sentenced to death.

In accordance with judicial practice, she would have heard her full name intoned by the Judge as he passed sentence on her and it must

have sounded very strange to her. For at least thirteen years her community had known her as 'Bill' and had become accustomed to the short,
strong and rather stumpy figure, always attired in men's clothes and
taking pride in the physically demanding work she'd done earlier in her
life. Since 1942 she'd been a bus conductress; and good at her job. She
had, said the General Manager of the Corporation Motors, 'a particular
reputation for kindness to the old and infirm.'

With the death, in 1943, of her mother, to whom she had been devoted
and with whom she'd lived, life became harsher for Bill; she took little
trouble with the house, substituted beer and cigarettes for proper meals,
often felt vaguely ill. Eventually her health broke down and she gave
up her job. It was becoming increasingly difficult to make ends meet,
difficult to stay out of debt. Someone who tried to help was Annie
Cook, a thirty-year-old woman with whom Bill fell painfully in love.
Heterosexual herself, Annie nevertheless recognized and accepted Bill's
lesbianism, accepted, too, the fact that Bill was in love with her. Even
though Annie refused Bill sexually, she did it in a way which preserved
Bill's dignity and their friendship.

As 1947 wore on, and Bill's health showed no sign of improving, her
financial situation became ever more desperate. Annie and her mother
could provide decent meals and a welcoming household, but it was her
own domestic bills which tormented her: she owed £8 13s 10d for an
electricity bill when she was arrested, and forty-eight weeks of rent
arrears.

It is sometimes suggested that the murder of Mrs Chadwick was not
in fact 'motiveless'. Mrs Chadwick read palms and the tea-leaves in the
bottom of cups, told fortunes in pubs, roamed widely during the day,
collected the rents from the little houses left her by a previous employer,
talked and listened. A woman well placed, perhaps, to hear things she
might later turn to her own advantage? Other people have suggested
that the older woman was a money-lender of a particularly harsh and
usurious kind and that, this time, she pushed a desperate client too far.
One elderly man, who knew Mrs Chadwick well and who was called as
a witness for the prosecution at Margaret Allen's trial, committed suicide
rather than give evidence. Possibly there were other undisclosed links
which yoked Margaret Allen and the woman she never denied killing.

In the days of capital punishment just three weeks separated sentencing from sentence. In fact Margaret Allen spent four-and-a-half months in prison because an appeal was lodged on her behalf, but not at her behest. She made her arrangements methodically, made a will leaving everything of which she died possessed to Annie Cook who eventually received a registered envelope containing a handful of personal things and four shillings and five-pence ha'penny.

During her final days Margaret Allen was much concerned to maintain her dignity and her courage. When Annie, who had visited her loyally throughout her imprisonment, saw her for the last time, she was told 'I'm going to have chicken for dinner and a few bottles before they put a rope round my neck.'

She added: 'It would help if I could cry but my manhood holds back my tears.'

'Darts'

from *Forties' Child* (1980)
TOM WAKEFIELD (1935–1997)

This warm and affectionate piece, so typical of its author, is a chapter from
Forties' Child, *an autobiography by the novelist, Tom Wakefield. Tom's great subject, and one to which he returned constantly in his novels, was friendship, and its power to transcend the divisions of gender, sexuality and age. He lamented the way in which it so often seems to be shamefully undervalued in modern life, relegated to an Also Ran of the emotions. In this passage, the adult, openly gay Tom looks back to a significant moment in his childhood when his mother and her friends furnished him with a strong example of solidarity for two other women, imperfectly comprehended but firmly held within the ties of female friendship.*

The Utic's Nest is a funny name for a pub. If a Utic had a nest then it must have been a bird. I'd never heard of a bird called a Utic and nobody else had, but that was the name of the public house just down the road from where we lived. If you asked anyone what a Utic was, they just shrugged their shoulders or shook their heads as though you were asking a daft or silly question. A pub was a pub and its name obviously was of little account or interest to its customers. I would never have gone there in the first place if my mother's working shifts had not been changed. She worked 'nights' in a factory in Darlaston. For some reason, she was required to work on a Saturday night. This gave her Wednesday and Thursday night free. It changed the lean social arrangements that my parents were limited to – the Saturday night at the Working Men's Club was now in abeyance.

It was substituted by a Thursday night visit to 'The Utic's Nest'. I suppose that in accordance with licensing laws children should have been barred entrance. They never were; the licensee did not seem at all uncomfortable when the local bobby came in for a pint. There were other children there besides me, either the policeman didn't mind or he chose not to see us. In any event, we were always limited to one bottle of Vimto and a bag of crisps. If you took little sips the bottle lasted all night. I never shared my crisps, nor did I join the other children who sat and talked quietly around a large table set apart in the end of the pub, well away from the bar. The pub only possessed one very long, oblong-shaped room and everything that went on happened in it. I usually sat to the right of my father, he on a chair, me on a stool. My mother always faced us, her back resting on the wall. The three or four couples that joined them at their table never varied much. Sometimes one of my aunties or uncles would join us, but they never stayed long. I would listen to the grown-ups talk, the men talked to men and the women talked to women.

Neither paid much heed to me, I didn't expect them to. Occasionally one of the men would say, 'Alright then Tom lad?' and nod his head. The women might say, 'You've got a Wakefield look but your mam's eyes.' There really wasn't much that I could say to these acknowledgments so I kept quiet. I was never bored. Other things happened at The Utic's Nest.

Each night a man would play the piano for a short time and at the end of his repertoire there would be a call for a song. It was always the same lady. And she always sang the same song. She was fat, older than

my parents, and her name was Mrs Welch. She was a widow. She wore
a black dress with sequins decorating its bosom. The song was called
'Love's Last Word is Spoken, Cherie'. She sang it beautifully and at the
end she never failed to wipe her eyes as she had moved herself to tears
by the quality of her own performance. Some of the women in the pub
cried a little too – but not my mother. She did clap though and would
say 'lovely voice, Elsie has a lovely voice.'

A darts match was also played. The Utic's Nest was part of a kind
of league. If other teams lost at The Utic's Nest there was always an
undercurrent of dissent or grumbling. Not that the game had been played
unfairly but on account of the four members who made up the darts
team. All of them wore trousers, all of them wore shirts. But two of the
players had trousers which buttoned down the side, no fly-hole in the
front. These two also had breasts, but their hair was short. They were
known as Billy and Mac. They were well liked at The Utic. They would
always greet my parents and often buy me an extra bag of crisps or
supply me with another bottle of Vimto. Sometimes, they would ruffle
my hair but they never said much. In fact, I hardly ever saw them a
yard apart from one another. They puzzled me.

If I wanted to know something, mostly I would ask my father. He
knew everything about everybody in the pub. I don't know what
prompted me to interrogate my mother. I half expected a curt reply. I
was surprised.

'Mam, those two, Billy and Mac, are they men or women?' She paused
and sipped at her milk stout, licked the froth from the top of her lip
and looked at me directly.

'They're good people,' she said.

'Are they men or women?' Other women around the table had heard
me repeat the question. I think they were as interested in her response
as I was.

'They're willdews,' she said.

'Willdews, willdews, what's a willdew?' She threw back her head and
chortled, this was rare for her and I thought that she had dismissed my
question with her mirth.

'Well, it's like this. They are ladies, they'll never be anything else.
But they won't marry because they live together in a bungalow. And

when they are at home it must be 'will yer do this or will yer do that'. Got it? So, they are willdews.' At this the other women laughed. I still did not understand but accepted the explanation. However, she did not let it end there. She addressed the other women.

'That's why the other teams get upset, well some of them do if they lose. Behave like bloody little kids, grown men, yes they do. I don't know why. Their lives are their own, as I say, they're good women.'

'Oh, I know that Esther, we'd never get ambulance drivers like those two ever again. They were ever so good when they took my mother to Stafford hospital. Do you know, they even took her in some flowers on the Sunday. Off duty they were, it was their day off. My mother said they were golden, yes, she said that to me about them before she died. And Esther, I think you're right, people often sling a bit of squitch in their direction – but they've no grounds for it. No, they wouldn't do anybody any harm. They are good, they mind their own business and lead their own lives. They'd help anybody yer know.' The other women nodded respectfully.

It was later that I noticed that when an opposing team lost, one or two of the losing men would say something nasty to Billy or Mac. Billy and Mac ignored the insults but the men did not get away free. One of the married women sitting drinking would hurl abuse at them, others would join in and Billy and Mac basked in their defence. After a time, no man dared say bad things to them. But my dad told me that Billy and Mac were only allowed to play in home games, not away games, not in other pubs. Darts was a man's game. It seemed that Billy and Mac could only fit in at The Utic's Nest. They were always there – every Thursday.

Reading between the lines and against the grain

from 'On Becoming a Lesbian Reader'
ALISON HENNEGAN (1988)

Young lesbian readers of the 1950s and early 1960s had to work hard to catch glimpses of other lesbians in books. Below are some of the solutions found by a very much younger me.

That I turned early to ancient Greece need come as no surprise. If there's one thing everyone knows about the Greeks it's that they were all That Way. Even *I* knew that much. Yet because they were so thoroughly dead, so safely Then rather than dangerously Now, even quite strict grown-ups seemed to regard the Greeks with relieved approval. These days I'm told it's 'elitist' to know classical Greek. If that means that the ever rarer ability to read it opens up a magnificently rich and vibrant world, a deeply desirable source of pleasure and delight, I'd agree, although it's always seemed to me a reason for keeping it on the curriculum rather than hissing it off. But in my early teens 'elitism' did not yet exist: unguilty, I headed hastily for a literature and a world which I confidently expected to find emotionally more congenial, more recognisable, more illuminating than my teenage present.

And so I did. That women's own voices were virtually silent, bar a few precious scraps of lyric poetry and the occasional verbatim transcript from a court hearing, did not then worry me. What I was looking for were strong and passionate emotions which bound human beings to members of their own sex rather than to the other. That the bonds depicted existed primarily between men didn't matter. In part this was because I spent at least half my adolescence 'being male' inside my own head: 'gender identity confusion' in today's terminology, or 'male identified', but neither phrase is right or adequate. I never for one moment thought I was a man nor wished to be. But somehow I had to find a way of thinking of myself which included the possibility of desiring women.

And just exactly how, you might well ask, did a passionate identification with an Achilles distraught with grief at the death of his beloved Patroclus help me towards a recognition that women, too, may desire women?

It did it by offering me a world free from the assumption that human completeness exists solely in the fusion of male and female. Implicitly, the *Iliad* – and Plato's Socratic dialogues, and the *Antigone*, and the Greek Anthology's paederastic love poems, and Theocritos's *Idylls*, and ... and ... and ... – refused to be bound by the belief that true psychological maturity, personal fulfilment and social worth existed only in heterosexuality, marriage and parenthood. Not that they despised those things, either: they simply declined to elevate them at the cost of all else. And that, for me, was freedom indeed.

I came to believe, and to a large extent still do, that hostility to homosexuality stems mainly from a widespread and deeply rooted desire for polarity. It's no accident that 'Opposites attract' is used neutrally or approvingly whereas 'Birds of a feather . . .', which asserts the attraction of like to like, is invariably used pejoratively. A dualistic belief in the Male and Female Principles underpins so much of our thinking, whether we're dealing with mediaeval cosmogonies or behavioural psychology, Renaissance theories of grammar or modern genetics. In sexual terms, it is most frequently translated into an implicit demand that we should desire and value Otherness, reject and despise Sameness or Self. Remember how long and how happily mainstream psychiatry condemned all homosexuality as basically 'narcissistic'. Remember too, with gratitude, how clearly the early gay liberationists recognised that a theory which damns as 'immature' the capacity to love a body formed in one's own image is a theory rooted in self-hatred.

[. . .]

Wherever I scented mutinous tendencies in an author, I helped them along a little by the creation of my own parallel text. And this was a liberty I felt as free to take with the Greats as with the Also-rans. Fanny Price was obviously never going to come to any good with Edmund so I gave her to Mary Crawford instead and ended *Mansfield Park* properly. Charlotte Lucas had to be saved from Mr Collins somehow and Elizabeth Bennett seemed to me to be the woman to do it. (Sometimes I let Darcy have Bingley instead. If I was feeling really kind I invented an entirely new character for him, someone with Bingley's integrity and Wickham's profile.)

If a male novelist seemed to be teetering on the brink of promising intimations I'd give him a helpful shove. *Our Mutual Friend* was so clearly improved and rang truer, if Eugene ended up with Mortimer, Lizzie with Bella. Miss Abbey, redoubtable publican of the Thameside Six Jolly Fellowship-Porters, is obviously a dyke and deserves a worthy lover. I gave her one. Clearly Steerforth should live *and* have David Copperfield who's anyway been madly in love with him from that first moment in the playground. Thus should the world be ordered and thus I ordered it. (By the time I came across Ronald Firbank I saw at once that he had made an art form out of doing pretty much the same thing: defiantly creating a world in which characters got the partners *he* wanted them to have, and stuff the rest of you.)

John Osborne, in a fit of pique, once said that reading *Gay News* made him feel as though he were looking at the world through the wrong end of a telescope. I knew exactly what he meant because that was my experience too as I read my way through endless heterosexual novels which never seemed to acknowledge *my* perspective on the world. Rewriting selected bits of Great Literature was my way of adjusting the picture.

I didn't always have to change the picture. Sometimes all I had to do was fill it in a little. As with school stories, for example. Like the good parent she was and is, my mother was worried to find the sixteen-year-old me still reading Enid Blyton's Malory Towers books. (I was also reading Dostoevsky, Stendhal and Flaubert, but still . . .) Recently browsing once more through Sheila Ray's *The Blyton Phenomenon* I noted that reading surveys carried out amongst schoolchildren reveal that it is those girls who are academic high flyers who go on reading Enid Blyton's school stories longest. The surveyors were surprised. I'm not. Schoolgirls who spend long hours in their bedrooms reading books are often schoolgirls who are desperately trying to escape from schoolboys and there's many a baby dyke amongst them. The much despised girls' school story invariably offered an enclosed community entirely governed and administered by women: none of this rubbish about healthy co-educational establishments in which – surprise, surprise – the Head Teacher just *happens* to be male. In these stories casual communication with the outside world is discouraged and made difficult. Flutters of excitement over inaccessible boys are briskly dismissed as 'silliness'. The teachers are qualified, proudly conscious of professional status and invariably dedicated to a career which they have chosen. Their single state is more a cause for satisfaction than regret. The books might seem repressive of female sexuality from a heterosexual viewpoint. From my lesbian one they were perfection. There was nothing I needed to filter out, nothing I had to work hard to ignore. All I had to do was add, provide, as it were, a subtext. So I did.

Two Legs Good,
Four Legs Better?

Animals often run women a close second in lesbian affections. Sometimes they almost win (witness the unnerving passion which Edith Cooper and Katharine Bradley, otherwise known as 'Michael Field', felt for their lordly dog, Whym Chow). For humans too much burdened by the intricacies and inadequacies of speech and introspection, the wordless communion offered by a loving animal is beyond price – something Stephen Gordon, the beleaguered hero/ine of Radclyffe Hall's The Well of Loneliness, *discovers in her long and precious partnership with her Irish hunter, Raftery. And sometimes animal affections actually seem to mirror lesbian loves, as with the little weasels and the fox terrier bitch encountered in the following pages. A warning: not all animals are what they seem, as you will discover.*

Sapphic weasels

from *Les Vies des dames galantes*
by ABBÉ DE BRANTÔME (?1540–1614)

People say that female weasels are touched with this sort of love, and
take pleasure in copulating with each other and living together; such
that, in hieroglyphics, women who made love with each other in this
way used to be represented by weasels. I have heard tell of a lady who
kept some as pets, and who had a taste for this love herself, and used
to enjoy watching these little creatures cohabiting.

The Ladies of Llangollen and 'Sapho'

*Fittingly, the Ladies of Llangollen called their much-loved dog 'Sapho' (as
did many other women in this period linked in loving female friendships,
including Irish friends of the Ladies themselves). This sad little item appears
in the accounts kept by the Ladies of Llangollen for 30 September 1791:*

Our precious and never to be forgotten little Sapho's *last* expense 4s. 6d.

'Daddy wouldn't buy me a bow-wow'
JOSEPH TABRAR (1857–1931)

*Things are not always what they seem. Joseph Tabrar's evergreen standard
from 1892 was originally advertised as 'A pretty little song for pretty little
children' and immediately became regarded as the special property of the
music-hall singer, Miss Vesta Victoria. But despite her childlike costume*

and characterisation, Vesta Victoria was already eighteen when she made this song famous, and her knowing impersonation of female childhood was part of that larger and nauseating late-Victorian phenomenon known as 'the cult of the little girl'. Until 1885, the age of female consent in England remained, as it had been in Shakespeare's day, twelve; it would take several stages of legislation before it reached its present age of sixteen. Clearly, there was genuine confusion in this period about when childhood ended and womanhood began.

But there is also an additional ambiguity about cats and dogs. Traditional sexual slang, in more languages than English alone, characterises dogs as male genitalia, cats as female ('Pussy', indeed). Singers working in the cabarets of Paris, including a number of lesbian ones, adopted this song, often using as a prop a stuffed toy cat which they stroked and fondled in a manner which made clear, even to the most unsophisticated, that here was a very precocious 'little girl' indeed. So now we can read the song's sub-text: 'I feel perfectly friendly towards the female genitalia, whether my own or someone else's, and show them physical affection, often; but I should like to extend my acquaintance to include male genitals, too. Sadly, Authority forbids at the moment. But, my day will come, and then you'll see!'

I

I love my little cat I do,
　　Its coat is oh! so warm,
It comes each day with me to school,
　　And sits upon the form.
When teacher says 'Why do you bring
　　That little pet of yours?'
I tell her that I bring my cat
　　Along with me because –

CHORUS

Daddy wouldn't buy me a bow-wow (bow-wow)
Daddy wouldn't buy me a bow-wow (bow-wow)
I've got a little cat, and I'm very fond of that,
But I'd rather have a bow-wow-wow, bow-wow-wow!

2

We used to have two tiny dogs,
　　Such pretty little dears,
But Daddy sold 'em 'cos they used
　　To bite each other's ears;
I cried all day – at eight at night
　　Papa sent me to bed;
When Ma came home and wiped my eyes,
　　I cried again and said:

Daddy wouldn't buy me a bow-wow (bow-wow)
Daddy wouldn't buy me a bow-wow (bow-wow)
I've got a little cat, and I'm very fond of that,
But I'd rather have a bow-wow-wow, bow-wow-wow!

3

I'll be so glad when I get old,
　　To do just as I please,
I'll have a dozen bow-wows then
　　A Parrot and some bees;
Where'er I see a tiny pet,
　　I'll kiss the little thing
'Twill remind me of the time gone by
　　When I would cry and sing:

Daddy wouldn't buy me a bow-wow (bow-wow)
Daddy wouldn't buy me a bow-wow (bow-wow)
I've got a little cat, and I'm very fond of that,
But I'd rather have a bow-wow-wow, bow-wow-wow!

(Unknown) Ladies and (unknown) dog

Two poems of Whym Chow
by 'MICHAEL FIELD'

Apart from each other and Sappho, the greatest passion of the Michael Fields was for their dog, Whym Chow, whom they made the subject of an extraordinary collection of poems, Whym Chow: Flame of Love *(1914). The Michaels' love for Whym Chow incorporated elements of their earlier paganism and their later Roman Catholic Christianity. As animal, Whym Chow incarnates a pre-Christian, almost primaeval natural power; as male, he, like Christ, becomes an acceptable embodiment of the male principle.*

'It is so old and a deep thing'

It is so old and deep a thing
The being fond of animals – so far
It goes back to when earth was first beginning,
Lay under forests dark as storm-clouds are,
Or from its ice menaced frail breath and motion
Of living creatures. Then, by many an ocean,
Lost to our planet now, man followed beast
As foe; and out of hatred came a love
For breath that feebly struggled as man's breath,
For loneliness of soul that could at least
Be faithful to the Voice of one above,
And listen for it through the woods till death,
And listen for it through the icy flaw;
Yea, come at last to worship at the door
Where dwelt the Voice, and at its human hearth
Find the one end to a world's trackless path.

God in His spaces overhead
Seeks not the powers and angels for His heart:
From these in passion ever is He parted,
And with our mortal ignorance hath part.

And in the solace of our upward glances
The truth of His own mystery prevails.
So is it when the creatures of the Earth
What was and shall be in ourselves reveal
From eyes that pierce us not; where love avails
To grasp what apprehension in its dearth
Can never judge. Oh, as our God, to feel
A being from below reach where in vain
Those of a race more equal scarce attain:
In sacred revelation to be caught
Be blessèd eyes even yet with chaos fraught!

'Full of the passions nurtured in the wild'

Full of the passions nurtured in the wild
And virgin places of the world, Whym Chow,
Thou camest to thy Mistress, as a child
Untameable of earth, and none knew how,
Save she, to mould thy untranslatable,
And native being, personality
Risen from primæval force and under spell:
A solitary creature that must be
Lone, till there lighted in its heart a star,
First love. O infinite and savage, yet
Of sweetest temper as those creatures are
That never had a hand on them nor let
Any save Nature's hand approach them near.
Thou wert far back from anything men write,
Far deeper in imagination's rear
Than books can delve or poet's lingering sight
Reach in the past of ages. Love alone
Threw on the dark of forests in thy soul
A flashlight to recesses never shown,

Where thou wert softly moving to one goal –
Love of thy Mistress, not of kind – a new
Compulsion from that Eros who began
Forth of God's breast the darkness to subdue,
And lead it to a bliss that stars should span.

Friendship
KATHERINE MANSFIELD (1888–1923)

*And here is another cat which seems to have got out of hand. Katherine
Mansfield, who was always strongly responsive to women and often erotically
drawn to them, wrote this poem in 1917, at a time when one particular
female friendship had ceased to be tame.*

When we were charming *Backfisch*
   With curls and velvet bows
We shared a charming kitten
   With tiny velvet toes.

It was so gay and playful;
   It flew like a woolly ball
From my lap to your shoulder –
   And oh, it was so small,

So warm – and so obedient
   If we cried: 'That's enough!'
It lay and slept between us,
   A purring ball of fluff.

But now that I am thirty
   And she is thirty-one,
I shudder to discover
   How wild our cat has run.

It's bigger than a Tiger,
  Its eyes are jets of flame,
Its claws are gleaming daggers,
  Could it have once been tame?

Take it away, I'm frightened!
  But she, with placid brow,
Cries: 'This is our Kitty-witty!
  Why don't you love her now?'

'A marriage-resisting fox terrier'

from *Unnatural Death* (1927)
DOROTHY L. SAYERS (1893–1957)

Marriage-resistance is not, it seems, confined to the human female. The animal kingdom has its dissidents, too, as Dorothy Sayers's aristocratic detective, Lord Peter Wimsey, discovers in this passage from Unnatural Death. *Anti-lesbian anxieties were gathering apace at this time, and the following year would see an unprecedented proliferation of novels – some hostile, some partisan – about sexual love between women, including, of course,* The Well of Loneliness. *Despite Sayers's own hostilities which become clearer as* Unnatural Death *unfolds, she did write at least one passionate love-poem to another woman, 'Veronica', which was deposited with the British Sexological Society.*

The rainy night was followed by a sun-streaked morning. Lord Peter, having wrapped himself affectionately round an abnormal quantity of bacon and eggs, strolled out to bask at the door of the 'Fox-and-Hounds.' He filled a pipe slowly and meditated. Within, a cheerful bustle in the bar announced the near arrival of opening time. Eight ducks crossed the road in Indian file. A cat sprang up upon the bench, stretched herself, tucked her hind legs under her and coiled her tail tightly round them as though to prevent them from accidentally working loose. A groom passed, riding a tall bay horse and leading a chestnut with a hogged mane; a spaniel followed them, running ridiculously, with one ear flopped inside-out over his foolish head.

Lord Peter said, 'Hah!'

The inn-door was set hospitably open by the barman who said, 'Good morning, sir; fine morning, sir,' and vanished within again.

Lord Peter said, 'Umph.' He uncrossed his right foot from over his left and straddled happily across the threshold.

Round the corner by the church-yard wall a little bent figure hove into sight – an aged man with a wrinkled face and legs incredibly bowed, his spare shanks enclosed in leather gaiters. He advanced at a kind of brisk totter and civilly bared his ancient head before lowering himself with an audible creak on to the bench beside the cat.

'Good morning, sir,' said he.

'Good morning,' said Lord Peter. 'A beautiful day.'

'That it be, sir, that it be,' said the old man, heartily. 'When I sees a beautiful May day like this, I pray the Lord He'll spare me to live in this wonderful world of His a few years longer. I do indeed.'

'You look uncommonly fit,' said his lordship; 'I should think there was very chance of it.'

'I'm still very hearty, sir, thank you, though I'm eighty-seven next Michaelmas.'

Lord Peter expressed a proper astonishment.

'Yes, sir, eighty-seven, and if it wasn't for the rheumatics I'd have nothin' to complain on. I'm stronger maybe than what I look. I knows I'm a bit bent, sir, but that's the 'osses, sir, more than age. Regular brought up with 'osses I've been all my life. Worked with 'em, slept with 'em – lived in a stable, you might say, sir.'

'You couldn't have better company,' said Lord Peter.

'That's right, sir, you couldn't. My wife always used to say she was jealous of the 'osses. Said I preferred their conversation to hers. Well, maybe she was right, sir. A 'oss never talks no foolishness, I says to her, and that's more than you can always say of women, ain't it, sir?'

'It is indeed,' said Wimsey. 'What are you going to have?'

'Thank you, sir, I'll have my usual pint of bitter. Jim knows. Jim!

Always start the day with a pint of bitter, sir. It's 'olesomer than tea to my mind and don't fret the coats of the stomach.'

'I dare say you're right,' said Wimsey. 'Now you mention it, there is something fretful about tea. Mr. Piggin, two pints of bitter, please, and will you join us?'

'Thank you, my lord,' said the landlord. 'Joe! Two large bitters and a Guinness. Beautiful morning, my lord – 'morning, Mr. Cobling – I see you've made each other's acquaintance already.'

'By Jove! so this is Mr. Cobling. I'm delighted to see you. I wanted particularly to have a chat with you.'

'Indeed, sir?'

'I was telling this gentleman – Lord Peter Wimsey his name is – as you could tell him about Miss Whittaker and Miss Dawson. He knows friends of Miss Dawson's.'

'Indeed? Ah! There ain't much I *couldn't* tell you about them ladies. And proud I'd be to do it. Fifty years I was with Miss Whittaker. I come to her as under-groom in old Johnny Blackthorne's time, and stayed on as head-groom after he died. A rare young lady she was in them days. Deary me. Straight as a switch, with a fine, high colour in her cheeks and shiny black hair – just like a beautiful two-year-old filly she was. And very sperrited. Wonnerful sperrited. There was a many gentleman as would have been glad to hitch up with her, but she was never broke to harness. Like dirt, she treated 'em. Wouldn't look at 'em, except it might be the grooms and stable-hands in a matter of 'osses. And in the way of business, of course. Well, there is some creatures like that. I 'ad a terrier-bitch that way. Great ratter she was. But a business woman – nothin' else. I tried 'er with all the dogs I could lay 'and to, but it weren't no good. Bloodshed there was an' sich a row – you never 'eard. The Lord makes a few of 'em that way to suit 'Is own purposes, I suppose. There ain't no arguin' with females.'

Lord Peter said 'Ah!'

The ale went down in silence.

[. . .]

Stephen and Raftery

from *The Well of Loneliness* (1928)
by RADCLYFFE HALL (1880–1943)

Stephen Gordon, is the hero/ine of what may claim to be the best-known lesbian novel of twentieth-century Britain – Radclyffe Hall's The Well of Loneliness. *Stephen has two enduring relationships in her life, neither of them with a lover. The first is with 'Puddle', initially her governess, later a friend, and herself, we eventually discover, a lesbian; the second is with Raftery, the Irish hunter whom Stephen's beloved father acquires for her when she is twelve. Stephen's wordless rapport with Raftery, who is so perfectly responsive to the language of his rider's hands and legs, brings her a communion and a love which surpasses anything she ever experiences with another human being.*

The hunter, when he came, was grey-coated and slender, and his eyes were as soft as an Irish morning, and his courage was as bright as an Irish sunrise, and his heart was as young as the wild heart of Ireland, but devoted and loyal and eager for service, and his name was sweet on the tongue as you spoke it – being Raftery, after the poet. Stephen loved Raftery and Raftery loved Stephen. It was love at first sight, and they talked to each other for hours in his loose box – not in Irish or English, but in a quiet language having very few words but many small sounds and many small movements, which to both of them meant more than words. And Raftery said: 'I will carry you bravely, I will serve you all the days of my life.' And she answered: 'I will care for you night and day, Raftery – all the days of your life.' Thus Stephen and Raftery pledged their devotion, alone in his fragrant, hay-scented stable. And Raftery was five and Stephen was twelve when they solemnly pledged their devotion.

*   *   *

Raftery was aged, he was now eighteen, so that lameness in him was not easy of healing. His life in a city had tried him sorely, he had missed the light, airy stables of Morton, and the cruel-hard bed that lay under the tan of the Row had jarred his legs badly.

The vet shook his head and looked very grave: 'He's an aged horse, you know, and of course in his youth you hunted him pretty freely – it all counts. Everyone comes to the end of their tether, Miss Gordon. Yes, at times I'm afraid it is painful.' Then seeing Stephen's face: 'I'm awfully sorry not to give a more cheerful diagnosis.'

[. . .]

So one morning she went into Raftery's loosebox, and she sent the groom Jim out of the stable, and she laid her cheek against the beast's neck, while he turned his head and began to nuzzle. Then they looked at each other very quietly and gravely, and in Raftery's eyes was a strange, new expression – a kind of half-anxious, protesting wonder at this thing men call pain: 'What is it, Stephen?'

She answered, forcing back her hot tears: 'Perhaps, for you, the beginning, Raftery. . . .'

[. . .]

Raftery stepped quietly into his horse-box and Jim with great deftness secured the halter, then he touched his cap and hurried away to his third-class compartment, for Stephen herself would travel with Raftery on his last journey back to the fields of Morton. Sitting down on the seat reserved for a groom she opened the little wooden window into the box, whereupon Raftery's muzzle came up and his face looked out of the window. She fondled the soft, grey plush of his muzzle. Presently she took a carrot from her pocket, but the carrot was rather hard now for his teeth, so she bit off small pieces and these she gave him in the palm of her hand; then she watched him eat them uncomfortably, slowly, because he was old, and this seemed so strange, for old age and Raftery went very ill together.

Her mind slipped back and back over the years until it recaptured the coming of Raftery – grey-coated and slender, and his eyes as soft as an Irish morning, and his courage as bright as an Irish sunrise, and his heart as young as the wild, eternally young heart of Ireland. She remembered what they had said to each other. Raftery had said: 'I will carry you bravely, I will serve you all the days of my life.' She had answered: 'I will care for you night and day, Raftery – all the days of your life.' She remembered their first run with the hounds together –

she a youngster of twelve, he a youngster of five. Great deeds they had done on that day together, at least they had seemed like great deeds to them – she had had a kind of fire in her heart as she galloped astride of Raftery. She remembered her father, his protective back, so broad, so kind, so patiently protective; and towards the end it had stooped a little as though out of kindness it carried a burden. Now she knew whose burden that back had been bearing so that it stooped a little. He had been very proud of the fine Irish horse, very proud of his small and courageous rider: 'Steady, Stephen!' but his eyes had been bright like Raftery's.

[. . .]

Long ago, it all seemed a long time ago. A long road it seemed, leading where? She wondered. Her father had gone away into its shadows, and now after him, limping a little, went Raftery; Raftery with hollows above his eyes and down his grey neck that had once been so firm; Raftery whose splendid white teeth were now yellowed and too feeble to bite up his carrot.

The train jogged and swayed so that once the horse stumbled. Spring-ing up, she stretched out her hand to soothe him. He seemed glad of her hand: 'Don't be frightened, Raftery. Did that hurt you?' Raftery acquainted with pain on the road that led into the shadows.

[. . .]

They took Raftery in an ambulance from Great Malvern in order to spare him the jar of the roads. That night he slept in his own spacious loosebox, and the faithful Jim would not leave him that night; he sat up and watched while Raftery slept in so deep a bed of yellow-gold straw that it all but reached his knees when standing. A last inarticulate tribute this to the most gallant horse, the most courteous horse that ever stepped out of stable.

But when the sun came up over Bredon, flooding the breadth of the Severn Valley, touching the slopes of the Malvern Hills that stand oppo-site Bredon across the valley, gilding the old red bricks of Morton and the weather-vane on its quiet stables, Stephen went into her father's study and she loaded his heavy revolver.

Then they led Raftery out and into the morning; they led him with care to the big north paddock and stood him beside the mighty hedge that had set the seal on his youthful valour. Very still he stood with the sun on his flanks, the groom, Jim, holding the bridle.

Stephen said: 'I'm going to send you away, a long way away, and I've never left you except for a little while since you came when I was a child and you were quite young – but I'm going to send you a long way away because of your pain. Raftery, this is death; and beyond, they say, there's no more suffering.' She paused, then spoke in a voice so low that the groom could not hear her: 'Forgive me, Raftery.'

And Raftery stood there looking at Stephen, and his eyes were as soft as an Irish morning, yet as brave as the eyes that looked into his. Then it seemed to Stephen that he had spoken, that Raftery had said: 'Since to me you are God, what have I to forgive you, Stephen?'

She took a step forward and pressed the revolver high up against Raftery's smooth, grey forehead. She fired, and he dropped to the ground like a stone, lying perfectly still by the mighty hedge that had set the seal on his youthful valour.

[...]

Before she left Morton that same afternoon, she went once more into the large, bare stables. The stables were now completely empty, for Anna had moved her carriage horses to new quarters nearer the coachman's cottage.

Over one loosebox was a warped oak board bearing Collins' stud-book title, 'Marcus,' in red and blue letters; but the paint was dulled to a ghostly grey by encroaching mildew, while a spider had spun a large, purposeful web across one side of Collins' manger. A cracked, sticky wine bottle lay on the floor; no doubt used at some time for drenching Collins, who had died in a fit of violent colic a few months after Stephen herself had left Morton. On the window-sill of the farthest loosebox stood a curry comb and couple of brushes; the comb was being eaten by rust, the brushes had lost several clumps of bristles. A jam pot of hoof-polish, now hard as stone, clung tenaciously to a short stick of firewood which time had petrified into the polish. But Raftery's loosebox smelt fresh and pleasant with the curious dry, clean smell of new straw. A deep depression towards the middle showed where his body had lain in sleep, and seeing this Stephen stooped down and touched it for a moment. Then she whispered: 'Sleep peacefully, Raftery.'

She could not weep, for a great desolation too deep for tears lay over her spirit – the great desolation of things that pass, of things that pass away in our lifetime. And then of what good, after all, are our tears, since they cannot hold back this passing away – no, not for so much as a moment? She looked round her now at the empty stables, the unwanted, uncared for stables of Morton. So proud they had been that were now so humbled; and they had the feeling of all disused places that have once teemed with life, they felt pitifully lonely. She closed her eyes so as not to see them. Then the thought came to Stephen that this was the end, the end of her courage and patient endurance – that this was somehow the end of Morton. She must not see the place any more; she must, she would, go a long way away. Raftery had gone a long way away – she had sent him beyond all hope of recall – but she could not follow him over that merciful frontier, for her God was more stern than Raftery's; and yet she must fly from her love for Morton. Turning, she hurriedly left the stables.

from *Inordinate (?) Affection: A Story for Dog-Lovers* (1936)
DAME ETHEL SMYTH (1858–1944)

The pioneer composer and redoubtable feminist, Ethel Smyth, had three great passions in her life: music, women and dogs. The women included Emmeline Pankhurst, Edith Somerville (of Somerville and Ross) and Virginia Woolf; the most important dogs in her life were all, rather confusingly, called Pan, and distinguished from each other only by numbers. In Inordinate (?) Affection, *Dame Ethel outlines what she calls 'A Dog-Lover's Philosophy', from which this extract comes.*

To my thinking the greatest blessing life can bestow, except perhaps the love and power of work, is the gift of winning and keeping affection. Yet, in this connection, wise words of a very dear friend of mine, one old enough to be my mother, often come back to me now: 'If the old feel like the young', she wrote, '*tant pis*; let them be silent!' And what she meant, I think, is that though when old age is your portion you may, and let us hope you will, love certain people dearly, a sense of the fitness of things warns you to be careful about demonstration. You must find some other way of bringing home to them that your affection is not only deep but warm; founded firmly on the rock of personality but also in its essence a fiery particle.

Now as regards your dog, although to make a fool of oneself is never permissible, not even in private, no such reticencies need cramp your style.

For instance, one of Pan's peculiarities was to march downstairs in front of you and suddenly sit down on one of the steps. Whereupon, if the mood happened to be on me, I would drop down on the step just below him, throw an arm round his firm, woolly body, bury my face in his fur, and ejaculate: 'Pan, I *do* love you so . . . *but don't lick my face.*'

Now suppose, though I allow it is improbable, one of my friends acquired this stair-sitting habit. I can think of one who might – a comely matron between forty-five and fifty (which is about the equivalent of eight years in a dog); or, to keep to Pan's sex, let it be a certain relation of mine, a portly fellow of about fifty, who is on the Stock Exchange, and as golfer affects curiously shaggy tweeds. We are attached to each other, and when one's handicap (in years I mean) is over seventy, it need not be added that the attachment is strictly platonic. Suppose that as you go down to breakfast an impersonally expansive mood of sheer gratitude for the boon of being alive comes over you, the sort of mood that made Schiller and Beethoven cry out in the Ninth Symphony: 'Be embraced, O ye millions! I kiss the whole world!'; a mood that can be induced, if on that day you are sensitively attuned, by almost anything; a ray of sunshine shooting at you through the branch of the birch tree, a charming letter from someone you are fond of, or even satisfactory news from the Bank concerning your balance will do it.

Now in such a mood of incandescent benevolence, could you, as elderly lady, encircle the Norfolk jacket of the figure on the step above you, hide your face on his shaggy shoulder, and ejaculate 'James! I *do* love you so' (omitting of course the latter half of the phrase as it would be addressed to Pan)?

I fear not. Even with my distant relation, James, it would be difficult to pull off this scene with ease and elegance. True, there is an old friend of mine, alas well over fifty now, who I know loves me, my devotion to whom would permit me to take almost any risk with him. But then he never comes down here, nor does he wear shaggy tweeds. Also it would make him feel rather uncomfortable. But how natural, how soul-satisfying to both parties is such an action in the case of one's dog! Doubtless grandmothers indulge in such effusions with their baby-grandchildren, but the lonely hard-working spinster I have in mind has presumably no such outlet for her emotions.

In all seriousness, it seems to me a pity to block up any sources of tenderness that advancing years have left us. Why become prematurely desiccated, why turn into a fossil if the presence of a dog may hinder the process? Luckily as long as life last nothing can debar us from the bliss of expending affection, and I think the love you bestow on your dog not only blesses him, the receiver, but yourself, the giver.

Elegy for a Cat
U. A. FANTHORPE

'Cats being the least moveable of all animals because of their strong
local predilections; they are indeed in a domesticated state the serfs
of the animal creation, and properly attached to the soil.'

Southey: *Memoir of the Cats of Greta Hall*

Yours was the needlework, precise and painful
As claws on a loved naked shoulder, that sewed us
Back into that Merthyr morning, when, terrorised by toddlers,
You mined under our alien gateway, claimed sanctuary
In a jacket pocket.

You were the first to join our outlandish outfit
On that hilltop housing estate, with the garage-in-name only,
Invisible agog neighbours, rhubarb corms from Aberfan;
You the first source of our logged jokes, with
Your ears akimbo,

Eyes so excited they retreated behind their withers,
Living a paw-to-mouth existence, elbowing your way
Up bodies like a midshipman up rigging,
Your whiskers wet with passion, sitting with one ear
In a human mouth, to keep warm.

I was never sure that English was your language,
Though you were probably just as dim in Welsh,
Vague about status, doglike coming to a whistle,
Running on white bandy-legs with a
Welcoming cluck.

You never took offence, were always ready
With an Eskimo kiss of your pink plebeian nose;
Set records for slow learning when we installed
The cat-flap; had no idea of the gravitas
Proper to cats.

Exiled in Gloucestershire, you domesticated
It for us, materialised on preoccupied laps, and,
Mozart-addict, rushed in filthy-footed from
Uprooting lupins, to settle yourself round Primo's collar
When duets began.

Now the heir's installed, she colonises
The outposts (both next-doors, and one further)
Where she's feasted and fêted. Such cunning
Is natural to your prudent race, in case
Of catastrophe,

And I see, dear dead one, how we severed you
From your own earth, how you chose us to be
Your territory. You are there quite often,
Dear tabby blur, in my bad eye's corner. We left you
Nothing to haunt but ourselves.

Haunt us still, dear first-footer,
First to live with us, first to confirm
Us as livers-together, you who took us so simply
For granted, translator of life into
The vernacular of love.

You who saw love, where innocent others
Saw only convenience.

Farewells

Παρθενον αδυφωνον
[the sweet-voiced maiden]
'Erinna, thou art ever fair'
'MICHAEL FIELD', after Sappho

*Erinna, an extremely promising young poet from the island of Lesbos and
one of Sappho's circle of pupil-friends, died young. Sappho mourned her in
a poem which forms the basis of this work by 'Michael Field', the sixth
poem in their 1889 collection* Long Ago, *inspired by and dedicated to the
memory and achievement of Sappho herself, the woman and poet they admired
above all others.*

Erinna, thou art ever fair,
Not as the young spring flowers,
We who have laurel in our hair –
Eternal youth is ours.
The roses that Pieria's dew
Hath washed can ne'er decline;
On Orpheus' tomb at first they grew,
And there the Sacred Nine,
'Mid quivering moonlight, seek the groves
Guarding the minstrel's tomb;
Each for the poet that she loves
Plucks an immortal bloom.
Soon as my girl's sweet voice she caught,
Thither Euterpe sped,
And, singing too, a garland wrought
To crown Erinna's head.

Sacred to the Memory of Mrs AMEY WORRALL
who departed this life September the 4th 1795 aged 60.
She was the only Daughter of GEORGE WORRALL Eſq^r
and MARY his Wife, many Years Inhabitants of this Town.
To enumerate her many excellent virtues and charitable donations
would be needleſs as they will ever ſpeak for themſelves, and are now
impreſſed with gratitude on the hearts of many who at this preſent
time feel the comfort of her kind benefactions. To theſe ſhe added the
moſt pure & unaffected piety which ſhone forth in every action of her
life, and has without doubt gained her a Crown of everlaſting glory
and happineſs. From the very earlieſt part of her life ſhe always ſhewed
the moſt diſintereſted and unſhaken friendſhip wherever ſhe profeſſ-
-ed it, but more particularly did ſhe ſhew the conſtancy of this heavenly
virtue in her long unabated attachment to her now ſorrowing friend
SARAH DELAMORE who with ſentiments of the utmoſt affection
and gratitude has cauſed this Monument as a testimony of her eſteem
and regard to be erected to her memory

This memorial tablet hangs in the parish church of St Peter and St Paul,
Wisbech, in Cambridgeshire. The woman it commemorates was unmarried:
'Mrs' was a courtesy title accorded in the eighteenth century to all women
of a certain age.

Elizabeth Carter on the death of
Catherine Talbot

Elizabeth Carter (1717–1806), translator, poet and scholar, first met Cath-erine Talbot (1721–1770), also a poet and essayist, in 1741. Even before that first meeting, Carter wrote: 'Miss Talbot is absolutely my passion; I think of her all day, dream of her all night, and one way or other introduce her into every subject I talk of.' An intense friendship rapidly developed between them, but one which was not without an endearing sense of self-mockery, as in this extract from a letter Carter wrote to Talbot:

People here are not in the least danger of losing their wits about you, but proceed as quietly and as regularly in their affairs as if there was no such person in being. Nobody has been observed to lose their way, run against a door, or sit silent and staring in a room full of company in thinking upon you, except my solitary self, who (as you may perceive in the description) have the advantage of looking half mad when I do not see you, and (as you know by many ocular proofs) extremely silly when I do.

The friendship ended only with Talbot's death, after a long and painful illness, in 1770. In the letters that follow, Elizabeth Carter writes to another friend, Mrs Vesey, about the final illness and death of Miss Talbot, and about her own feelings as she struggles to come to terms with her loss and achieve Christian submission to the Divine Will.

Clarges Street, *Jan.* 15, 1770

You will be so kindly solicitous about me, my dear Mrs. Vesey, when you see in the papers a confirmation of the reality of my apprehensions about my dear Miss Talbot, that I cannot forbear writing you some account of myself. I am tolerably well, and my spirits, though low, are very composed. With the deepest feeling of my own unspeakable loss of one of the dearest and most invaluable blessings of my life, I am to the highest degree thankful to the Divine goodness for removing her from the multiplied and aggravated sufferings, which in a longer struggle with such a distemper, must probably have been unavoidable. The calm and peaceable sorrow of tenderness and affliction, sweetly alleviated by the joyful assurance of her happiness, is a delightful sentiment compared with what I have suffered for these last two or three months.

Two or three days before her death she was seized with a sudden hoarseness and cough, which seemed the effect of a cold, and from which bleeding relieved her; but there remained an oppression from phlegm which was extremely troublesome to her. On the ninth this symptom increased, and she appeared heavy and sleepy, which was attributed to an opiate the night before. I staid with her till she went to bed, with an intention of going afterwards into her room, but was told she was asleep. I went away about nine, and in less than an hour afterwards she waked; and after the struggle of scarcely a minute, it pleased God to remove her spotless soul from its mortal sufferings to that heaven for which her whole life had been an uninterrupted preparation. Never surely was there a more perfect pattern of evangelical goodness, decorated by all the ornaments of a highly improved understanding, and recommended by a sweetness of temper, and an elegance and politeness of manners, of a peculiar and more engaging kind than in any other character I ever knew.

I am just returned from seeing all that was mortal of my angelic friend deposited in the earth. I do not mean that I went in ceremony, which, had it been proper, would have been too strong a trial for my spirits, but privately with two other of her intimate friends. I felt it would be a comfort to me, on that most solemn occasion, to thank Almighty God for delivering her from her sufferings, and to implore his assistance to prepare me to follow her. Little, alas! infinitely too little, have I yet profited by the blessing of such an example. God grant that her memory, which I hope will ever survive in my heart, may produce a happier effect.

Adieu, my dear friend, God bless you, and conduct us both to that happy assembly, where the spirits of the just shall dread no future separation! And may we both remember the awful truth, that we can hope to die the death of the righteous only by resembling their lives.

Clarges Street, *Feb.* 13, 1770

It was not till yesterday, my dear Mrs. Vesey, I received your kind
enquiry after me. I am greatly obliged to you for the solicitude you
express about me, and I ought not to delay giving you some account of
myself. Do not be uneasy for me; I shall do very well. Never did my
mind feel a more peaceful calm, than, I thank God, it enjoys at present.
My spirits indeed are not lively, nor can I yet bear mixed companies;
but I do not withdraw myself from the society of my friends; and though
I am not capable of any high degree of pleasure, my thoughts are
perfectly awake to the innumerable and unmerited blessings which I
enjoy, and I hope no deprivation will ever make me forget how sensibly
I should feel the loss of any of those which remain. Under these restrictions I believe you will not accuse me of indulging any unreasonable
grief, by fixing my attention as much as possible on the dear object who
has engaged it for so long a course of years. While she was in a mortal
state I was accustomed to look up to her as the most perfect pattern of
goodness I ever knew; and now my thoughts pursue her into the world
of glorified spirits with more awful impressions: and I cannot help considering her sometimes as more present to my mind than when the veil
of corporeal obstruction confused her view. There is no describing the
various sentiments with which this idea strikes me – From the whole of
what I feel on this affecting subject, I find reason for thankfulness to
Him who 'gives and takes away,' with equal goodness to all, whose
inconsiderate folly does not counteract and disappoint the gracious purpose of all his various dispensations, to the children of men. Pray for
me, my dear Mrs. Vesey, that I may not incur this guilt. – I have been
laying open my internal state in a very unreserved manner: it will at
least help you to discover that though I am deeply affected my mind is
not unhappy; and at this I know you will kindly rejoice. You have too
much feeling, I am sure, not to be pleased to hear that poor Mrs. Talbot
submits to her affliction with perfect resignation, and is wonderfully
supported under it. [. . .]

To Love
'MICHAEL FIELD'

This poem was written by Katharine Bradley, one half of the poet 'Michael Field', when the other half, her niece and lover, Edith Cooper, lay mortally ill.

The poem is more ambiguous than at first it seems. Who is 'I' – and who is 'she'? In one reading it seems as though the living Katharine here ventriloquises the thoughts of the dying Edith, who had almost 'detached' herself from the lover-aunt who will survive her, but realises that to do so would be to commit an offence against Love. This time, at least, Edith is able to return by an effort of will. (The word 'creature' is used with its full meaning, 'created being': one human creature – 'created being' – should not seek to keep another creature's soul from its Creator.) But Love, naturally, urges the soul back to its human beloved. In another reading, Katharine, the older partner, has detached herself from the dying Edith, perhaps to protect herself from the pain of loss, but is recalled by Love.

It seems entirely fitting that there should be such confusion between 'I' and 'she' in a poem written at a time when the conjoined identity of 'Michael Field', a poet made up of two women who were also lovers, is about to be sundered irrevocably by the death of one of them. As in much of the writing of the Michael Fields' last years, after their conversion to Roman Catholicism, there is a tension between their earlier Pagan Love Gods (Eros and Aphrodite) and Christian Love (God and his son, Christ). This poem pleads for some acceptable fusion of the two – everlasting life at one with the beloved in a way which fuses metaphysical notions of perfect union with altogether more corporeal ones.

> I had detached myself, I had grown free –
> A creature must not hold me on the rack,
> I broke from her, I left her on her track
> Of doom and bore to God. Love smiled on me
> Fecund from His infinity,
> And caught my chains and bade me hurry back
> To that lone figure, that she might not lack

One minute's daily assiduity.
O Love, O Majesty – and is it thus –
I may pour nard upon her head and weep?
That I may cover her with tears as rain?
Die for me that the grave I may not keep,
As if we were one breathing cherish us
Give us the loving of our lips again!

Feast of Santa Lucia
Dec. 13th, 1913

Edith Sichel and Mary Coleridge

To Mary
EDITH SICHEL

Edith Sichel was for many years an extremely close friend of Mary Coleridge, a number of whose poems appear in this book. Her grief at Mary's death in 1907 was intense and after it she wrote numerous poems, including this one, to and about her dead friend.

Sichel shared a cottage for 'six happy summers' (1888–1894) with Emily Ritchie, who, in 1918, published privately a memoir of her: Edith Sichel: Letters, Verses and Other Writings. *Sichel undertook prison visiting at Holloway, which exhausted her, and gave away half her income each year. She lived a life of considerable self-denial and frugality, but did not uphold asceticism as a virtue in itself.*

I asked the stars where Mary dwelt —
  The light they gave was but their own.
Remote they shone, a gleaming belt;
  They made me colder, more alone.

I asked my faith where Mary dwelt —
  She spread white wings on upward way;
I could not see her where I knelt —
  It seemed a pointless task to pray.

I asked my heart where Mary dwelt —
  My heavy heart so full of woe —
And as I questioned it I felt
  That here was something I could know.

For with the rush of tears that welled
  From deeps below to heights above,
I dreamed at last where Mary dwelled,
  Since there, as here, her home is Love.

August 1907

Friendship was a passion for Edith, just as she said, in a letter written in Autumn 1907, it had been for Mary Coleridge. Emily Ritchie's memoir included this testimony to Edith Sichel's qualities as a friend.

It would be difficult to say to how many Edith was *l'amie idéale*. Although her range of friendship was always widening, and especially in those years when she grew closely intimate with some of Mary Coleridge's friends, these words of one who knew her well define truly the nature of her relation to all those she loved: — 'Each of her friendships was clear-cut as a separate jewel; no one ever entered so fully into each detail of her friends' lives.

Just so did Edith write of Mary's own gift for friendship, in the letter to Violet Hodgkin, the second of those which appear below.

[*To A.C.F.*]
(*after Mary Coleridge's Death*)

1907

Her love had not times or seasons, suns or moons, it only deepened. . . .
God help us to live more sweetly for her dear sake. . . . I do not feel
memory binds us more to earth. It seems to me more like the first link
of the chain which vanishes out of sight. . . . It sometimes feels as if I
had been drowned in a strong tide and had left something mechanical
here as me. I have a strange *desorienté* sense that my real me is not here
but away – *where* I do not know. The sense is so strong that sometimes,
when I am walking or moving, I have to dwell on the physical sensation
of it to make me feel *here*.

[*To Violet Hodgkin*]

Autumn 1907

We must thank God that Mary compels us to grieve with our faces
towards the sunrise and not towards the West. I am so glad that you
are going on as she would wish. Life does not stop because one great
part of it has grown so much larger. . . . And why are we mortal and
all playing at the tedious screen game, when we have such forces within
us, as free as air and as strong as love. . . . It was a kind of realised law
of friendship by which she largely lived. The more I think the more I
see that, instinctively, she showed to each one she loved, the bit of her
that was most theirs. The one who had most selves perhaps got more
of her facets, but each of us had the same Mary and a different Mary. . . .
She saw her own soul in all our eyes and, standing by it, the soul
of the person she was looking into. It was – is – a kind of radiant
self-identification.

Coda

Of Mermaids
from *Feminist Fables* (1981)
SUNITI NAMJOSHI

But if a mermaid sang passionately enough, then it would be all right? She could be singing for the soul she didn't have or singing simply because she was curious and was wondering what her voice sounded like, or singing because she was vain and knew damn well that her voice was good. Anyhow, if she was concentrating, surely then it would be all right? And no drunken sailor would club her as she sang and immediately become tearful because he'd wanted a woman, and not just a thing that wasn't even alive and that smelled like a fish, and was probably an extension of his own mood.

from *Sybil: The Glide of her Tongue* (1992)
GILLIAN HANSCOMBE

The Prophetical Songs

14

I might (says Sybil), if pressed, construct the
narrative of how the love of women undercuts a
multitude. You know how life's invented. For every
she, a he made mad and lordly. But that's just
seeing. Underneath the sea, where there's believing,
are the mermaids breathing as we dream. I've heard
how our days since earth began are numbered and
batched in secret. At times, even I forsake my

women. But now let's admit how things are. Whoever says she's his may do so for his heart's
content. We're not here to spend ourselves in
repudiation. (She, to herself only, murmurs her desire.)

Sybil's Pre/Texts

3

Being dykes, we adore in the dark, feel well within
our walls. History never penetrates us straight, nor
cleaves us navel to chaps

                     it seeps in sideways enters
in whispers oozes when we're distempered craves
(that is) attention. We pick what we can seed and
garden by night.

             We know our one anothers; we can
see each secret eye, each set of hardened hands/and
the ears pricked, scanning the static. (Fellow gallants
and gardeners, giants, lovers, fellow followers, we
ripen one by one and two by two.)

             Being dykes, we show each other
cities (not ours) decked with paintings (not about
us) filled with families (whose blood we share but
who regret).

          Being dykes, we're not to be trusted.

                     Our cause is rude.
But watch: we know alchemy, turn base things into
gold.

from *The Interloper* (1996)
by GILLIAN HANSCOMBE

My lover grieves for myths unmade, the unmended speech of
chroniclers, the passing of privilege, purpose, time, and probity; for
the music of the spheres, for the band of fixed stars.

    – I can be no help, I say; – I am sacred to Artemis, at least for a
while.

    – I am writing in sand, says my lover. – See how the patterns
collude and collapse, conform and contrast; see how the stories weave
in and out of each other.

    – Is that your version? I ask. My lover stares, then carefully,
kindly, kisses my lips, my hands.

The philosophy of Dame Evangeline Musset

from *Ladies Almanack* (1928)
DJUNA BARNES (1892–1982)

*From the vantage point of the late 1920s, Dame Evangeline Musset (very
recognisably based upon Barnes's friend Natalie Clifford Barney) looks back
with considerable satisfaction on a lesbian life well spent.*

'In my day,' said Dame Musset, and at once the look of the Pope, which
she carried about with her as a Habit, waned a little, and there was seen
to shine forth the Cunning of a Monk in Holy Orders, in some Country
too old for Tradition, 'in my day I was a Pioneer and a Menace, it was
not then as it is now, *chic* and pointless to a degree, but as daring as a
Crusade, for where now it leaves a woman talkative, so that we have
not a Secret among us, then it left her in Tears and Trepidation. Then
one had to lure them to the Breast, and now,' she said, 'You have to
smack them, back and front to ween them at all! What joy has the
missionary,' she added, her Eyes narrowing and her long Ears moving

with Disappointment, 'when all the Heathen greet her with Glory Halleluja! before she opens her Mouth, and with an Amen! before she shuts it! I would,' she said, 'that there were one Woman somewhere that one could take to task for Lethargy. 'Ah!' she sighed, 'there were many such when I was a Girl, and in particular I recall one dear old Countess who was not to be convinced until I, fervid with Truth, had finally so floored her in every capacious Room of that dear ancestral Home, that I knew to a Button, how every Ticking was made! And what a lack of Art there is in the Upholstery Trade, for that they do not finish off the under Parts of Sofas and Chairs with anything like the Elegance showered upon that Portion which comes to the Eye! There should,' she added, with a touch of that committee strain which flowed in a deep wide Stream in her Sister, 'be Trade for Contacts, guarding that on which the Lesbian Eye must, in its March through Life, rest itself. I would not, however,' she said, 'have it understood that I yearn with any very great Vastness for the early eighties; then Girls were as mute as a Sampler, and as importunate as a War, and would have me lay on, charge and retreat the night through, as if,' she finished, 'a Woman, be she ever so good of Intention and a Martyr, could wind herself upon one Convert, and still find Strength in the Nape of her Neck for the next. Still,' she remarked, sipping a little hot tea, 'they were dear Creatures, and they have paced me to a contented and knowing fifty. I am well pleased. Upon my Sword there is no Rust, and upon my Escutcheon so many Stains that I have, in this manner, created my own Banner and my own Badge.'

Acknowledgements

The editor and publishers are grateful for permission to include copyright material as detailed below. Although every effort has been made to trace all copyright holders, in a tiny number of instances this proved impossible. The editor will be happy to rectify any omissions in future editions.

Illustrations

'An exact Representation of Mrs Charke walking in the Ditch at four Years of Age, as described by herself in the first Number of the Narrative of her own Life, lately published', 1755 engraving.

Putative portrait of Abigail Masham; reproduced by permission of the British Library, Add. MS 20818, fo. 65.

'Sappho' (A Study), by Simeon Solomon (1862), reproduced by permission of the Tate Gallery, London 2000.

Cartoon of the Ladies of Llangollen © Kate Charlesworth 1986.

'Laura started from her chair' © Martin Ware 1980.

Portrait of Radclyffe Hall, by 'Matt', from *T.P.'s Weekly*, 1926; reproduced by permission of the British Library.

'I will now sing a short song . . .' © Jo Nesbitt 1981.

Texts

TOM AITKEN
'Sapphics' © 1990 Tom Aitken.

JANE BOWLES
Extract from *Two Serious Ladies*, from *The Collected Works of Jane Bowles*, by Jane Bowles. Copyright © 1966 by Jane Bowles. Copyright renewed © 1982 by Paul Bowles. Reprinted by permission of Farrar, Straus and Giroux, LLC (for the USA); and by permission of Peter Owen Ltd.

JANE CHEYNE
'The Angry Curs', by kind permission of the Bodleian Library, Oxford, from MS Rawl. poet. 16. I am grateful to Dr Jane Stevenson for drawing my attention to this item.

SALLY CLINE
'Changes' © 1988 Sally Cline; this poem first appeared under the name of 'Daisy Kempe' in *Naming the Waves: Contemporary Lesbian Poetry*, edited by Christian McEwen (London: Virago Press, 1988).

CLEMENCE DANE
Extract from *Regiment of Women* © 1917 Clemence Dane; by permission of Laurence Pollinger Ltd, and the Estate of Clemence Dane.

C. M. DONALD
'Father and I went for a walk' and 'When we lie together', from *The Breaking-up Poems* © 1988, Christine Donald; 'Poor old fat woman' and 'I expect you think', from *The Fat Woman Measures Up*, © 1986 C. M. Donald; 'At my new school', from *Ten or So* © 1993 C. M. Donald.

EMMA DONOGHUE
'Title Story' © 1999 Emma Donoghue.

CAROL ANN DUFFY
'Small Female Skull', from *Mean Time*, by Carol Ann Duffy, published by Anvil Press Poetry in 1993.

MAUREEN DUFFY
'Unfathered the child clings to the wall of the heart', from *Lyrics for the Dog Hour*: Copyright © 1968 Maureen Duffy. Reprinted by kind permission of Jonathan Clowes Ltd, London, on behalf of Maureen Duffy.

HAVELOCK ELLIS
Two lesbian case-studies from *Sexual Inversion* 1897; © François Lafitte, and reprinted with his generous permission.

U. A. FANTHORPE
'At Averham', Copyright U. A. Fanthorpe, from *A Watching Brief* (1987), reproduced by permission of Peterloo Poets; 'Elegy for a Cat', Copyright U. A. Fanthorpe, from *Neck-Verse* (1992), reproduced by permission of Peterloo Poets.

ELLEN GALFORD
'Meeting Angela Thirkell' © 1990 Ellen Galford; a version of this piece was first published in *The Women's Press Bookclub Catalogue*, October–December 1990.

RADCLYFFE HALL
Extract from *The Well of Loneliness* by Radclyffe Hall (Copyright © 1928 by Radclyffe Hall; copyright renewed © 1956 by Una Lady Troubridge) reprinted by permission of Brandt & Brandt Literary Agents Inc., and A. M. Heath & Co., Ltd.

GILLIAN HANSCOMBE
'I might (says Sybil)' and 'Being dykes, we adore in the dark', from *Sybil: The Glide of Her Tongue* © Gillian Hanscombe 1992 (Melbourne, Australia: Spinifex Press, 1992); 'My lover grieves', from *The Interloper* in *Conversations of Love* (Penguin, Australia, 1996) © Gillian Hanscombe 1996.

ALISON HENNEGAN
'On Becoming a Lesbian Reader' © 1988 Alison Hennegan, from *Sweet Dreams: Sexuality, Gender and Popular Fiction*, edited by Susannah Radstone (London: Lawrence and Wishart, 1988). 'The Manhood of Margaret Allen': this redaction of various accounts of this case © 2000 Alison Hennegan.

JOHN CAM HOBHOUSE
Extract from the diary of John Cam Hobhouse: from the British Library, BL Add. MSS 56541.

A. E. HOUSMAN
'The weeping Pleiads wester', from *More Poems* from *The Collected Poems of A. E. Housman*, copyright © Barclays Bank Ltd, © 1964 by Robert E. Symons, © 1965 by Henry Holt and Co. Reprinted by permission of Henry Holt and Company, LLC. With acknowledgements to The Society of Authors as the literary representative of the Estate of A. E. Housman.

ESTHER ISAAC
'Last Mango in Paris', 'Scan' and 'Tattooed' © Esther Isaac, 1999.

ANNE LISTER

Extracts from *The Diaries of Anne Lister* © 1988 Helena Whitbread, and reprinted with her kind permission.

COMPTON MACKENZIE

Extraordinary Women © Compton Mackenzie 1928; with acknowledgements to The Society of Authors as the literary representative of the Estate of Compton Mackenzie.

MARIE MAITLAND

'As Phebus in his spheris hicht'; from a manuscript in the Pepys Library, 2251, ff. 78ᵛ–79ᵛ, Magdalene College, Cambridge, and reprinted by kind permission of the Pepys Librarian. I am grateful to Georgia Brown for alerting me to this work, and to Jane Stevenson for providing me with a transcript of the original text.

ROSEMARY MANNING

The Chinese Garden © 1962 Rosemary Manning; by kind permission of Lis Whitelaw.

KATHERINE MANSFIELD

'Friendship', with acknowledgements to The Society of Authors as the Literary Representative of the Estate of Katherine Mansfield.

SUNITI NAMJOSHI

'The Example', 'Misfit', 'I see you what you are' and 'Of Mermaids', from *Feminist Fables* © 1981 Suniti Namjoshi.

RUTH PITTER

'The Strawberry Plant' was first published in *A Trophy of Arms* (London: Cresset Press, 1936; New York: Macmillan, 1936); it is reproduced on page 83 of *Collected Poems*, by Ruth Pitter (London: Enitharmon Press 1996).

ADRIENNE RICH

Poem XX of 'Twenty-One Love Poems', from *The Fact of a Doorframe: Poems Selected and New, 1950–1984*, by Adrienne Rich. Copyright © 1984 by Adrienne Rich. Copyright © 1975, 1978, by W. W. Norton & Company, Inc. Copyright © 1981 by Adrienne Rich. Used by permission of the author and W. W. Norton & Company, Inc.

D. L. SAYERS

Unnatural Death (HarperCollins) © 1927 Dorothy L. Sayers.

E. J. SCOVELL

'A Girl to Her Sister' © 1946 E. J. Scovell, *Collected Poems* (1988), published by Carcanet Press Ltd.

MARY SHELLEY

Extract from a letter, by kind permission of the Bodleian Library, Oxford, MS Shelley adds. c.6, fols. 53–4.

DAME ETHEL SMYTH

'A Dog-Lover's philosophy', from *Inordinate (?) Affection* (Cressett Hutchinson), © 1936 Ethel Smyth.

GILLIAN SPRAGGS

'Spring Landscape from a Train' © Gillian Spraggs 1985.
Translations: from *Fables of Phaedrus*; from Ptolemy's *Tetrabiblos*; two epigrams on Philaenis by Martial; from *Familiar Colloquies* by Erasmus; 'Which expounds the most exalted nature of love' by Sor Juana; from *The Interpretation of Dreams* by Artemidorus; 'I Sing the Light of Agido' by Alcman: all © Gillian Spraggs 1999.

JOSEPH TABRAR

'Daddy wouldn't buy me a bow-wow', words and music by Joseph Tabrar © 1892; reproduced by permission of Francis Day & Hunter, London WC2H 0EA.

ANGELA THIRKELL

Cheerfulness Breaks In (Hamish Hamilton, 1940) © 1940 Angela Thirkell; *Private Enterprise* (Hamish Hamilton, 1947) © 1947 Angela Thirkell; *County Chronicle* (Hamish Hamilton, 1951) © 1951 Angela Thirkell: reprinted by permission of Penguin U.K. and the Estate of Angela Thirkell.

TOM WAKEFIELD

'Darts', chapter 8 of *Forties' Child*, Routledge and Kegan Paul © Tom Wakefield 1980.

Author Index

Title Index

General Index